RELUCTANT REBELS

Reluctant Rebels

COMPARATIVE STUDIES
OF REVOLUTION
AND UNDERDEVELOPMENT

John Walton

1984

COLUMBIA UNIVERSITY PRESS

New York

Library of Congress Cataloging in Publication Data

Walton, John, 1937–
  Reluctant rebels.

  Bibliography: p.
  Includes index.
  1. Revolutions—Developing countries—Case studies.
  2. Insurgency—Developing countries—Case studies.
  3. Peasant uprisings—Developing countries—Case
  studies.   4. Economic development—Political aspects—
  Case studies.   I. Title.
  JC491.W24   1983   303.6'4   83-7698
  ISBN 0-231-05728-8
  ISBN 0-231-05729-6 (pbk.)

Columbia University Press
New York   Guildford, Surrey

Clothbound editions of Columbia University Press books are Smyth-
sewn and printed on permanent and durable acid-free paper.

For Casey
and the fellowship of Davis

Contents

Preface

LIKE SO MANY things in life, this book was born in a moment of escape. Less dramatic than some, my escape was from years of occupation with the question of why underdeveloped countries remain desperately poor—why, when they do change, they seem to get worse in a new way. Earlier work on politics and development, mainly in Latin America, impressed me with the obstinacy of social and economic institutions, the slow progress of change toward what I chose to think of as development. Under the weight of these ill-formed questions and gloomy answers, in the summer of 1976, I began traveling to Europe, East Africa, and Central America, reading and musing along the way. I soon realized what people unschooled in the mysteries of dependency theory knew better—that the poor nations are changing daily in incremental and occasionally revolutionary ways. Before long I was asking myself why, in certain times and places, revolutions do come about and transform the nature of underdevelopment.

Naturally, the "literature" was an obvious place to look for answers, but I soon found myself confounded by its idiosyncrasies. My naive questions focused on the origins of contemporary struggles ("Why Rhodesia?") and their fates ("Whither the Tupamaros?"), but the literature instructed me that most of these events were not revolutions at all. At first it was not clear what they were (perhaps movements, as in national liberation movements), but the catchall categories that kept popping up were revolt and rebellion. Relieved, probably unburdened by the irrelevance of all those famous revolutions, I turned to the nature of revolts and their causes. Here I was delighted to find harmonies between the accumulated discoveries of research on underdevelopment and the lively study of peasant revolts. There was only one drawback. The revolts I was beginning to learn about (starting with Mau Mau in Kenya and reaching out to Asia and Latin

America) were not peasant affairs—at least not exclusively so. In fact, they appeared very much like the celebrated historical revolutions. This took me back to the theories that, confusingly in my judgment, made so much of the different worlds of revolution and all those lesser commotions of "mere" revolt.

That conundrum led me into the analysis and, I hope, the solution developed in the introductory chapter. Explorations in the zone of revolutionary theory are dangerous and arduous, but rewarding to survivors. The species of revolution are so varied that one encounters repeated efforts at definitional purity (China and Cuba, *sí;* Algeria and Indonesia, *no*), many based on unrealistic criteria. A more unsettling form of unreality is the abstract theorizing convinced of timeless formulas that predict revolutions, often from the dubious viewpoint of individual psychology. They recall to me what Arthur Stinchcombe's book on *Constructing Social Theories* calls "explications of the logic of social theorizing which analyze arguments no serious student of society would bother to make." Where this kind of work creates no special obstacle to deft analyses, it shades into another obstructive tendency sometimes called the "mirror image problem." Downright silly psychologizing may lead others who know better to reify something vaguely called a "structural approach," which, if it excludes anything but individual psychology (e.g., if it denigrates process, consciousness, or culture), leans to another kind of myopia. Stress by some on the moral economy (E. P. Thompson's phrase, which has been put to good use with peasant societies) leads others to adopt a too exclusive political economy preoccupied with materialistic rationality. Economic explanations are decried in a campaign to replace them with the verities of politics, and so forth.

In this book I have avoided such "approaches" not for the sake of rapprochement, but because the study is empirical. Culture, society, politics, and the economy are all important in different ways. This is not to say that the book is eclectic in purpose. On the contrary, it advances an interpretation of revolution and its causes and consequences that is distinctive by contrast to much that is written on the topic. In the end it suggests imagery for the revolutionary process that is contrary to many popular notions and theoretical premises— not to mention the rhetoric of proponents and critics of revolution. The story told in the following pages shows that images based on a cataclysmic encounter of mobilized social classes and the denouement of social and political order all yield under empirical assault to a view of revolution as a steady historical process whose "brief and fragile" (in the words of Barrington Moore) eruption owes more to political calculation than to inexorable social forces and whose very real transformative impact, nevertheless, merges again with the adapting tenets of social organization.

A prefatory word is fitting about my own leanings concerning the value of revolutions and liberation struggles—not as testimony, but as a frank recognition of perspective. Generally, I favor them. Whether this distorts the analysis others will have to judge. I can judge that it colors the analysis in the sense that I tell the story more from the standpoint of the revolutionary movements, their grievances and ambitions, than, say, from the perspective of colonial administrations or foreign investors. Such a perspective does not imply error— both cops and robbers have something valid to say about the crime problem, cowboys and Indians about the land problem—provided we are clear about perspectives and social bases. Researchers invariably take sides, and the interests of objectivity are better served by recognizing this fact and complementing it with other perspectives than by pretending to an impossible impartiality. In that sense I have also tried to complement the story with other viewpoints. The more I work with this material, the more I find myself, sometimes unwittingly, viewing it much as a dramatic tragedy in which partisans, well intentioned by their own lights, are fated for collective disaster. The same sense of events taking control is plot for the dramatist and theory for the social scientist.

Methodologically the book belongs in the tradition of artisan research (a happy phrase I found in the book *Captain Swing* by Eric Hobsbawm and George Rudé). It is mainly historical work, although it relies occasionally on my own research and, more, experience in the field. In artisan fashion my job has been mainly to put things together, indeed, to *re*search the developmental experiences of the societies and to join a synthesis of these to a reappraisal of revolutionary theory.

For some time I imagined that the main title of this work was my own inspiration. In fact, long before penning it I had read, and forgotten, the article by Romana Pahlilanga-De Los Reyes and Frank Lynch, "Reluctant Rebels: Leasehold Converts in Nueva Ecija," *Philippine Sociological Review,* 20 (January and April 1972). No doubt their apposite phrase lingered in my subconscious until coaxed out by the histories that I analyze. As V. S. Naipaul (*New York Review of Books,* December 16, 1982) says of another such instance, Conrad's "creative borrowing" from Flaubert, "writing seeds writing"; I am grateful to have harvested this kernel.

In addition to many essential works cited in the footnotes, I have made ample use of expert colleagues. Early summaries of the analysis were presented to a Working Group on Latin American Urbanization whose intercontinental meetings were supported by the Social Science Research Council. From this group I received the valuable advice of my collaborator for many years in other ventures, Alejandro Portes, and my friends Manuel Castells, Jorge Hardoy, Larissa Lomnitz, Bryan Roberts, Paul Singer, and Oscar Yujnovsky. Friends and coworkers who read an earlier draft of the manuscript and provided line-by-line commentaries on matters from history to style include Cynthia Brantley, Walter Goldfrank, and Judith Stacey. Gary Hamilton gave me the same careful editorial advice and many refreshing ideas in the continuing course of our fruitful work together.

Charles Tilly's work inspired my understanding of how these materials should be assembled and what they meant. His reading of the draft manuscript provided the encouragement I needed and an unerring set of suggestions on how to present the case. I am especially grateful for his efforts to see that it was published. Howard Becker has never read this work, although I owe to our long friendship much of what I know about social research and professional deportment.

Portions of the manuscript have been retyped so many times I have lost track of many who helped. Some are by now engaged in other pursuits, but I am grateful that Wava Fleming is here and so skilled. Beverly Lozano contributed the maps. Thanks also to Addison-Wesley Publishing Co., Inc., for permission to reprint a figure from Charles Tilly's *From Mobilization to Revolution,* and to Delacorte Press/Seymour Lawrence for permission to reprint Alastair Reid's translation of "El Pueblo," from *Pablo Neruda: Selected Poems,* translated by Alastair Reid, edited by Nathaniel Tarn (copyright © 1970 by Anthony Kerrigan, W. F. Merwin, Alastair Reid, and Nathaniel Tarn; copyright © 1972 by Dell Publishing Co., Inc.).

Davis, California
December 1982

That man I remember well, and at least two centuries
have passed since I saw him;
he traveled neither on horseback nor in a carriage—
purely on foot
he undid
the distances,
carrying neither sword nor weapon
but nets on his shoulder,
axe or hammer or spade;
he never fought with another of his kind—
his struggle was with water or with earth,
with the wheat, for it to become bread,
with the towering tree, for it to yield wood,
with the walls, to open doors in them,
with the sand, constructing walls,
and with the sea, to make it bear fruit.

I knew him and still he is there in me.

The carriages splintered in pieces,
war destroyed doorways and walls,
the city was a fistful of ashes,
all the dresses withered into dust,
and he persists, for my sake,
he survives in the sand,
where everything previously
seemed durable except him. . . .

Pablo Neruda
"El Pueblo"

RELUCTANT REBELS

CHAPTER ONE

National Revolts: A Framework

LIKE THE ACT, the subject of revolution must be approached with great caution. It is simultaneously alluring in promise and dangerous in pursuit, a province of remarkable scholarship and partisan romanticism, widely analyzed and little understood. With some justification revolutions have been construed both as the cataclysmic events that shape eras of human history and as incremental, even accidental, occurrences in the steady unfolding of historical forces. Impatient with the desultory pace of social science, radical critics seize on revolution as the most consequential of intellectual pursuits, while world-weary cynics and complacent technicians content themselves with the continuities of pre- and postrevolutionary society: "Revolution is a fiercely and inevitably contentious topic."[1]

Despite these pitfalls one is drawn to the subject of revolt and revolution, particularly in endeavoring to understand the contemporary Third World. For more than a decade the best theory and research on underdevelopment have argued grimly the abject nature of dependence, the inexorable mechanisms of neocolonialism, the subtly penetrating forces of multinationalism, and the seeming omnipotence of capitalist ideological hegemony. Yet nations and peoples do revolt: yesterday in Algeria, Angola, and Cuba; today in Nicaragua, Iran, and El Salvador; perhaps tomorrow in Southern Africa or the Middle

East. Anyone confident in the last decade's progressive contribution to a general understanding of the underdeveloped world should be profoundly curious, if not theoretically shaken, by these events. With only a few exceptions the study of underdevelopment has emphasized all of the repressive and cooptative obstacles to progressive change to the exclusion of revolutionary alternatives whose conditions may be bred in the same process. Consequently, students of underdevelopment often find themselves in the same position as governmental agencies unwittingly confronted with revolutionary shocks to former allies and, in retrospect, possessed of no other explanation than a notion that tensions must have mounted to the point of exploding.

Recent work on the nature of dependency and underdevelopment gives us valuable insights on the continuing condition of backwardness. Yet these elegant explanations of persistent poverty tend to rise above the circumstances of struggle and resistance that also continue and, in occasional concrete settings, reverse the expectations of this curiously deterministic "radical" thinking. Colin Leys speaks eloquently of the peculiar bias.

One way of seeing this is to note the heavily economistic character of most underdevelopment theory. Social classes play an important part, yet rather abstractly and passively, not as protagonists in intensifying struggles providing its central dynamic. Political power, control of the state, is also seen to be important, but again somewhat abstractly, not as a pervasive dimension of the struggles between classes and of structures of oppression which permit one class to exploit another, and which indeed are bound up with the very formation and development of classes. Imperialism features in underdevelopment theory too, of course, but once more, in a rather disembodied form. . . . The real contemporary history of the third world . . . tends to be treated in underdevelopment theory as part of the supplementary context, rather than as central. The significance of all this is that in one critical respect underdevelopment theory tends to resemble 'development theory'—it concentrates on what happens *to* the underdeveloped countries at the hands of imperialism and colonialism, rather than on the total historical process involved including the various forms of struggle against imperialism and colonialism which grow out of the conditions of underdevelopment.[2]

The study of revolution has evolved in an altogether different direction, seldom interacting with the sociology of development. Research on social protest presents a great diversity of foci and explanations for the facts of rebellion as well as much ambiguity about what actually constitutes a revolution. Seemingly kindred analyses range from descriptive accounts of guerrilla warfare and national liberation movements to definitionally hidebound treatments of "classical revolutions." The former tend to be atheoretical, while the latter are confined to a few watershed events of the distant past.

Contemporary revolutionary activities that resonate with the popular imagination seem to escape our theoretical grasp, to become lost somewhere between scholarly treatment of great transformations such as the French Revolution and historically denatured instances of riot and coup. Associated with these very narrow to diffuse conceptions of revolutionary phenomena are causal theories that range from the formation and function of the state to the social psychological vexations of relative deprivation. Accordingly, the topical and engaging activities of the Basques, Eritreans, Katangese, Kurds, Moluccans, Palestinians, Tupamaros, Zimbabweans, and many others are somehow outside the purview of any sociology of revolution unless or until they transform some social order or succumb to trivialized accounts of their psychic discontents.

Obviously, the matter cannot be left at this seeming impasse. To do so would not only exclude from theoretical embrace a wide range of consequential, if somewhat exotic, historical events, it would also deprive us of a convenient window on social organization since

> social conflict, ranging from riots to revolutions . . . dramatize crucial aspects of social structure because they are here strained to the breaking point. . . . Certain important problems cannot be studied at all except in and through such moments of eruption, which do not merely bring into the open so much that is normally latent, but also concentrate and magnify phenomena for the benefit of the student, while—not the least of their advantages—normally multiplying our documentation about them.[3]

If available concepts and theories of revolution prevent the realization of these potential benefits, then we must build a better foundation.

Associated with the problems of definition, theory, and substantive focus is a more fundamental reason for the present separation of developmental and revolutionary theory. Based as it is on only a few historical transformations, revolutionary theory avoids the study of major protests that are not historically distant or patterned along classical lines of struggle and resolution. If, for a variety of developmental reasons, modern revolutions present a different complexion and follow a novel path, they are relegated to a theoretical limbo—out of bounds for revolutionary theory but within the bounds of no equally rich analytic tradition. These, then, are the twin sources of estrangement between developmental and revolutionary studies: an ironically deterministic idea of dependency unaffected in its prognoses by class struggle; and a very exclusive conception of the struggles that qualify for the attentions of revolutionary theory.

The elements of a more discerning theoretical approach begin to appear as we turn from the classical experiences of revolution to the conditions of underdeveloped countries. As a first step we may entertain the suggestion that there is a difference between what various authors call "early and late" or "center and periphery" revolutions and, further, that "for revolutions in the new states, new concepts and theories must be elaborated." [4] The distinctive attribute of these modern revolutions is that they take place under conditions of imposed intrasocietal underdevelopment and intersocietal dependency. In such circumstances the most anguishing social conflicts are without precedent in earlier revolutions.

Basic problems arise from the tension between ideological pressures and high aspirations for building a national society and structural limits on the capacities for transcending the internal and external confining conditions in which the national leaders find themselves. . . . The outcome in almost every case is uncertain, not only because contemporary revolutions are more difficult to discern and analyze, but because, beyond internal and external polarization, revolution has ceased to be (if it ever was) either a single dramatic event or an instant cure-all. Revolution has become a far more elaborate process that involves a very long-term struggle within and between increasingly more complex societies. [5]

Unlike the classical portrait of a revolution, these new national revolts are not especially rapid or basic transformations of social and political structures. Nor do they necessarily involve transfer of power to a new class, as opposed to long-term and continuing struggles in which nationalistic classes and political factions may coalesce in opposition to others aligned with metropolitan interests. National liberation movements may be a part or a stage of these long-term revolutionary struggles to the extent that they aspire to social transformation beyond the elimination of foreign oppression. This characterization of contemporary national revolutions helps dispel conceptual confusion deriving from attempts to force-fit on them classical (early) conceptions of revolution that would denegrate liberation movements because of their manifest, short-term aims or questionable "success" in the blatant sense of directly seizing and reorganizing state power. Of particular relevance here, "It is unfortunate that the experiences of countries which had been involved in decades of struggle for nationhood, that finally succeeded in sending the imperialists packing were made light of by the last minute rush of colonizers to grant independence to all in the consciousness of the bankruptcy of colonialism.''[6]

This book is concerned with rebellion and underdevelopment. It endeavors to understand the conditions in which poverty and inequality come to be viewed as unacceptable rather than inevitable and in which groups within a peripheral society organize in political and violent struggle for alternative ways of development. In addition to their intrinsic interest, these national or developmental revolutions merit closer attention for several reasons. First, they may represent the more common form in which revolutions of the twentieth century appear. That is, both the locus and the dynamics of modern revolutions may be more typically centered on the peripheral areas of the world economy struggling for development. Second, because national revolts are more numerous and temporally accessible, their study promises to extend the empirical terrain of revolutionary phenomena. Similarly, to the extent that reformulated concepts and theories of rebellion are developed in this area that draw on analyses of classical revolutions, there is the possibility of extending and generalizing revolutionary theory. And finally, this approach beckons to an integration of revolutionary and developmental studies—those natural allies that suffer serious weakness in isolation.

This book is also about the contemporary history of the Third World, the process whereby concrete struggles arise to challenge the whip of underdevelopment, not simply what happens *to* these countries as a result of dependency and colonialism. It is a comparative historical study of three major revolts in the developing world of the mid-twentieth century: the Huk rebellion in the Philippines, the Violencia in Colombia, and the Mau Mau revolt in Kenya. The Huk rebellion germinated in the first imposition of American colonialism in Asia at the turn of this century and, like the Chinese revolution, matured in opposition to invading Japanese armies. Presaging the Vietman War, it engaged broad segments of the Philippine populace in a military and political struggle for national liberation immediately after World War II. The Colombian Violencia was an enormously destructive conflict, rivaled in Latin American history only by the Mexican revolution, and culminating in the imposition of a fragile political peace so characteristic of Latin America today. The Mau Mau revolt in Kenya was, perhaps, the most chronicled and prototypical anticolonial rebellion in modern Africa and continues to symbolize the struggle for independence on that continent.

The study, therefore, deals with a species of rebellion that has been largely ignored in revolutionary theory—one that convention is reluctant to call a true revolution yet cannot dismiss as a coup or transitory insurrection. The term *national revolts* will be used to designate these occurrences. The intention here is not to carve out a special province within some spectrum of revolutionary events or to develop a special theory of revolt. On the contrary, the central *hypothesis* in this study is that beyond the several twentieth-century developments that are consensually termed revolutions (e.g., the Russian, Chinese, Mexican, Cuban), national revolts are more common—facilitating comparative study and generalization—and sufficiently similar in their origins and trajectories to those major events that they belong to the same class, suggesting, in turn, broader application of a refined theory of revolution. The hypothesis, of course, cannot be established by definitional fiat or a priori judgments about the historical processes producing revolt and revolution. Empirical treatment of the issues requires a reformulation of some standards, concepts, and theoretical perspectives.

Conceptions of Revolution and Revolt

As a first step toward refining the tools of this inquiry we need a term to designate contemporary revolutionary movements in the developing world, events variously and imprecisely labeled developmental revolutions, liberation movements, peasant wars, popular insurrections, civil wars, and so forth. It would seem prudent to avoid the term *revolution* precisely for the grandiose connotation that it carries. Although more on this issue follows, for the time being it is advisable to employ a less reactive term that does not invite immediate demur to the effect that an allegedly revolutionary process lacked the cataclysmic proportions deserving the name.

Briefly stated, this study is about class fights over the policies and beneficiaries of development. More elaborately, the object of analysis in what follows is the "national revolt" defined as a process involving violent conflict between mobilized class and status groups and the state, of an extended duration, on a national (or at least non-local) scale, and based on cultural, social, political, and economic issues whose mediation transforms the state and society. National revolt designates a broad class of events and processes that vary from sustained insurrection to revolution as it is customarily understood. Yet, this eclectic convenience is only one among several advantages that the concept provides by contrast to the problems associated with customary distinctions between revolts and revolutions.

Let us consider briefly the conventional posture on these matters. With respect to the notion of revolution Skocpol's formulation is the most recent and compelling:

> **Social revolutions are rapid, basic transformations of a society's state and class structures; and they are accompanied and in part carried through by class-based revolts from below.** Social revolutions are set apart from other sorts of conflicts and transformative processes above all by the combination of two coincidences: the coincidence of societal structural change with class upheaval; and the coincidence of the political with social transformation.[7]

This definition reflects two important theoretical considerations. First, Skocpol emphasizes a *concrete*, if *"complex* object of explanation,"* in preference to the vagueness of social protest or collective violence. Second, the revolutionary phenomenon as a complex and coherent object includes more than those acts of insurgency and social mobilization seeking redress. It also includes the reaction and "transformation" of the state in the face of class upheaval—the interplay of these forces. So far, the formulation accords with the purposes of this study.

But what of the question of revolts? Implying a fourfold property-space, bounded presumably by the case of no conflict, two forms of less-than-revolutionary events are identified: "In contrast, rebellions, even when successful, may involve the revolt of subordinate classes—but they do not eventuate in structural change. Political revolutions transform state structures but not social structures, and they are not necessarily accomplished through class conflict."[8]

In other words, class struggles without transformative consequences (rebellions) and reorganizing coups (political revolutions) are not revolutionary in the complete sense—a point well taken, despite the fact that it raises difficult questions since these changes are matters of degree. Now, depending upon what one intends by basic transformations of social and political structures, this definition could be construed as sufficiently catholic to include among revolutions those kinds of national revolt that will concern us here. However, Skocpol (and many others who follow this convention) makes it clear that true social revolutions include only those "rare but momentous occurrences in modern world history" such as took place in France, Russia, China, Mexico, and Cuba. If this were simply a matter of semantic convention, with one preferring to reserve the designation *revolution* for a few great events and another choosing to apply it more broadly, there would be no quarrel, assuming that both agreed that the events themselves were of a piece—comparable theoretical objects differing only in "scope" or momentousness. But the difference is much more than semantic. At the heart of the issue are empirical and theoretical differences.

In support of the revolution-rebellion distinction Skocpol explains: "The rationale is my belief that successful social revolutions probably emerge from different macro-structural and historical contexts than do either failed social revolutions or political transformations that are not accompanied by transformations of class relations."[9]

Presumably this applies equally to the "rebellions, even when successful" mentioned previously. The fundamental point in this discussion is that the observation is impressionistic, representing no more than an unsupported empirical claim providing the concept as defined with greater purity than empirical fact may warrant (as is hinted by the words *belief* and *probably* in the passage). The empirical material in this study, as well as comparison with kindred analyses of revolt and revolution, takes as problematic whether the historical and structural features of national revolts bear sufficiently strong similarities to successful revolutions to justify their treatment as a single theoretical object, or whether they emerge from different contexts, as Skocpol maintains. Others, of course, hold the former position, namely, that there is no theoretical justification for treating societies and revolutions such as in China, Cuba, and Algeria as (truly revolutionary) phenomena distinct and in a separate category from the struggles in other peripheral countries: "These countries share a continuity of situation and experience, that of peripheral status in a relation to the central, industrial societies, which, combined with economic development, justified the adoption of a common theoretical perspective."[10] The argument can only be settled through empirical study, particularly of national revolts, their contexts of emergence and their effects, which may then be compared with the better known revolutionary experiences.

Apart from this issue centered on the generality of the causes of revolution, Skocpol places equal emphasis on *outcomes* with respect to class relations and the state. Again, she prefers an exacting (perhaps restrictive) criterion for the kind of outcome that would qualify a class struggle as a revolution: a "basic transformation" of class relations and the state. The important advantage of this approach is to embrace the entire *process* of revolt, particularly involvement of the state as an actor influencing the direction of events. However, since transformations are matters of degree, a question arises as to how much amounts to "basic."

But this too is an empirical question. If a popular insurrection produces a new ruling class, how much reorganization of the state would qualify as a revolutionary transformation? Conversely, how much change in state and class structures without the replacement of rulers might be judged to accomplish basic revolutionary objectives? This approach founders on the exceptional ambiguity of what constitutes "success" and easily lapses into historical convention in lieu of conceptual precision—revolutions are those major conflagrations that have been awarded the title by victors and historians.[11] The dilemma is even more serious. Definitional preconceptions that restrict the empirical purview of the revolutionary process rule out the possibility of accounting for those variations in outcome that probably relate to the revolutionary situation itself. As critics argue,[12] by some criteria even the great revolutions fail with the emergence of bourgeois tendencies or new class inequalities, while mere revolts often succeed in bringing about independence or reforms of land and labor. There is no point to the a priori separation of these potential outcomes since their transformative implications and sources of variation invite explanation. The question of success should be left to empirical determination within a more generous definition of the revolutionary process.

Other authors have pursued the revolution–revolt distinction along different lines. Hagopian is instructive in this regard since he explicitly mentions certain "false or uninteresting criteria of distinction," including the success–failure dichotomy, the level of violence, the amplitude or geographical scope, and the socioeconomic results. Revolt is construed as

the angry violent expression of the refusal of an individual or group to continue in its present condition. . . . [But] revolution is an acute, prolonged crisis in one or more of the traditional systems of stratification (class, status, power) of a political community, which involves a purposive, elite-directed attempt to abolish or to reconstruct one or more of said systems by means of an intensification of political power and recourse to violence . . . the differences between revolt and revolution, however, are qualitative [involving] (1) the stakes of the uprising, (2) the function of ideology, and (3) the role of leadership. We have argued that the stakes of revolution are the abolition or reconstruction of one or more of the systems of stratification in society. In simple revolt none of these systems as structures is threatened by serious attempts at reconstruction, let alone by complete abolition.

Revolts are virtual prisoners of the reigning set of values, and therefore cannot mount a full-scale attack on the institutionalized systems
of stratification that are both cause and effect of these values. The
short-run impact of revolt on the structure and function of social and
political institutions is therefore indirect and marginal.[13]

Although this formulation allows the inclusion of a greater number of contemporary instances of revolution (e.g., Bolivia, Rwanda,
Zanzibar), it combines problems of empirical preconception with
overinclusiveness. It is questionable, for example, whether revolts lack
high stakes (at least from the standpoint of participants), articulate
ideologies, coordinated leadership, or a measurable impact. By these
standards most sustained movements of social protest would qualify
as revolutionary, whereas revolts would comprise only ephemeral occurrences of angry collective behavior. Moreover, historians would
question the extent to which revolutions are predicated on a radical
new set of values (as opposed to threatened old ones) or the "complete abolition" of traditional systems of stratification. A cogent object of explanation gets lost in an otherwise persuasive effort to avoid
the success–failure dichotomy.

If, in some key respect, the difference between these two approaches is in Skocpol's stress upon *successful* social transformations
and Hagopian's upon concerted (elite-directed) *attempts,* a complementary alternative is provided by Stinchcombe, who would go no
further than trying to account for a *predisposition* or readiness for
revolution.

Rather than explaining the occurrence of revolution, a sociological
theory ought to try to explain the occurrence of a "revolutionary
situation." Whether or not a change in the ruling powers of a society
takes place by means of violence depends both on the predisposing
characteristics of the social structure and on concrete military and
political situations at given historical times. The flow of historical
events, the disposition of troops at particular times, the political loyalty of strategic groups, the tactical genius of revolutionary or governmental leaders are all situational variables which a sociological
theory ought not explain. But it is possible to outline the conditions
under which the means of political conflict tend to become unlim-
ited.[14]

Like Hagopian, Stinchcombe disputes the idea that the important
facets of revolutionary phenomena attach to whether or not a movement succeeds in taking power or totally transforming the social
structure, since these results depend upon circumstantial or strategic
considerations unrelated to the structural evolution of revolutionary

forces. Unlike Hagopian, whose solution is to relax the conceptual grip to the point of losing the object, Stinchcombe prefers to reconceptualize the theoretical object itself. Ironically, however, Stinchcombe retreats from the singular term *revolution* because it is implicitly understood as the successful replacement of ruling powers through violence (as the military and strategic considerations in the passage suggest), rather than as measurable impacts or transformations of class and state structures. About a similar formulation Tilly notes, "The insistence on armed force and on actual transfer of power eliminates many instances in which competing observers see something revolutionary."[15]

Consequently, others will persist in the attempt to explain full-fledged revolutions as opposed to generalized explosive situations in which the political constraints on the use of violence have eroded; they want to take the matter further into the realm of particular outcomes. This is true particularly of recent critical thinking about revolution that identifies the response of the state to mounting social tensions (the revolutionary situation) as a key determinant in the subsequent course of events: "Perhaps the largest single factor in the promotion of revolutions and collective violence has been the great concentration of power in national states."[16] Both positions have merit. Stinchcombe is correct in arguing that the revolutionary situation is a cogent object of explanation apart from the circumstantial exigencies of its resolution. But Tilly and Skocpol are also correct in stressing that the more complete statement of the revolutionary process, including the role of the state in some transformation, can also be a valid theoretical object—albeit a less general one. The real snag that Stinchcombe properly tries to avoid and others are caught on is the question of successful ("true") revolution.

Is there a ready solution to this problem? The answer is yes and no. Choices about the inclusiveness of one's concept of revolution are unavoidable, but the elements involved in the choice can be clarified. In this I follow Tilly's suggestion:

No concept of revolution can escape some such difficulties, because no conceptualizer can avoid such choices. Nevertheless, we can clear a good deal of conceptual ground by means of a simple distinction between *revolutionary situations* and *revolutionary outcomes*. Most significant disagreement about the proper definition of revolution falls somewhere along these two dimensions.

Varieties of revolt and revolution, Tilly says, can be located along these dimensions where revolutionary situations are characterized by multiple sovereignty ("when a government previously under the control of a single, sovereign polity becomes the object of effective, competing, mutually exclusive claims on the part of two or more distinct polities")[17] and revolutionary outcomes by the displacement of one set of power holders by another. Combining the two dimensions, Tilly produces figure 1.1[18] indicating more and less revolutionary possibilities.

For present purposes this formulation accomplishes a useful effect in its recognition of a general field of rebellious activity whose varied forms become matters of degree and, fundamentally, of inves-

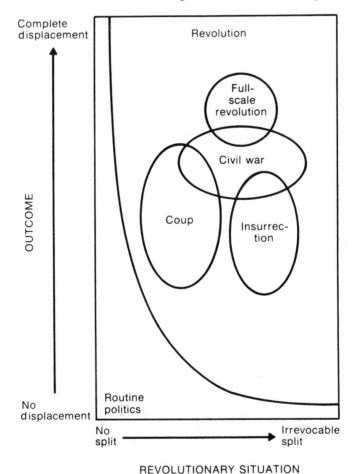

Figure 1.1. Situations and outcomes in different types of power transfers.

tigation. The outcome dimension I shall modify since the replacement of policies (i.e., reforms) rather than power holders is normally of greater interest. Similarly, to avoid confounding these dimensions with the long-run effects of revolt and revolution the outcomes here must be distinguished from what Tilly calls "further structural changes." Nevertheless, these points are minor by contrast to the clarifications involved. In terms of the definition that introduced this section, national revolt designates the entire field of insurrectionary processes that lie beyond the (inevitably qualitative) bounds of routine politics.

Restating the focus of this study in light of the foregoing considerations, *national revolts* are protracted, intermittently violent, nonlocal struggles involving large-scale mobilization of classes and status groups that become recognized claimants of rival sovereignty and engage the state in responses with the effect of transforming social and state power in the development process.

Returning to the issue of success, state responses may take many forms from immediate to phased-out (colonial) abdication, efficacious reforms of the economy and polity, attempts at concession and cooptation, or straight repression. National revolts and their outcomes are determined in this interplay of mobilized groups and state responses endeavoring to negotiate some solution, whether for safe passage out of the fray or some concession that ensures the retention of renegotiated power. But, as we have emphasized, national revolts are elaborate and long-term struggles. Massive mobilization quelled by a minor concession is both unlikely and unrevolutionary. National revolts do produce transformations of social and political structure, though not necessarily desirable ones, as witnessed by harsh repression and the creation of new coercive (and less legitimate) power in garrison states. Equally important are those negotiated responses that lead, perhaps gradually, to new political leadership and structural changes designed, sometimes disingenuously, for a more nationalistic and distributive developmental policy.

The initial results and continuing efforts of twentieth-century national revolts place most of them in an unsatisfactory position along a continuum of efficacious development as a result of their own limited potential and the balance of power among negotiating parties both domestic and foreign. Still, these considerations allow us to clearly distinguish national revolts from short-lived protests, localized rebellions, sectarian movements, and the like since all the latter do not involve broad geographic and class mobilization, national developmental objectives, rival sovereignty, and systemic responses. Moreover, although national revolts constitute new phenomena requiring treatment with reappraised theories and concepts on an equal footing with classical revolutions, there are doubtless many historical and theoretical parallels between the two, suggesting the possibility of future syntheses and the much needed advance of revolutionary theory as a whole.

Revolutionary Theory

The conceptual issues reviewed here as well as the position taken on national revolts are closely bound with causal theories. From the wealth of theoretical thinking about revolution the focus here is necessarily reduced by the relevant themes of underdevelopment, structural change, class and status groups, violent struggle, rival sovereignty, and the role of the state. Although these suggest an ambitious range of theories, they distinguish the inquiry from others that address general social transformations (e.g., the industrial revolution) or the social psychology of individual (participation in) rebellion.

This perspective accords with the cogent criticisms of revolutionary theory provided recently by Aya and by Skocpol.[19] To summarize the latter's classification, "aggregate-psychological" theories reduce the explanation of social movements to the presumed verities of individual psychology—including the dubious claim that relative deprivation regularly produces aggressive or violent action under a specifiable set of circumstances. Theories of "systems/value-consensus" rarefy the concrete circumstances that may generate revolutions and establish no connection between value conflicts and revolutionary activity. And "political conflict" theories correctly shift the locus of causation to the political sphere, but minimize economic forces and indiscriminately absorb all forms of conflict into an overly generalized explanation. Marxist theory is the best start on a structural explanation, but requires critical emendation concerning the role of social classes and the state. An adequate social structural approach must rely on historical and comparative analysis, give prominence to global and national economic influences that shape institutional structures, and place special emphasis on the role and autonomy of the state acting in mutual causation with economic and class structures.

Under the broad canopy of social structural theory four complementary approaches help orient this critical inquiry. Each contains insightful ideas and fertile hypotheses that invite evaluation in the context of national revolts. The theories are reviewed not for purposes of facile refutation, but because they represent some of the best contemporary work on explaining revolution.

The first of these approaches, whose origin lies in the study of Third World underdevelopment, is the peasant revolt thesis. National revolts are construed as fundamentally rural-based peasant wars or agrarian revolutions.[20] Concerned with underdevelopment, these explanations appropriately proceed from a recognition of the importance of the global economy, or what Wolf calls "North Atlantic capitalism." This system penetrates Third World societies and their agricultural economies through processes that disrupt traditional forms of social organization, converting land from an object of customary rights and obligations into a commodity, and labor from subsistence and petty commodity production into proletarianized wage dependency. The result is to devastate the moral economy of the peasantry and to threaten and radicalize the artisan class and the middle peasantry.[21] Recent refinements suggest that the export economy may produce a variety of agrarian rebellions, ranging from reformist protests over commodity prices and working conditions to nationalist and socialist revolutionary movements, depending upon particular combinations in the organization of land, capital, and wages.[22] This argument has been richly developed historically and has held up under rigorous empirical evaluation.[23]

Although the peasant revolt thesis is a valuable supplement to the Marxian emphasis on the industrial proletariat, it is equally conjectural in its singular attribution of revolutionary potential. Moore has shown in great detail the links between rural and urban society in the classical revolutions.[24] The contribution of urban politics to great social revolutions has been documented in the cases of France and the United States.[25] Hobsbawm's analysis of the evolution of rebellion from primitive to modern forms attests to the interaction of rural and urban forces and the increasing importance of the latter.[26] In the case of the Chinese Revolution these rural–urban linkages have proven to be so clearly patterned that some speak of the urban origins of this later, rural revolution.[27] Similarly, urban and rural elements combine in distinct if varied ways in modern revolutions such as Algeria, Malaya, Vietnam, and many others that have been critically analyzed from this standpoint.[28]

It should be added that an alternative bias has recently entered the field in the faddish concern with the "new" urban guerrillas.[29] Although far less sophisticated or theoretically developed than the peasant revolt thesis, this approach offers a valid, if singular, emphasis. Thus we encounter rival approaches seriously maintaining convictions that the conditions for modern revolution arise only in the cities or exclusively among the peasantry.[30] Curiously, no less an authority than Gramsci is cited as the inspiration for both Scott's argument that the peasantry is the most important agent of modern revolution *and* Tilly's more plausible analysis of rural–urban links.[31]

Two tendencies in analyses of the role of the peasantry seem to cloud explanations of national revolts. The first pits the peasantry against urban workers, viewing the former as somehow more important, always the prime mover or "the crucial insurrectionary ingredient in virtually all actual (i.e., successful) social revolutions to date."[32] In its strongest form this position holds,

> It is abundantly clear that the peasantry, not the proletariat, has constituted the decisive social base of most, if not all, successful twentieth century revolutions. In China, Vietnam, Mexico, and Angola the massive participation of the peasantry so overshadowed the participation of other social elements that it becomes possible to speak of *peasant* revolutions . . . (although Cuba and Algeria seem exceptions). In neither case, moreover, did the urban proletariat make anything like the contribution one might expect from a reading of orthodox Marxist theory.[33]

Yet historical evidence refutes this statement and supports another generalization—that these two classes act within a revolutionary field including others (e.g., rural wage workers, artisans, shopkeepers) *and* that their relative contributions vary across time and place. The sense in which any one of these classes is "crucial" appears largely rhetorical. What is needed here is a theory that can direct inquiry toward an explanation of the differential role of classes under specified circumstances, rather than partial theories that place their bets on false or incomplete alternatives.

A second tendency treats the peasantry as central, yet curiously residual—a kind of powder keg always ready to explode if other circumstances (e.g., a breakdown of repressive force) or actors (e.g., marginal elites or urban workers) provide the incendiary spark.

> By definition, peasants are invariably subjected to nonreciprocal claims on their production. . . . Peasants always have grounds for rebellion against landlords, state agents, and merchants who exploit them. What is at issue is not so much the objective potential for revolts on grounds of justifiable grievances. It is rather the degree to which grievances that are always at least implicitly present can be collectively perceived and acted upon.[34]

On one hand, this position lends itself to a simple additive or mechanical explanation in which exogenous sparks produced by the "political factor" interact with "the structurally given insurrectionary potential of the peasantry to produce the full-blown social-revolutionary situation that neither cause alone could have produced."[35] On the other hand, a wealth of peasant studies show that their condition is far from "structurally given" but involves many reciprocal claims and varies between relative and absolute prosperity and immiseration according to identifiable historical influences[36] (including the conditions of participation in the global economy emphasized in the foregoing theories).

The peasant revolt thesis is informed by a remarkable literature and is valid as far as it goes. Certainly the incorporation of predominantly agrarian societies into the world economy is devastating to the peasantry, and the many excellent studies of this change are in substantial agreement on the structural consequences of the process. However, fundamental theoretical difficulties arise when the very real rural effects of incorporation are considered in isolation from equally obvious urban and "systemic" effects and when only the former are traced in their revolutionary implications.

One may argue persuasively for the revolutionary potential in agrarian society created by incorporation into the international system through the devices of monetization of subsistence and petty-trading economies, the proletarianization of a labor force, and the expanding importance of commodities. However, the same agency of change produces massive urban migrations, the realignment of urban hierarchies, and qualitative changes in the urban economy and labor force— such as the destruction of craft and artisan industry. These changes, in turn, may produce "urban involution" or overcrowding of the tertiary sector, the creation of urban export industry, and the introduction of foreign imports and comprador trade.[37] Ignoring these collateral and interrelated changes stemming from the expansion of global capitalism truncates the understanding of revolutionary action by anticipating it theoretically only in the form of agrarian revolt. Hence, it may come as a surprise, disconfirmation, or anomaly for theories of peasant rebellion when confronted with the abundant facts of urban insurrection. Yet *both* may be anticipated, and perhaps causally linked, in a more holistic world systems perspective to be considered momentarily. In this sense it is significant that Wolf concludes his extraordinary study of twentieth-century peasant wars with the observation that

> **the peasants rise to redress wrong: but the inequities against which they rebel are but, in turn, parochial manifestations of great social dislocations. Thus rebellion issues easily into revolution, massive**

movements to transform the social structure as a whole. The battle-field becomes society itself, and when the war is over, society will have changed and the peasantry with it.[38]

Building on this insight, the investigation that follows is sensitive to the systemic character of influences stemming from the international political economy—the manner in which rural and urban structures evolve in tandem. By emphasizing the interaction of agrarian and urban transformations that contribute to revolutionary situations, I do not wish to exaggerate their present divorce or imply any special liabilities in the peasant studies. Nevertheless, since Marx's forceful theoretical statements identifying the proletariat as the only truly revolutionary force, and the eager chorus of recent writers that seems to delight in refuting such pronouncements, the peasant revolt thesis has assumed questionable generality. It is certainly the bias of much development policy (e.g., land reform to quell peasant unrest) and penetrates scholarly thinking to the extent that such an acute (and influential) observer as Eric Wolf is led to a theory of revolution rooted in the "middle peasantry" despite his own evidence of a collateral urban impetus (especially in his Algerian and Russian cases). Moreover, even when these different social bases are given equal attention, the logic of their combination tends to be additive rather than focused on interactive manifestations of a broader transformation. In sum, it is one thing to ask why peasants rebel and quite another to assay their contribution to national revolts.

These observations introduce the second theoretical approach. Many of the external causes of uneven development identified in studies of peasant revolt are synthesized and applied to broader social and political structures in work on the "modern world system."[39] Articulation of the world economy and local society has enormous consequences, but they vary according to a number of considerations of time and place. Three such considerations deserve emphasis. First is the question of time, or what some authors call "world time,"[40] which connotes stages in the development of the world system and how the "same" practice (e.g., trade) may have very different meanings and consequences depending upon when it takes place in the chronological development of the system. Second are the changing patterns of competition and exigencies of the evolving world system itself—whether, for example, core states are trying to enhance their position by ensuring a stable flow of raw materials from the periphery or whether they are more concerned with cultivating new markets. Third are the unique resources of peripheral societies that provide them with more or less autonomy in negotiating the terms of incorporation or its resistance. Patterns of underdevelopment and revolutionary potential vary along these dimensions.

International forces affected the early revolutions in European societies,[41] but they are far more constraining on national revolts. National revolts are shaped decisively by conflicts over the aims of development policy, the fate of displaced segments of the population, and struggles within the political leadership over nationalist versus dependent paths of development—conflicts that arise mainly in the nexus of penetration and incorporation by the world system.

Strictly speaking the world systems perspective does not provide a theory of revolution as opposed to an emphasis on the broader context in which national revolutions are "made possible" and, therefore, some of the elements that merit inclusion in that theory. For example, Wallerstein treats in detail the local factors contributing to the Netherlands Revolution, including fears among the nobility that it had been abandoned by the prince, the rise of town governments and urban commercial interests, and the growing influence of Protestantism. One way of interpreting the revolution is to see it as an assertion of self-control by locally dominant groups.

Another way to interpret it is to say that because after 1559, Spain, France, and England balanced each other off, the Netherlanders had the social space to assert their identity and throw off the Spanish yoke. This was particularly true after the defeat of the Spanish Armada in 1588. It was not that any of the countries stood for the independence of the Netherlands. Spain did not want to lose part of her dominions. France, although it wanted to weaken Spain, vacillated because of the implications for the internal religious struggle in France. England wanted to get Spain out but not let France in, and preferred therefore Netherlands autonomy under nominal Spanish sovereignty. The point however is that this conflict within the world-system, this weakening of Spanish world dominance, made it possible for the bourgeoisie of the United Provinces to maneuver to maximize *its* interest.[42]

Peripheral societies in the contemporary world system find themselves in a position analogous to the Netherlands of the sixteenth century. Not only are the core powers struggling for dominions or allies, they are heavily invested in local economies. That involvement goes some distance toward explaining the nature of underdevelopment, which is the central issue in national revolts. Nevertheless, the world systems *perspective* is just that, a broad angle of vision allowing us to identify forces that only come alive in concrete historical settings. Like the peasant revolt thesis, this perspective adds a valuable ingredient to a more discerning approach.

A third theoretical approach based on political conflict is best represented in Tilly's work as previously introduced. Having addressed the conceptual problem of revolution with a combination of revolutionary situation and revolutionary outcome continua, the theoretical question then centers on the proximate causes of multiple sovereignty and power transfer. Tilly is fully cognizant of the world system and "longer historical view" that traces revolutionary causation to "the rise and fall of centralized states, the expansion and contraction of national markets, the concentration and dispersion of control over property." But his explanation is cast at the middle range of political contention, providing a necessary complement to theoretical integration.[43]

Since revolutionary situations and outcomes may develop independently (or do not determine one another), their proximate causes must be sought in separate sets of conditions. Multiple sovereignty characterizing a revolutionary situation depends first on the appearance, or better the mobilization, of contenders advancing alternative exclusive claims to control of the governing polity. This may be occasioned by conflict within dominant classes or by increased suffering. Second, there has to be a commitment to the alternative claims advanced on the part of significant segments of the population. Ironically, this is often a result of government action stemming from its sudden failure to meet obligations (e.g., employment or protection) or unexpected demands on the population (e.g., taxes or conscription). Mobilization arising from these first two conditions is not necessarily revolutionary or counterrevolutionary, something that depends upon the coalitions potential rebels make and whether through those they seize some portion of government in a manner that is honored by others outside the coalition. Third, revolutionary situations are caused by governmental inaction through an unwillingness or incapacity to suppress alternative claims.

Revolutionary outcomes are also analyzed in three sets of conditions. First, the greater extensiveness of the revolutionary situation increases the likelihood of a transfer of power. Second, however, the coalitions formed between members and challengers of the polity may work against basic changes in power relationships. Much depends upon the negotiations and stability of coalitions. Finally, few extensive transfers of power are accomplished without disaffection in the armed forces of the polity. Tilly is prudently cautious about the permanent consequences of a revolution or revolt, particularly those "further structural changes" involving a redistribution of resources or improvement in the general quality of life. Such uncommon results are traceable to the extent of structural alteration occurring under multiple sovereignty and of transfer of power among classes.

The final theoretical approach summarizes some of the previous themes at the level of social class and the state, moving squarely into the realm of general revolutionary outcomes. Moore's work exemplifies this approach, particularly his earlier book that accounts for the social and economic conditions of modernization that led different nations along the paths of democratic, fascist, and communist political systems.[44] The first and last of these outcomes were revolutionary in bourgeois (England, France, United States) and peasant (Russia, China) forms. To simplify greatly, the conditions separating these trajectories involved the opportunity and vitality of emerging capitalist classes, the extent to which commercialization invaded agriculture and undermined feudal arrangements of land and aristocratic power, the extent to which peasant communities survived this onslaught, the relationships between the state and the landed aristocracy and merchants, but fundamentally the political mechanisms that accomplished surplus extraction in economic modernization.

Although the theory of peasant revolution is heavily indebted to Moore, before much of it was written he observed,

The shortcoming of all these hypotheses is that they focus too much attention on the peasantry. A moment's reflection on the course of any specific preindustrial rebellion reveals that one cannot understand it without reference to the actions of the upper classes that in large measure provoked it. Another noticeable feature of rebellions in agrarian societies is their tendency to take on the character of the society against which they rebel. . . . Before looking at the peasantry, it is necessary to look at the whole society.[45]

History concerned with the whole society discovers that revolutions arise from characteristic alignments between urban and rural groups. The potential for peasant revolution exists in precapitalist agrarian institutions and peasant communities that are neither bound to the upper classes nor undermined by commercialization.

Whether or not this potential becomes politically effective depends on the possibility of a fusion between peasant grievances and those of other strata. By themselves the peasants have never been able to accomplish a revolution. . . . The allies that peasant discontent can find depends upon the stage of economic development that a country had reached and more specific historical circumstances . . . [among

those a] major revolutionary ally was the urban crowd in Paris . . .
[and] without urban leaders it is unlikely that the peasant could have
organized the Red Army.[46]

The French Revolution demonstrated the converse, where "no matter
how radical the city was, it could do nothing without the help of the
peasant."[47]

Recent works have extended this approach. Skocpol's comparative study of the French, Russian, and Chinese revolutions is distinguished by its treatment of the state as an actor (rather than an arena)
in the unfolding of potentially revolutionary events. Tilly and Moore
both comment on the fact that the state may be responsible for initiating a revolutionary chain of events, but Skocpol's fuller account
demonstrates many of the national and international circumstances
that explain the state's disastrous management of the crisis.[48]

Summarizing the theoretical orientation that informs this study,
the focus is on national revolts understood (hypothesized) as a causally
unitary field including phenomena that vary by degrees of contestatory situations and power outcomes from insurrection to revolution
within the development process. The approach effects a merger of
developmental and revolutionary theory as necessary allies in the explanation of modern rebellions, thereby turning the first from its grim
certainty of underdevelopment and the second from its classical exclusivity. Four theoretical perspectives on revolution (peasant revolt,
world systems, political conflict, and social class and the state) provide the necessary integration of issues and questions to apply on new
terrain for the purpose of evaluating old explanations and, when it is
called for, generating new ones.

Comparative Method

The comparative historical method employed here has a close affinity
with the theoretical orientation. Obviously, the intent is to study and
compare a set of national revolts that represent major, perhaps even
prototypical, processes according to the earlier definitional criteria of
scope, duration, and socioeconomic import. I have pursued a case
study design in the belief that only through detailed historical comparisons are we likely to reveal the essential causes and critical comparative dimensions of the revolutionary process. Broad comparisons
of a large number of countries or regions based on aggregate social
indicators may be justified for specific descriptive purposes or, con-

ceivably, for analytic use somewhere down the line. At present, however, they involve serious problems of validity, typically relying on newspaper or periodical accounts for their evidence of "social protest"[49] and tending to minimize the constraints of this method by recourse to formalistic, ahistorical, and psychological theorizing.[50] By contrast, the comparative study design allows depth, validity, and construction of appropriate theoretical categories, based not on unconstrained or esthetic choice of cases but on their strategic selection with respect to certain theoretical dimensions.

These considerations require, of course, cases that are amply documented. Beyond that, the criteria for selecting revolts involves theoretical issues and fertile comparisons that recommend cases spanning the major geographical reaches of the Third World (Africa, Asia, and Latin America), particularly as these reflect distinctive continental experiences of underdevelopment and different patterns or "moments" of the interplay of world systemic and indigenous social factors. It is important that differences exist in the timing and nature of colonialism as well as in the process by which independence is achieved. In that much the design parallels the work of Adas, who "intentionally selected examples that differ widely in terms of geographical location, sociocultural context, the nature and timing of European colonial penetration, and the patterns displayed by the movements themselves."[51] Concern for modern national revolts and the fortuitous and explosive historical events in the Third World since World War II recommends a period extending from the late 1940s into the 1960s. It would be valuable, too, for the case studies to reflect differences in their trajectories and manner of resolution. Differences on this account would enable explanation of contrasting patterns of struggle and degrees of transformation. Finally, a number of potential cases are excluded for lack of documentation or because they seem relatively minor events, do not fit the contours of national revolts (e.g., ethnic and separatist movements), or have been frequently studied as instances of "true" revolutions (e.g., Algeria, Cuba, Vietnam). The latter consideration is not a principled one but is recommended by the practical necessity of comparing a manageable number of cases, the desire to plow some fresh ground, and the relative ease with which available explanations of those revolutions could be compared.

These considerations resulted in the choice of the Huk rebellion in the Philippines, the Colombian Violencia, and the Mau Mau revolt in Kenya. Despite long histories, the critical revolutionary events took place from the late 1940s through the 1950s. Although all three have been treated elsewhere as instances of peasant rebellion, their histories suggest the possibility of urban and national upheaval in which the global political economy played a decisive role. In that sense they become critical case studies for prevailing theory and the surest route to theoretical refinement, if it can be shown that events once thought to be explained by a particular theory, despite some inconsistencies, in fact follow more directly from a broader theory that also eliminates the inconsistencies.

The revolutions were acted out on very different colonial terrains. In the Philippines U.S. imperialism had replaced and altered the earlier Spanish colony. In Colombia the Iberian conquest 400 years earlier had created a classical colonial society that, nevertheless, evolved with independence after 1820 and twentieth-century neocolonialism. Kenya experienced a much briefer (c.1880–1963) era of British rule and the distinctive features of settler colonialism. Despite these differences in the process of incorporation into the world system, and others based on indigenous socioeconomic organization, the cases provide many instructive parallels. They illustrate similar patterns of underdevelopment, land use, labor control, urban growth, regionalism, and nationalist politics—parallels that are sufficiently strong and general reflections of underdevelopment to suggest that the cases are theoretically comparable as wombs of revolution.

They also moved along different trajectories. In a complex sense explored later, their successes varied. The Mau Mau revolt was followed by important economic and political reforms culminating in national independence. The Colombian Violencia produced a new National Front government whose political reforms led to changes in economic organization. The Huk rebellion was the most effectively repressed in a process that led to major changes in the state and its dependent alliance with the United States. These different outcomes invite comparative explanation in terms of peripheral status, the nature of the revolution and counterrevolution, and, generally, the lineup of forces in the conflicts.

Those familiar with the relevant histories, particularly the Colombian, may question its inclusion among these experiences of national revolt. It seems quite different. By the 1940s Colombia was far removed from colonial domination, and the Violencia is legendary among modern instances of vendetta, fratricide, and localized civil war. The full rationale for its inclusion must await chapter 3, where the several forms of violent conflict are recognized. I shall argue that among those forms the most pervasive, the kind that did more to let loose the others, grew out of class and political struggles over the control of the state and the benefits of developmental policy. The issues that animated the greatest part of this complex struggle were national rather than local, and they clearly divided classes and mobilized groups seeking to transform the state. The Colombian case is different from the others, just as they all are from one another, but deeper parallels that emerge in the conclusions of this analysis seem to sustain its comparative logic.

Concerning certain foci and limitations of the study, first, it does not attempt to follow a positivist logic or quasi-experimental design, comparing these cases with similarly situated societies, or "negative cases," that experienced little or no revolutionary movement. When judiciously executed such a design can be instructive.[52] However, that effort is beyond the scope of this study and not entirely appropriate since, unlike Wolf's study of victorious peasant wars,[53] the focus is not on three cases of similar revolutionary outcomes but on three distinctive processes of national revolt that followed rather different courses and produced different results. Comparable "negative cases" are not easily conceived or really germane, although it is desirable to compare these three with a broader range of cases and trajectories in the spirit of Moore's analysis of the different routes to democracy, socialism, and fascism. Consequently, in the concluding chapters we shall have occasion to compare the causes and outcomes of these revolts with other modern revolutions and with changes in nonrevolutionary Third World countries.

Nor is this a study of the strategy and practice of revolution. Attention will focus on the historical development and causes of revolt rather than the details of military engagements. Nevertheless we shall not eschew the activities of real people engaged in risky and indeterminate struggles for the illusory precision of broad historical-comparative generality. I shall attempt to steer a course between the twin obstacles flagged by two of the foremost revolutionary historians: Hobsbawm, who notes that "the danger of this type of study lies in the temptation to isolate the phenomenon of overt crisis from the wider context of a society undergoing transformation,"[54] and Moore, who cautions, "There is a tendency, I believe, to over-emphasize the underlying long-run social trends behind revolutionary outbreaks as well as dramatic peaceful changes, and to under-estimate the importance of control over the instruments of violence—the army and the police—and the significance of decisions taken by political leaders."[55]

In summary, this study provides a historical and comparative analysis of strategically selected national revolts generated in different circumstances of underdevelopment within the global system and resolved in distinctive ways. It is suggested that these cases represent a new form of revolution by contrast to the imagery, concepts, and theoretical explanations provided by treatments of classical revolutions. Rather than having our thinking dominated by antiquated models that exclude or denigrate major contemporary events, I shall speak of national revolts as distinctive kinds of social conflicts in today's developing world. Once properly conceived and compared in full historical context, the explanation of national revolts proceeds from three fundamental assumptions: that they are *inter*societal phenomena shaped in critical ways by the global political economy; that they are intra*societal* phenomena rather than rural or urban, peasant or proletarian affairs; and that they are caused and shaped by the interplay of state and society, economy and polity. And, again, these provide hypotheses whose utility depends upon the comparative histories.

The Inquiry

Three chapters that follow provide the historical material essential for understanding backdrops, causes, and consequences of the national revolts. Under the latter headings the next two chapters synthesize and compare cases using the framework sketched and in light of the pertinent theories. At bottom all the rest of this book is an excursion of inductive theory building. Accordingly, the raw material in chapters 2, 3, and 4 is developed in the character of a theoretical narrative.[56] I have attempted, of course, objectivity and reasonable thoroughness in the case studies. In the hope for serendipity, which seems to have been rewarded, I have tried to let the narrative flow in its own direction once the theoretical terrain was charted. Yet I do not pretend that the data speak for themselves or speak to other theorists in the same tones. My arrangement of the material and my interpretation of its significance reflect the concerns outlined in the previous sections.

Because the cases were selected to illuminate experiences of underdevelopment and encounters with the changing world economy, the histories endeavor first to describe the evolution of colonialism— the brand of colonialism involved with its reception by the indigenous society. The cases differ in this respect, but not in the general headings under which effects are measured and contrasts established. The theoretical narrative suggests that in each case the important questions are when colonialism occurred, who did the colonizing, with what motives, how the precolonial society was organized, what the institutional arrangements for implementing colonialism were, how effective they were, what the reactions of local society was, and how these arrangements changed owing to internal contradictions and external shifts in the world system. Second, the histories describe the origins and evolution of the popular movements, the struggles for and after independence, that fostered the revolts. Revolutionary movements develop in interaction with the trials of underdevelopment and the constraints of the colonial or postcolonial state.

Thus far the evidence and the argument it will inform are cast at two levels of analysis, the world system and the local society. The first level consists of those broad historical influences (e.g., conquest, mercantilism, market integration) that are transmitted from the dominant states to the emerging (and underdeveloping) Third World in roughly uniform ways. The second level shows how the pressures emanating from capitalist production in the core produce different results in peripheral societies depending upon their own exploitable resources, social organization, and a score of other circumstances. Much theorizing about revolution relies upon evidence gleaned only at the second level and therefore runs the risk of spuriously interpreting local reactions as fundamental causes. Conversely, analyses cast exclusively at the level of global influences on revolution "may help to explain its occasion, but not its character."[57] Briefly, these are the salient concerns that guide the selection and narrative of the historical evidence.

Implicit in all of this is the ambition to evaluate theory. The great virtue of case studies is the opportunity they provide for fine-grained, comparative assessments of theoretical propositions. Within the limits of the three-case research design, some of the notions previously reviewed hold remarkably well, others not at all, and new ones appear as the whole enterprise moves toward reinterpretation. For the moment this means that the uninnocent histories are organized to answer questions such as: who revolts (peasants, urban workers, both, neither), in what sorts of economic and social conditions, and under what banner (class interest, political rights, cultural values).

Moving from an interpretive presentation of historical case studies to the evaluation and reformulation of theory requires an intermediate step taken here in elaboration of the framework based on revolutionary situations and outcomes. Accordingly, once the empirical foundation has been laid, chapter 5 analyzes the extent to which multiple sovereignty attended each national revolt and, therefore, the degree of its revolutionary situation. Forecasting the conclusions, each case qualifies as a revolutionary situation. Rival claimants enjoyed sovereignty in different geographical regions and among various sections of the populace. The revolutionary situation was most advanced in Kenya, intermediate in Colombia, and least in the Philippines. The rest of the chapter explains why.

In a parallel analysis chapter 6 assesses the amount of displacement of ruling groups and of old politics. The magnitude of revolutionary outcomes assumes, through no contrivance, the same order among the three cases. National revolt in Kenya produces the greatest amount of change with independence and local government. Colombia experienced moderate progressive reforms, and the Philippines changed least, becoming in ways more regressive through counterrevolution. The sense in which these changes may be labeled degrees of success is subtle, depending upon what other standards are employed—whether, for example, the question is how the changes differed from the past or from what might have been. The revolts produced important changes, some progressive, and some new forms of inequality. Nowhere was there a "basis transformation" bringing forth liberty, equality, or much less brotherhood.

Does this prove that national revolts are beyond the pale of revolutionary analysis? I shall argue the contrary on two counts. The first is that the outcomes just described are not qualitatively different from the fruits of other revolutions that, for circumstantial reasons, may or may not be awarded that title. The second is more theoretical and holds that the causes of these national revolts are the same as the causes of those celebrated events that custom leads us to call revolutions.

The causal argument is the principal subject of chapter 5. Having established that revolutionary situations exist in degrees, the question becomes how they arise. Contrary to the wisdom of theories about "modernization" and political development, each of the societies has a long history of protest that by the 1920s had become articulated in such modern forms of political organization as ethnic associations, labor unions, and political parties. Their advent corresponded roughly to the time at which the terms of incorporation into the world economic system shifted from commercial adventurism to essential exploitations in the strategies of core nations. Characteristically those strategies involved the creation of export agriculture in the periphery that would provide a stable flow of raw materials to the core at the same time it generated a narrow, but increasingly dependent, internal market for core exports. Among the sectors of the colonial economy affected (e.g., mining, crafts), agriculture was critical in these rural societies as incorporation led to a series of catastrophic changes: alienation and concentration of land, coerced wage labor, and related forms of primitive accumulation. One theoretically salient consequence was increased urban migration—the literal creation of urban poverty and a proletariat divided between the new service and the informal, subsistence economies. But these new urban groups were intimately and institutionally linked to rural society through such mechanisms of dependent development as labor registration, absentee ownership, and the export motif linking the fields that grew fewer subsistence crops to the docks where costly imports including food were exchanged for the surfeit of a few local products.

The exploitation of this system was felt most keenly in particular export regions and among selected social classes. As the peasant revolt thesis suggests, it was indeed the middle peasantry that suffered most among rural classes and organized early. But the middle peasantry had its urban proletarian equivalent comprised, among others, of transportation workers, service sector personnel, and public functionaries. Not only did these urban and rural groups form their own political alliances, they were sometimes aggregated as a matter of state policy. The grievances experienced by these groups had similar origins in the political practice of underdevelopment and their organizers recognized that fact as it facilitated coalescence of the popular movement.

Economic exploitation played an enormous part in the development of these movements, perhaps the major part if such a calculation can be validly made—which I doubt. For economic grievances cannot be separated from the cultural forms in which they are experienced and understood, nor from the political forms in which they are expressed. Each of the national revolts was the product of a popular movement begun in response to the methods of primitive accumulation and nurtured in the increasing disruption occasioned by economic reorganization for the ends of dependent capitalism. Yet the resistance mounted by the popular movements was fundamentally cultural and political. One important discovery in the case studies is that each national revolt was immediately preceded by a sharp reversal in the economy *coinciding with* an abrupt cancellation or repression of political gains that the popular movement had achieved *within* the legal norms of conventional politics. Under this counterpunch from the ''system,'' the popular movements reeled into a revolutionary situation as an aroused political consciousness shifted support to the claims of rival sovereignty. Economic grievances were necessary conditions, but their mobilizing potential was only realized in the sufficient conditions of political organization rooted in cultural tradition.

The final revolutionary pass came when the ruling group, dimly recognizing the revolutionary situation, attempted to suppress it with officially initiated violence. That decision was not blindly reactionary or unrelated to other strategic considerations. It coincided with special crises of modernization faced by the ruling groups, occasions in which internal economic contradictions and externally proffered opportunities required a dramatic shift in policy which these weak states could only hope to effect through a realigned and reconsolidated coalition of interests. The ruling groups reasoned, or intuited, that an attack on the popular movement would vouchsafe the alliances necessary for achieving their version of economic modernization. Of course they miscalculated, but much less in their reading of coalitional strategies than in their ignorance of the strength and disposition of the popular movement. Having attempted, and seemingly succeeded, with the system's own rules for redress, having played fair only to meet with violent bad faith, the movements' reluctant turns to rebellion were invigorated with moral justification.

In the concluding section of chapter 5 this scenario of revolutionary causation is compared with some of the more durable theories, including some designed to explain classical revolutions. In many ways the events and their causal significance are the same. For example, the alienation and concentration of land, proletarianization of small-holders, organic connections among the peasantry and urban proletariat, the national organization of popular resistance, and other causes in different combinations—all are as germane to the revolutions in France, China, Russia, Mexico, Algeria, and Cuba as they are to the national revolts in Colombia, Kenya, and the Philippines.

After assessing the magnitude of revolutionary outcomes in chapter 6, the analysis endeavors to explain why Kenya's national revolt produced greater change than the mildly progressive reform in Colombia or the reaction in the Philippines. Coincident results in the sense of identical rankings of the three cases on the degree to which a revolutionary situation existed and the degree of change, obviously, suggests that more extensive revolutionary situations produce greater displacement of ruling groups and policies. But this is no mere tautology, since the concepts are separately defined and measured. It is a fact that calls for its own explanation. That is, no logical necessity requires that an advanced revolutionary situation should finally produce important postrevolutionary results, especially ones of a redistributive sort. Indeed, the irregularity of such an association is a favorite chestnut of critics of revolution from Burke to Chaliand.[58]

The association is analyzed according to the "internal" and "external" circumstances of each national revolt (recognizing the superficiality of this dichotomy). Internally the key circumstance was the structure of class power and the extent to which it was altered as a result of the struggle. In the Philippines the old structure of power dominated by landowners and agribusiness was, if anything, enhanced by the defeat of the Huk rebellion. Kenya, at the other extreme, experienced a major transfer of power from the white settlers and colonial administration to African groups and the bureaucracy of an independent state. Although far from egalitarian, the new arrangement of class power was more diversified. In the intermediate case Colombia's old elite, while retaining political power, introduced reforms that they desperately hoped would end the Violencia.

These outcomes are all the more understandable in view of external constraints. The Kenya colony had become a British albatross by the 1950s. England wanted to retain the economic advantages of trade and investment while withdrawing from costly colonial governance. Similarly, the economic stake of the United States in Colombia was never great by contrast to other Latin American countries, and there were no objections to liberalizing reforms provided the "communist guerrillas" were held down. Not so in the Philippines, which continues to be a vital stone in the ring of U.S. defenses and economic colonies. National political elites and agricultural interests joined military and "aid" missionaries from the United States to ensure the continuity, indeed the fortification, of class rule. The critical condition here is "a tolerant or permissive world context."[59]

As these fragmentary observations suggest, revolutionary outcomes are sometimes meager, bringing us back to the issue of successful revolution. Some may argue that the case studies (or perhaps one or two of them) do not merit treatment as revolutions because of their compromised outcomes—they did not produce, after all, basic transformations. Or did they? My response involves several points, including the earlier argument that many problems are avoided if we define revolution as "an *attempt* . . . to seize state power on the part of political forces avowedly opposed not merely to the existing regime but to the existing social order as a whole."[60] Second, of course, is the argument based on the causal unity of "true" revolutions and "mere" revolts, however individual cases are classified. This I believe is the strongest argument since it is supported empirically and carries the theoretical advantage of suggesting explanations of greater and lesser success. Finally, I shall argue at the end of chapter 6 that the outcomes in the three cases of national revolt are *not* meager by contrast to the fruits, sometimes bitter, of revolutions that merit the name. Although I think it fruitless to belabor what is a "basic transformation," I do not see how Kenya's independence or Colombia's National Front (both safely regarded as directly, if not singularly, the result of national revolt) can be considered anything else. But the clearest resolution of the problems comes when we turn all this critical accumen on the results of revolutions that "deserve the name." Did the shift in class power and the redistributive effects of reform in Mexico go all that further than in Kenya, enough to justify their separation into categories prefaced by "true" and "mere"? In the end I argue not only that it is unfair and invalid to make such distinctions, it is unnecessary.

The issue of nomenclature can be taken a step further by inquiring into the circumstances in which national upheavals are labeled revolution, rebellion, and revolt.[61] Depending upon who wins and the political consequences of how they characterize their victory, very similar struggles are later designated as *the* revolution or this or that revolt in the political lexicon. For example, the political consolidation of Kenya after Mau Mau required that the momentousness of the "revolt" be downplayed since its tribal and anti-imperial character would surely have made it difficult to reconcile white Kenyans and the plurality of minority tribes to the new government. What uncritical historians and politicians facing other problems accept today as African revolutions do not differ qualitatively.

Lest this conceptual matter cloud our vision, I want to conclude on another note from chapters 6 and 7, where it is clear that revolutions and national revolts do make a difference and sometimes even a difference for the better. The argument is simple: more people share more of the goods of society than before. That result is far from guaranteed and always has to be balanced against the new forms of inequality that revolution brings. In some cases, and here I would include the Philippines, the latter overshadows the former, and only sentimental reasons suggest that the revolution was for the better. I expect that the most constructive words this book has to say about revolutions come in connection with what kind of imagery we should have about them and what we should expect from them. National revolts are complex and highly contingent events that belie deterministic or timeless mechanistic models of explanation. The imagery and appropriate explanatory theme, like "the experience of twentieth-century revolution is . . . a matter not of plucking the ripe fruits of protracted and ineluctable processes of social development, but rather of contriving not to miss a bus which may set out only once, if indeed it sets out at all."[62]

Notes

1. Dunn, *Modern Revolutions*.
2. Leys, *Underdevelopment in Kenya*, p. 20.
3. Hobsbawm, "Social History," p. 39.
4. Hermassi, "Toward a Comparative Study," p. 222.
5. *Ibid.*, pp. 226–27.
6. *Ibid.*, p. 232.
7. Skocpol, *States and Social Revolutions*, p. 4.
8. *Ibid.*
9. *Ibid.*, p. 5.
10. Hermassi, "Toward a Comparative Study," p. 223.
11. Aya, "Theories of Revolution Reconsidered."
12. Chaliand, *Revolution in the Third World*.
13. Hagopian, *The Phenomenon of Revolution*, pp. 1, 10–11.
14. Stinchcombe, "Social Structure and Organizations," p. 169.
15. Tilly, *Mobilization*, p. 190.
16. Tilly, "Does Modernization Breed Revolution?" p. 445.
17. Tilly, *Mobilization*, p. 190.
18. *Ibid.*, p. 198.
19. Aya, "Theories of Revolution Reconsidered"; Skocpol, "Explaining Revolutions."
20. See Hobsbawm, *Primitive Rebels;* Wolf, *Peasant Wars;* Alavi, "Peasants and Revolution"; Scott, *Moral Economy;* Paige, *Agrarian Revolution*.
21. Hobsbawm, *Age of Revolution;* Moore, *Social Origins;* Rudé, *Paris and London;* Alavi, "Peasants and Revolution"; Wolf, *Peasant Wars*.
22. Paige, *Agrarian Revolution*.
23. Hobsbawm, *Primitive Rebels;* Moore, *Social Origins;* Paige, *Agrarian Revolution;* Chirot and Ragin, "Market, Tradition, and Peasant Rebellion."
24. Moore, *Social Origins*.
25. Hunt, *Revolution and Urban Politics;* Nash, *Urban Crucible*.
26. Hobsbawm, *Primitive Rebels*.
27. McDonald, *Urban Origins of Rural Revolution;* Kau, "Urban and Rural Strategies."
28. Wolf, *Peasant Wars;* Stenson, "Communist Revolt in Malaya"; White, "Vietnamese Revolutionary Alliance"; Tilly, "Town and Country."
29. Oppenheimer, *Urban Guerrilla;* Moss, *Urban Guerrillas*.
30. Oppenheimer, *Urban Guerrilla*.
31. Tilly, "Town and Country"; Scott, "Hegemony."
32. Skocpol, *States and Social Revolutions*, pp. 112–13.
33. Scott, "Hegemony," p. 267.
34. Skocpol, *States and Social Revolutions*, pp. 114–15.
35. *Ibid.*, p. 117.
36. Scott, *Moral Economy*, is the most compelling account of the moral economy and changing fortune of peasant society.
37. Slater, "Colonialism"; McGee, *Urbanization Process;* Walton, "Accumulation and Comparative Urban Systems."
38. Wolf, *Peasant Wars*, p. 301; emphasis added.
39. Wallerstein, *Modern World-System; Modern World-System II:* Kaplan, ed., *Social Change*.
40. Eberhard, "Problems in Historical Sociology"; Hopkins, "World-Systems Analysis."

41. Hobsbawm, *Age of Revolution;* Skocpol, *States and Social Revolutions.*
42. Wallerstein, *Modern World-System,* p. 210.
43. Tilly, *Mobilization,* pp. 207, 200–22.
44. Moore, *Social Origins.*
45. *Ibid.,* p. 457.
46. *Ibid.,* pp. 479–82.
47. *Ibid.,* p. 92.
48. Skocpol, *States and Social Revolutions.*
49. Paige, *Agrarian Revolution;* Gurr, "Civil Strife."
50. Gurr, "Civil Strife"; Feierabend, Feierabend, and Nesvole, "Social Change and Political Violence."
51. Adas, *Prophets of Rebellion,* p. xxiii.
52. Cf. Skocpol, *States and Social Revolutions;* Moore, *Injustice,* ch. 10.
53. Wolf, *Peasant Wars.*
54. Hobsbawm, "Social History," p. 39.
55. Moore, *Injustice,* pp. 82–83.
56. Stinchcombe, *Theoretical Methods in Social History.*
57. Thompson, *English Working Class,* p. 543.
58. Edmund Burke, *Reflections on the Revolution in France;* Chaliand, *Revolution in the Third World.*
59. Goldfrank, "Theories of Revolution."
60. Lasch, quoted in Aya, "Theories of Revolution Reconsidered," p. 43; emphasis added.
61. Aya, "Theories of Revolution Reconsidered," p. 46 and fn. 32; Wuthnow, "On Suffering, Rebellion, and the Moral Order."
62. Dunn, *Modern Revolutions,* p. 233.

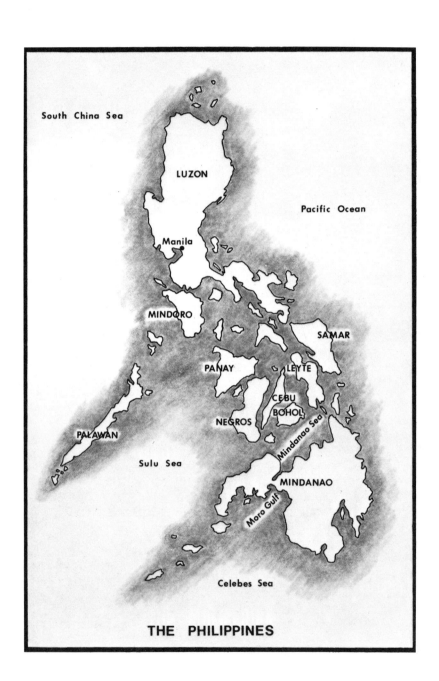

South China Sea

LUZON

Pacific Ocean

Manila

MINDORO

SAMAR

PANAY

LEYTE

CEBU

BOHOL

NEGROS

PALAWAN

Mindanao Sea

Sulu Sea

MINDANAO

Moro Gulf

Celebes Sea

THE PHILIPPINES

CHAPTER TWO

The Huk Rebellion

IF NATIONAL REVOLTS are broadly contestatory processes, not the least of the dispute surrounds exactly what name the whole commotion should go by. Revolts often go by many names coined by contestants in the struggle and in its subsequent interpretation. To the victors may go the more or less exclusive copyright to the revolution's name and all that it implies for what the fuss was about. For example, insurgent victories and the effort to consolidate them in a new social order may result in defining the events that led to this pass as "revolution," although defeat or compromised victories may be designated as "rebellion" in the hope of restoring some form of order—all quite apart from the character or momentousness of the preceding events.[1] Doubtless this is another part of the conceptual problem, which I shall return to later, and the fact that history records so few "revolutions."

The Huk rebellion, accordingly, is an interesting misnomer. The term *Huk* is an abbreviation for another abbreviation, "Hukbalahap," referring to the Philippine native language (Tagalog, the most common of a variety) phrase, Hukbo ng Bayan laban sa Hapon, meaning the People's Anti-Japanese Army. However, what is commonly referred to as the Huk rebellion is the postwar movement that grew out of the Hukbalahap resistance and was designated by its participants as the HMB, signifying Hukbong Mapagpalaya ng Bayan, or People's Liberation Army. Although I shall follow convention here, it is important to keep in mind that where authorities chose to define their task as one of putting down a vestigial rebellion from the days of Japanese occupation, other participants renamed postwar activities as a distinctive new stage of national liberation.

The Huk rebellion had its origins in a long history of protest and revolt beginning with Spanish colonization in the late sixteenth century and continuing, after U.S. conquest, into the 1920s and 1930s, as the frequency of organized revolt increased and moved from local and provincial to national levels. The Huk rebellion itself spanned roughly the years 1946–1953. At its peak, between 1949 and 1951, the revolution attracted some 15,000 armed guerrilla fighters and, perhaps, a half-million sympathizers and provisioners in the villages and cities.[2] The first figure is low if one accepts others estimating more than 8,000 casualties and 14,000 captured and surrendered between 1950 and 1956.[3] With some exceptions the movement was concentrated in the most populous zones of the island republic, the area of Central Luzon, including Manila and four fertile agricultural provinces devoted mainly to rice and sugar cultivation.

Although the movement flourished in these largely peasant zones, it was joined by tenants, small-holders, and rural wage workers, especially in the sugar mill centrals. Moreover, the HMB was explicitly linked at various times and in varying degrees with national political movements and parties, the national (urban and rural) labor movement, and the Philippine Communist Party (PKP). The HMB was concerned with and mobilized around a variety of issues ranging from land tenure and tenant crop-shares, wages, and labor conditions to global concerns in the presence of U.S. colonial policy (free trade and the sugar-export economy)—all summarized in the nationalistic drive for complete independence. Although many of the events of the Huk rebellion centered on matters directly related to agrarian organization (since the society was largely rural and the economy based mainly on agricultural export), the ultimate origins of these problems lay at the intersection of national politics and neocolonial dependence on the United States. The conditions and policies associated with dependency affected acutely the various classes of the agrarian economy. But they also affected the urban and industrial sectors, which were involved at various times both directly and indirectly in the revolt.

Incorporation of the Philippines into the world economic system began in the late sixteenth century with Spanish colonization. The

ILOCOS NORTE

CAGAYAN

ABRA

MOUNTAIN PROVINCE

ILOCOS SUR

ISABELA

LA UNION

San Fernando

Baguio

NUEVA VIZCAYA

San Carlos

PANGASINAN

San Jose

La Paz

NUEVA ECIJA

ZAMBALES

TARLAC

Tarlac

Arayat

PAMPANGA

San Fernando

BULACAN

BATAAN

Cavite

Quezon City

Manila

Santa Cruz

CAVITE

LAGUNA

CAMARINES NORTE

BATANGAS

QUEZON

THE PHILIPPINES: Luzon
Principal Areas of
Rebel Activity

form of this incorporation shifted in the 1820s with the final collapse of the Manila galleon trade and the independence of Mexico from Spain, which severed the key link from the Philippine–Spanish chain of trade. Although the islands remained under Spanish rule (with brief British occupations of Manila begun in 1762–1764), the early nineteenth-century transformation of the economy was initiated by English and Chinese traders. The major reorientation of the Philippine economy toward export production was not a Spanish innovation. In response to this challenge, however, Spain adopted a series of measures to encourage local development and export. Throughout the balance of the nineteenth century what had once been an entrepôt economy turned increasingly to the export of agricultural commodities, importing machinery and British textiles, as trade flows shifted away from China to England and the United States.[4]

The wholesale incorporation of the Philippines came with U.S. possession in 1898 as a result of the Spanish American War. Beginning in 1896 and continuing through the early years of U.S. rule, Philippine nationalist forces engaged in an unsuccessful war of independence. The decisive transition from Spanish rule was marked by Admiral Dewey's Battle of Manila Bay (May 1898) and the subsequent taking of Manila with the aid of Philippine independence forces (August 1898)—encouraged to believe, by their own accounts, that the United States was only interested in their freedom from Spain. By the Treaty of Paris (December 1898) the islands were acquired along with Guam, Puerto Rico, and a Spanish promise to abandon Cuba, in exchange for U.S. $20 million—suggesting the dubious connection between the Caribbean spoils of war and colonial ambitions in the Far East. Billed as the purchase price of the islands, the money was actually designated for payment of the debt Spain had incurred in suppressing the independence movement and to overcome any objections from European creditors to this new imperial role of the United States. Following military occupation in early 1899, the United States fought a three-and-one-half-year war of "pacification" against the popular forces of Philippine independence and resistance in a campaign that presaged the Vietnam War with destruction of native villages and civilian population sympathizers.[5] The significance of these relatively recent events that provide the context of rebellion must be sought among the unusual patterns of colonialism in the Philippines.

The colonial society encountered by the forces of American occupation was a rather special type by contrast to the more typical products of Spanish rule and Creole independence in Mexico and the

Andean region. Colonialism in the Philippines was less rapacious, indigenous society less thoroughly penetrated and Hispanized, although mestizoization occurred among the Filipino and Chinese upper class. In the Philippines, Spaniards adapted more to precolonial social organization and the precapitalist economy than they did in Mexico and Peru. Precapitalist agriculture and sharecropping systems were maintained and modified with changes toward individual ownership and large estates. Native principals retained some of their wealth and political power and were used by the Spaniards as brokers in dealings with the population of cultivators. An astounding datum in the annals of Spanish colonial penetration was that by the end of the first colony in 1900 only an estimated 10 percent of the population spoke Spanish.[6] This contrasts with the former colonies of the Americas, where a large majority were Spanish-speaking by 1900, with the exception of isolated Indian communities. These observations suggest the uniqueness of Spanish colonialism in the Philippines, but they do not mean that it was benign.

The centerpiece of Spanish colonialism, the economic raison d'être of the colony, was the Manila galleon trade between China and the Orient (e.g., India) and Acapulco (and beyond to Europe), in which, via Manila, the silks, spices, and porcelain of the East were exchanged for Mexican silver and gold.[7]

The galleon trade occurred between 1565 and 1815 and was the decisive factor in the development of the colony as a commercial entrepôt of decadent luxury, boom-or-bust fortunes, and essentially unproductive activity—by contrast to the promotion of opportunities for trade of indigenous products and for industry. The colonial economy produced little new wealth in preference for the exchange of commodities (and the speculation in commercial ventures that that entrained) and the influx of foreign goods that not only discouraged new local enterprise but displaced traditional industries such as textiles. By 1600 the galleon trade began to deteriorate, and efforts to revive the port in the 1750s failed because Spain chose not to open it to international free trade, thus losing advantages to British Singapore and Hong Kong.

The tradition of the Galleon monopoly was clearly incompatible with the new order to things. A memorial, drawn up in 1805 by royal treasury officials at Manila, was to contain this indictment of the ancient trade: "It is well known that the proceeds from the Galleon commerce have been of little benefit to agriculture and industry in the Philippines. Instead of realizing the great advantages that were promised by the fertility of these lands, the stream of silver which

has poured in from New Spain has only had the effect of rendering sterile those very advantages. For the profits are only divided among a small number of real merchants, a few of their hangers-on, some persons with influence in Manila, and the intermediaries in Mexico. The result is that, instead of promoting the welfare of the farmers and the artisans and of the other poor classes of those islands, it has been prejudicial to the state and to its inhabitants."[8]

Yet the indigenous population experienced colonial domination in ways that went beyond neglect and unfulfilled opportunities stemming from the commercial enclave economy. Outside Manila two Spanish institutions governed parts of the countryside. First, royal land grants, the *encomiendas*, were important in the early years, although they had declined by the middle of the eighteenth century.[9] The trustees of these lands, or *encomenderos*, directly exploited the natives by drafting labor and exacting tribute. Local village (*barangay*) society practiced traditional agriculture on communal land, although the use of sharecroppers was known as one of the privileges of the local governing stratum. The Spaniards concentrated this stratum into *caciques*, or local bosses, by appointing them tax collectors. Private ownership was introduced in a situation that allowed the *caciques* to extend their own land, driving former freeholders into the increasingly typical position of tenancy.

The second and more pervasive institution was the friar estates. In the Philippine countryside, which is to say everywhere except Manila, the clergy was more powerful than the colonial administrators because there were far more priests and because they played a greater role in creating a subject colony. In their pioneering capacity the priests were exempted from monastic vows and allowed to form religious corporations that acquired large tracts of land through purchase and outright land-grabbing that began to supplant the *encomiendas*, not to mention the communal holders. Adapting traditional practice for broader use, the friars propagated tenancy and sharecropping on estate lands. Lessees, or *inquilinos*, paid a fixed rate for the use of the land and, as intermediaries, themselves retained the sharecropping tenant, or *kasama*. In the late eighteenth century growing consumer demand in Manila and the opportunities in export trade led *caciques* to join the friars in this arrangement, which originated with the large haciendas. These practices "vastly extended landlordism. . . . Tenancy and commercialization of the economy together intensified and spread out from the Manila Bay core area."[10] The "underlying propulsive factor" in this wholesale reorganization of rural society was "the growing linkage of the country to world capitalism" created by British and Chinese traders.[11]

Land-grabbing and sponsorship of an exploitative tenancy system by the friar estates were parts of a broader set of abuses that became the chief target of native rebellions. The freebooting friars exacted taxes, tribute, exorbitant rents, forced labor, and personal services. People were denied commons privileges (e.g., grazing, wood gathering, fishing) on the land that had been usurped. Using funds donated to the church for "pious works," the clergy played an important role in commercial life, financing trade ventures to China and India, shippers on the galleon trade, and even the colonial government, in much the same capacity as a commercial bank and insurance company. The very arrival of Spanish intruders in 1565 prompted resistance that claimed the life of Ferdinand Magellan, but as colonialism took root, native revolts were motivated by the heavy extraction of taxes and tribute (especially during colonial wars), forced labor, conflicts with the friar estates over land, church domination, and the suppression of native religion. Phelan describes 5 "major uprisings" between 1580 and 1762, Crippen mentions 16 from 1601 to 1744, and others estimate more than 100 during the entire colonial period; Constantino's description of the early risings is most complete, documenting their cultural bases and growing political sophistication.[12] Cultivators on the *encomiendas* fought soldiers who came to collect tribute. In 1583 natives of Pampanga on the main island of Luzon were sent to work the modest gold mines of Ilocos and not allowed to return for the planting season. Famine in the following year spawned a revolt and an aborted plan to enter Manila and massacre all Spaniards. On the small island of Bohol in 1622, 2,000 people rose, burning four villages and their churches supervised by the Jesuits. Most of these revolts had nativistic wellsprings and traditional deities that exempted people from tribute. Economic grievances were expressed in religious wars and millenarianism.

But the pattern of resistance began to change in at least three important ways. First, the very success of heathen conversions led the people to adopt features of the Catholic religion in support of their protests. Second, divide and rule tactics of the Spaniards were partly successful in creating a privileged class of native chiefs and their followers from the more prosperous agricultural areas of Luzon, who joined Spanish soldiers in suppressing their fellows. Third, the Hispano-Dutch War of the Cloves from 1609 to 1648 increased demands for agricultural surplus and labor tribute just as it deepened class divisions and economic exploitation. The naval conflict, for example, required woodcutters, shipbuilders, and crews raised by manpower levies on the villages. As a result the new rebellions began to divide indigenous groups in struggles that combined class and religious motives. Some of these were nonrevolts in which opportunistic chiefs mobilized their forces to bargain for Spanish concessions in the new elite of *principales* (e.g., the office of village mayor and the *indulto de comercio,* or monopoly of local commerce). But others were vigorous and sustained, like the Boholano resistance, which survived for eighty-five years (1744–1829) in cohesive mountain communities that adopted their own Catholic faith.

A line can be drawn from this form of resistance to twentieth-century rebellions, a line running through the Tayabas revolt of 1841. In 1839 a man named Apolinario de la Cruz, later known as Brother Pule, attempted to join a monastic order in Manila but was denied because he was a native. He promptly founded the lay brotherhood Cofradía de San José, which attracted many adherents to its spiritual offices and its militant opposition to the friar estates. The Cofradía's retaliatory policy of admitting only "pure-blooded" natives aroused the unknowingly accurate suspicion among the Spaniards that this was a political organization. Growing resistance to estate tax and tribute led the friars to call for military forces, which attacked the brotherhood's fortifications, dispersing to the mountains its members and executing Pule. But the movement, which drew its special vitality from a blend of economic, racial, and religious passions expressed in "protopolitical" organization, would be heard from again in its Colorum sect descendants.[13] The changing character of native resistance, of course, grew out of transforming class and economic structures: "We now see the beginnings of mass movements with class content directed against foreign and local exploiters and putting forth demands of an egalitarian nature."[14]

With the termination of the galleon trade around 1815, liberalized commercial activity ended the islands' isolation from the world economy. The influence of British long-distance trade penetrated local society through Chinese merchant middlemen in what some called an Anglo–Chinese colony flying the Spanish flag. The Chinese brought new wares, including English and Indian cottons, and, through foreign firms now allowed to do business in Manila, provided the opportunity for cash crop exports. Directly two important consequences followed. First, the Chinese and Chinese mestizos grew rapidly as an influential minority and as a powerful, if interstitial, social class controlling local commerce and much investment capital. Second, the economy shifted decisively toward an export orientation in tune with world capitalist demand. Previous exports of tortoise shells, birds' nests, and shark fins were fogotten in the rush to indigo, tobacco, rice, coffee, and Manila hemp (abaca) sold in large quantities for marine cordage to the U.S. Navy. But the future giant of these new export crops was sugar. Prior to 1850 sugar was grown only in garden plots for domestic use and sale to traveling Chinese merchants. With the opening of new ports, the British consul in the southern island city of Iloilo, a Scotsman named Nicholas Loney, began selling on credit sugar-refining equipment, which he promised local planters could be paid for from future profits. Indeed, profits boomed. One southern island that produced 14,000 piculs (a Chinese unit, equal to 133 pounds) in 1859 raised its production to 618,120 piculs in 1880 and to almost 2 million by 1893.[15]

The new prosperity came with certain costs and dislocations. As suggested previously, this was the occasion of vast land concentration and the rise of large haciendas that based their production on tenant sharecroppers, many of them forcibly converted from freeholding. Moreover, the acreage devoted to subsistence crops, particularly rice, declined, resulting in food shortages and importation of staples. The same surge of imports brought English textiles, which helped destroy the leading local industry of traditional weaving. The prosperous enterprises were dominated by foreigners and the native ruling class that became the large landowners, while the costs were visited upon the peasantry and new wage workers. The latter half of the nineteenth century saw the beginning of modern underdevelopment—the emergence of a dependent society divided sharply along lines of class, race, and power. But the seeds of revolutionary nationalism were growing apace.

Nationalism mounted in direct measure with the number of people who considered themselves "Filipino." Throughout Spanish America a distinction of status was drawn between the *peninsulares* from Spain and the *insulares* of pure Spanish ancestry born in the colonies. Initially, in the racial and elitist hierarchy, only the creole *insulares* enjoyed second place as Filipinos after the *peninsulares;* all others were known as "Indios," "Tagalogs," and other indigenous language groups. But three hundred years of Hispanization liberalized the status of Filipino as it was appropriated first by Spanish mestizos, then the native upper class, and finally by Chinese mestizos to the extent that these groups adopted the cultural bearing of the *peninsulares.* The strongest single force uniting the growing numbers of Filipinos was religious nationalism—secularization of Catholicism in the creation of a Philippine Independent Church. The unifying importance of secularization stemmed from the paradox that people acquired deep Christian convictions at the same time that they came to regard the friars as the principal agents of suppression.

As a political movement Philippine nationalism can be dated from 1872 and the odd circumstances of the Cavite mutiny. The mutiny itself was of little note: on January 20 at the arsenal in Cavite a group of 200 soldiers and dockworkers mutinied in protest against the withdrawal of their exemption from paying tribute. Cancelation of that privilege was a small part of a broadly reactionary policy brought by the first new provincial governor since the restoration of the Spanish monarchy in November 1870. The stern resolve of Governor Izquierdo (the man's name adding more irony since it also means "left" in Spanish) was aimed at curbing such flagrant lapses of colonial discipline as the demand for secularization. Yet the unsuspecting mutineers were caught in the reign of terror that followed. The authorities pointed to Cavite as the precursor of an attempt to overthrow Spanish rule and retaliated against political liberals and religious reformers with imprisonment and exile. Virtual martial law was established, and three priests were executed in front of a crowd of 40,000: "The summary execution of the three popular priests, more than any other act of suppression, aroused in the masses a fierce hatred of the Spanish. . . . [They] became the first religio-nationalist martyrs."[16] Cavite and 1872 mark the beginning of a new nationalist political consciousness among creoles, mestizos, and natives joined now as Filipinos. The unwitting mutiny also put the Philippine Independent Church in the mainstream of the people's movement.

During the 1880s and 1890s the movement was for reform. Ideologically it drew on Spanish liberalism, and the main propaganda effort came from sympathetic groups in Madrid and Barcelona. The leaders of the reform movement were generally wealthy, and their program leaned heavily on assimilation. Of course, they advocated secularization, but they also wanted local control of the economy in lieu of colonial administration and the friars, greater political autonomy, perhaps representation in the Spanish Cortes as a province. José Rizal, a medical doctor and respected novelist, symbolized the reform movement and gave it organizational form in the Liga Filipina, which he established in 1892. For his effort Rizal was promptly exiled, despite the Liga's unthreatening aims of mutual aid and self-help. Others, particularly Andres Bonafacio, continued the reform work until it became clear to some that peaceful agitation was futile. Bonafacio led the Liga's radical faction into a new and secret Katipunan society, which now, for perhaps the first time since the Spaniards had stepped ashore 327 years earlier, proposed national independence—separation, not assimilation.

In urban and rural areas the Katipunan grew rapidly with the convergence of several sources of revolutionary nationalism. Rizal's novels on the suffering of common folk and the propaganda press were published in Tagalog and voraciously read by a strategically placed audience. The urban labor force had expanded from a few hundred in 1850 to 20,000 in 1882, mainly stevedores and workers in the five cigar and cigarette factories created as a government monopoly. An economic depression from 1891 to 1895 aggravated their poverty, while falling prices of sugar and hemp spread gloom in the countryside.[17] The small but significant group of Filipino professionals was denied government employment. Rizal's banishment, and his execution once the revolution he did not support started, added personal resentment to economic woes. By 1896 Katipunan commanded the allegiance of 30,000 Filipinos from urban and rural origins, middle-class professionals, workers, and peasants:[18] "The grievances of each class flowed together to form one common stream of national protest. Conditions were ripe for the advent of a revolutionary movement. Bonafacio and his group were, therefore, able to organize the Katipunan with a wider mass base."[19]

The Philippine revolution against Spain failed for various reasons, including tactical errors and a split in the leadership that invited repression. On the first point, accounts differ concerning how a Spanish friar came into possession of vital documents on the size and organization of the secret society (perhaps the sister of a member disclosed their existence or a printer betrayed the movement). At all events, the news that a revolution was in the making engendered another reign of terror that dwarfed the response to the Cavite mutiny. Literally thousands were arrested and publicly executed including Rizal, who was innocent of the affair and at the time en route to Cuba to serve as a physician in the Spanish army. But the official view guiding the repression held that only educated Filipinos could have organized the revolutionary movement on such a broad scale. This half-truth led to the jailing and execution of moderates and nonrevolutionaries, while Bonafacio and his associates, including the formidable Emilio Aguinaldo, fled to reorganize in the provinces.

Immediately the rebels decided to establish a revolutionary Philippine Republic with its own General Assembly, to declare a national uprising, and to attack government garrisons. The split in Katipunan leadership arose over the political and military initiatives of the Bonafacio and Aguinaldo factions of the movement. Aguinaldo led his own troops in several brilliantly successful engagements with the Spanish army, while Bonafacio's men were regularly defeated. Flushed with victory, the Aguinaldo faction issued decrees in the name of a provisional government in liberated areas and began to doubt the effectiveness of the Katipunan organization. Dispute and misunderstanding led to a convention dominated by Aguinaldo supporters that chose him as president of a reorganized revolutionary government. Bonafacio's demotion to a ministerial position in this government led him to challenge its legitimacy and the dominant faction, in turn, to arrest and execute him for disloyalty. The split was disastrous. Bonafacio's moral leadership and mass following was lost in the face of military counteroffensives by the Spanish. The war dragged to a stalemate. In December 1897 Aguinaldo agreed to peace terms that included vague words about reform and the very concrete sum of 800,000 pesos, which Aguinaldo and nineteen associates took with them in exile to Hong Kong. But the absence of celebrated leaders did not stop the revolutionary struggle of the masses, which continued well into the American occupation that followed.

Inevitably historical interpretation is divided over whether Aguinaldo betrayed the revolutionary spirit of Bonafacio (who refused compromise) and Katipunan, or whether he retreated under the best bargain possible at the time to fight another day.[20] Perhaps the better interpretation is more transcendental. Aguinaldo is a historical replica of Conrad's Nostromo—both gallant revolutionaries, common men whose heroism made them very uncommon leaders of the people. Yet both longed more for the esteem and equality of their colonial superiors denied them by custom and the circumstances of birth. In the end both took their reward in colonial treasure, as unsatisfying as it was destructive.

The Philippine insurrection coincided with the far-flung implications of the Spanish American War. With Spain in retreat in the Caribbean, the United States, casting an eye on opportunities in the Pacific, had dispatched Admiral Dewey to Hong Kong, where his representative contacted the exiled revolutionaries. Although historical inquiry has failed to produce the smoking gun of promised independence, it is clear that Aguinaldo's forces were enlisted for the decisive advantage in taking Manila in the mistaken belief that their liberation came in the bargain.[21] When Aguinaldo pressed for a written commitment from the United States to Philippine independence he was told by one of Dewey's captains, "The United States is a great and rich nation and does not desire colonies."[22] Mistakenly the

Americans were trusted. The only motive for Philippine cooperation in the fight against Spain was independence.

A far cry from independence, the American invasion was followed by a colonial war of pacification that finally put down the insurrection begun against Spain and redirected at American occupation. In 1902 the U.S. Congress passed the Organic Act incorporating the Philippines as a territory and providing for tutelary self-government that (according to the Jones Act of 1916) would pave the way to full independence at some future date as the United States deemed attainment of sufficient political maturity. Most important, and consistent with the confessed commercial aims of the emerging colonial policy, the Underwood Tariff Act of 1913 created complete free trade between the United States and the Philippines.

At this early point in the development of its interdependence with the global economy, U.S. imperialism involved some special attributes. Industrialists at home warned direly of an impending domestic crisis of consumption given unparalleled expansion of productive capacity and, therefore, an urgent need of new markets. Meanwhile military analysts envisioned the advantages of bases in the Far East, where a watchful eye might be kept on Japan. Yet, arrayed against these interests were the respectable forces of the Anti-Imperialist League and domestic agricultural groups, particularly the sugar beet and cane producers. U.S. policy, with its twin tenets of free trade (especially sugar for manufacturers) and scheduled decolonization (at least in its formal trappings), was very much a resolution of these contending domestic forces as they shifted in strength over time and interacted with the political realities of the Far East and the development of Philippine nationalism. Military, industrial, and sugar interests on both sides of the Pacific established the context of political conflict and compromise.[23]

Against this historical backdrop, the Huk rebellion had its mediate causes in events of the 1920s and 1930s. It must be understood as continuous with protest movements among peasants, agricultural workers, and urban labor that gained momentum in this period, moving from local disputes to national political movements.[24] American occupation did nothing to quell the pattern of rebellion based on tenant exploitation, factory conditions, and the Philippine Independent Church.[25] The first large demonstrations under American rule were the Colorum uprisings, constituting three separate revolts between 1924 and 1931. Although these were officially regarded as instances of religious fanaticism among descendants of the Cofradía sects responsible for the 1841 Tabayas revolt, they had advanced far beyond the proto-political aims of that incident. The Colorums were independent religious orders that combined Catholicism with traditional beliefs among the lower classes, whose theology and mobility within the church were proscribed. As the movement grew, new orders began to appear in the cities. The movement "was both rural and urban based" and "membership was almost always confined to the peasantry and the urban proletariat."[26]

Politically they had high ambitions: "The Colorums talked incessantly about *libertad* and Philippine independence."[27] Economically they sought relief from usury, heavy taxation, and land-grabbing and the elimination of tenancy. In concrete actions they protested abusive treatment at the hands of the landlord-sympathizing Philippine Constabulary (or PC, an American creation) and seized and burned land titles, debt records, and tenancy contracts. Peasant actions were complemented by labor strikes in the sugar centrals and protests by urban workers in Manila, where Colorum sects flourished. Although their armed revolts were easily suppressed, the movement provided a bridge from isolated rebellions of a defensive cast after the defeat of independence to modern political party organization.

Political and economic development in the 1930s provided the basic contours and most of the ingredients for revolution. As we shall pursue in detail momentarily, the industrialization of sugar under lucrative, if narrowly beneficent, U.S. trade relations took root during the decade with devastating implications for traditional agrarian social organization. The labor movement grew in size and organization with the formation of unions, labor syndicates, and national confederations. Colonial policy, in response to these developments and the new constituencies they created for aspiring political leaders, underwent important changes as the Philippines became a U.S. Commonwealth in 1935. Commonwealth status meant a constitution modeled closely along the lines of that of the United States as well as greater autonomy and salience for local electoral politics. The dominant Nacionalista party was composed of factions led by Senate President Manuel Quezon, Sergio Osmeña, and Manuel Roxas, all vying for leadership of the promised nation-to-come through the advocacy of competing plans that would achieve full and rapid independence at minimal risk to U.S. trade concessions and maximal gains in national prestige value.

The most dramatic peacetime precursor to the Huk rebellion was the Sakdal (meaning "to accuse" or "to strike") nationalist movement of the early 1930s and uprising of May 2–3, 1935, by some

"65,000 partially-armed peasants. . . . Sakdalism marked the transition from blind rustic protest on the one hand to the later well-organized and near-successful [Huk] rebellion on the other."[28] Sakdalism was an independence movement that combined organizationally the concerns of the peasantry and urban middle class. The Sakdal political party was founded by Benigno Ramos, a formerly well-placed civil servant and editor of a newspaper bearing the party's name. Sakdal's popularity among provincial readers soon identified Ramos with the cause of the common *taos*, the poor "Filipinos of heart and face." The Sakdal party stood for "complete, absolute, and immediate independence," elimination of poll and revision of land taxes, investigation of friar lands, formation of an all-Filipino army, teaching of native dialects in the public schools, legal aid to the poor, reduction of salaries of high officials, and increases for lower civil servants, workers, and soldiers.[29] It also linked explicitly for the first time Philippine underdevelopment and the colonial policies of the United States.

Campaigning on these issues in the 1934 House of Representatives, provincial, and municipal elections, the party scored surprising victories against the Nacionalistas in the primaries, owing, perhaps, to their appeals for land reform and denunciations of the national political influence of rural bosses, or *caciques*.[30] In light of these victories the Quezon and Osmeña factions of the Nacionalistas closed ranks in an election of the same year for delegates to a Constitutional Convention to act on the Tydings–McDuffie Law and the commonwealth status it promised. The Sakdalists boycotted that election as "a thinly disguised technique to perpetuate oligarchic controls on a foundation of American bayonets"[31] and set about plans to block the national plebiscite scheduled for May 14, 1935, on the convention-endorsed Tydings–McDuffie Commonwealth Act.

In the spring of 1935, while Ramos repaired to Japan to discuss his plans with anti-American sympathizers, Sakdal party activists mounted a vociferous campaign against the plebiscite, formulating at the same time plans for a violent counteroffensive to the certain repression by Nacionalistas. Somehow they managed to convince their supporters that a show of insurgent force would win an easy victory for independence, aided, if need by, by the intervention of Japan. The result was a massive attack on constabulary and government headquarters in a dozen or so provincial towns of Central Luzon that, after some frantic hours, was suppressed with the death and wounding of more than one hundred men. Assuming Sakdal leaders anticipated the futility of armed insurrection, the revolt is explained in the dilemma posed by their party goals and the realities of the political situation. Unquestionably, they hoped to achieve partial success as a step toward a larger objective. Widespread violence could frustrate the plebiscite, hinder the establishment of the commonwealth, make manifest the opposition of a large group of Filipinos to the Tydings–McDuffie Law, and perhaps lead the United States to modify its views on Philippine independence.[32]

While none of these tactical objectives was achieved, with the adoption of the commonwealth that year, other long-term influences for change were set in motion. An official inquiry into the causes of uprising, though leaning toward an explanation based on autocratic caciquism and peasant gullibility, nevertheless recognized publicly for the first time the desperate plight of tenant farmers and landless agricultural workers. Socioeconomic conditions were officially acknowledged as contributory and in need of reform. Concrete reforms followed including laws for improvements in the terms of tenant crop-shares and loans, public acquisition of estates and land redistribution, legal representation for peasant claims, and a panoply of measures associated with ''President Quezon's Social Justice Campaign [that] grew in part out of his desire to win back alienated rural elements.''[33] Labor was affected by many of these reform measures and subsequently experienced its greatest gains in organization.[34]

Perhaps most important, Sakdalism created a new political climate in which popular forces came to appreciate their own efficacy and potential in opposition to the landlord-dominated legislature and the opportunistic Nacionalista party. Electoral politics became an increasingly effective method of redress. Subsequently, a Popular Front socialist coalition not only organized at the grass roots, but won many important local offices in 1937 and 1940.[35] Although these changes were doubtless accompanied by a retrenchment of conservative landlord–constabulary interests, the 1930s produced a political renaissance in the loosely knit coalitions of peasants and workers that would figure decisively in the postwar revolution. By the end of the decade, Philippine politics could be summarized by commonwealth ties to the United States, a promise of their steady withdrawal, Nacionalista party factions competing for stewardship of that transition, and the incipient but determined organization of popular forces.

Parallel to these changes in the polity were fundamental developments in the dominant sugar economy. As colonial ties and American investment grew in the 1920s and 1930s, agricultural production expanded dramatically, with increasing proportions destined for export to the United States. Several critical facts must be considered here. First, historically, where the bulk of Philippine exports had gone to Europe and Asia and only 13 percent to the United States at the turn of the century, by 1940 more than 80 percent of trade was with the United States.[36] Similarly, "By the late interwar period the Philippines was sending three-quarters of its exports (by value) to the United States and obtaining two-thirds of its imports from the metropolitan country."[37] Second, among export commodities agricultural products, of course, dominated with 85 percent of the total value, led by sugar (40 percent of the total value of all agricultural commodities) and followed at some distance by coconut products and hemp.[38] Third, from the earliest recorded national figures in 1906, through 1940, sugar production increased nearly tenfold (from 136,614 "short tons" to 1,214,080). And finally, in the period of the early 1930s leading up to the commonwealth agreements, sugar production increased very rapidly (some 81 percent from 1931 to 1934). This was a result of the "quota race"—increased production anticipating an import quota to be set by the United States (in consideration of her own domestic producers) based on recent "average" production levels in the Philippines.[39]

In short, the economy experienced a huge quantitative stimulus to sugar production prompted by U.S. ties and the politics of independence. But equally important were qualitative changes in the organization of sugar production stemming from the fact that export demand and prices favored milled or centrifugal over the more primitively processed *muscovado* sugar. Sugar production became industrialized. In the early years the main island of Luzon had few sugar centrals due to its historical pattern of agrarian organization characterized by relatively small holdings and very high rates of tenancy.[40] The mills also required sizable investments of capital. Initially the sugar central and plantation-like production was confined to Negros Occidental, which had favorable natural conditions combined with a smaller and less densely settled population. However, given the great incentives to profit in U.S. trade, as well as the production advantage of proximity to Manila, by the 1920s industrialized sugar production had begun in Central Luzon—particularly in the provinces of Pampanga and Tarlac, where centrals much larger than those of Negros were built, sometimes with U.S. capital.

The consequences of these changes included a series of disruptions in the agrarian economy that contributed heavily to rebellion. Primarily: (1) there was greater pressure on the land for conversion to sugar production and efficient use of expanded milling capacity; (2) tenancy arrangements were less efficient for this production (at least, certain tenants were), leading to an increase in evictions; (3) a greater demand for seasonal wage labor in the mills and company fields that could be recruited only from former tenants and small-holders (encouraged by pressures on the land to sell); (4) therefore, the number of wage workers increased; (5) incentives for greater ef-ficiency undermined the moral economy of customary landlord–ten-ant relations and reciprocal services, especially since investment in the centrals was a significant capital risk for conventional landlords, who therefore had less discretion in the making of loans and ex-change of services with tenants:

> **Farmers milling with centrals wanted less tenant labor. Several of them began to rely more on tractors, obviating some of the service of their tenants. Moreover, the planters' milling expenses were higher, as much as 50 percent of their total harvest. While the greater selling price of centrifugal sugar and the availability of better markets may have justified milling with a central, the margin was not such to favor dividing returns with a large number of tenants working expanded fields. The bigger planters also had to make heavier outlays for greater numbers of harvest workers, particularly given the demand of the central for only the best grades of cane. And a number of planters had invested heavily in the construction of the centrals, mortgaging their land to raise the necessary cash. With their property in jeop-ardy, the landowners' margin of leeway to carry old and faithful tenants, even if they had worked the same land for years, was se-verely reduced. The new need was for efficient workers, not loyal retainers. Under such circumstances the traditional tenant system be-came something of an anachronism;** [41]

(6) the concentration of landholding increased, altering the class structure as well as leading to an "overcrowding" of tenants who now competed for plots to work under increasingly less attractive landlord terms; and (7) in general, the standard of living of peasants and agricultural workers either deteriorated or remained unchanged, while "the centrals created a new crop of planter millionaires . . . who profited enormously from the investment in the booming sugar industry. But the wealth did not filter down to the lower classes . . . economic development became more uneven." [42] As one U.S. high commissioner observed of the times,

> **Where great quantities of sugar cane were produced, thousands of Filipinos worked under disgraceful conditions and often for less than a living wage. They had to fight poverty all their lives, whereas the owners of the estates, living in Manila, grew inordinately rich and profited heavily from the free entry of their sugar into the United**

States. Here was a pernicious social problem—the indefensible and shocking contrast between the rich, lordly landowners living in Manila and the impoverished workers in Pampanga.[43]

The changes in the agrarian sector and their contribution to a revolutionary situation require two interpretive comments in view of the theoretical temptation to view the Huk Rebellion exclusively in terms of the peasantry.[44] First, between the global economic situation represented by U.S. neocolonial policy and the conditions of Philippine rural social organization, the crucial choices for the development of the sugar industry were made in the arena of national politics. Particularly, these decisions were a product of the struggle for national leadership among such personages as Quezon, Osmeña, and Roxas—factional leaders interested in claiming for themselves the victory of phased independence, while at the same time trying to boost the permanent U.S. sugar quota as high as possible. These domestic political considerations interacted with strong sentiment in the United States for granting full independence with reduced quotas plus tariffs protecting mainland sugar producers. Quezon, the preeminent political figure of the time, managed a delicate balance of advocates for immediate independence (e.g., the Sakdals and Popular Front) and the gradualist sugar interests, themselves split between millers and planters.[45] Quezon's developmental policy was a temporary resolution of a class struggle. Had he been less successful, or had the Osmeña or Roxas factions succeeded in more precipitate moves toward independence—and certainly had the Sakdal revolt been more successful—the pattern and consequences of uneven economic development could have been different.

Second, the general policy emphasis on sugar export and import of U.S. manufacturers had discernible impacts on other sectors of the economy: failure to develop national manufacturing; destructive competition with native industries (e.g., weaving); and a reduced capacity to create new urban jobs or adequately reward existing ones. Agricultural export conditioned developments in labor and the urban economy that would contribute to the revolutionary situation.

Prerevolutionary labor conditions were changing nearly as dramatically as the peasant situation, particularly in the expansion and politicization of worker organizations. This was aided by the fact that the Philippine labor sector is officially organized at the levels of both worker confederation and governmental responsibility so as to include agricultural workers in the same category with urban and industrial labor.

Philippine labor problems are products of a colonial agrarian economy. As such, they are tied with the whole social and political development of the country. They combine the problems of rural workers bound to the soil and those of modern wage earners. The so-called agrarian question occupies the forefront of labor struggles in the Philippines . . . hence there is no such thing in the Philippines as a farmer movement independent of and distinct from the labor movement.[46]

Thus, for example, Quezon's Social Justice Campaign aimed to "win back alienated rural elements" after the Sakdal revolt included labor reforms that affected equally rural and urban confederations—the right of unions to organize and bargain collectively and the establishment of a Court of Industrial Relations to mediate labor disputes. Speaking of the "new unionism" of this period and its increasing militance by 1936, Crippen suggests, "The best indication of what was happening was the growth of a new kind of labor movement—which, because of the nature of the Phillippine economy, involved the countryside as well as the cities."[47]

The first modern labor union in the Philippines was organized by printers in 1902 (Unión Obrera Democrática Filipina). Although trade unionism was legally recognized "by indirection in 1908" with the creation of a government Bureau of Labor, Wurfel describes the period 1901–1907 as one of "trade union repression," followed by an era of "passive recognition" until 1935. In the second period, unions proliferated, with the 31 registered entities in 1919 that embraced 42,000 workers growing to 145 unions and 90,000 members by 1924. Prior to 1930 there were no national federations of labor, but the fledgling movement was inspired by socialist internationalism, and direction was provided by three strong unions, the stevedores from the Manila waterfront, the National Labor Union of Manila industrial workers, and a federation of agricultural and general workers in the southern islands.[48]

The first triumph of the new unionism came in the mid-1930s attendant to Sakdal agitation with the recognition of unions, collective bargaining, and the new Court of Industrial Relations. Among urban labor, such as the 8,000 cigar workers who staged the largest strike in Philippine labor history to date, "strikes and lockouts reached their prewar peak in 1934."[49] The labor movement in general was fortified by a series of peasant confederations coalescing around the General Workers' Union (AMT), National Peasants Union (PKM), and National Society of Peasants of the Philippines (KPMP). One compilation of protest incidents among peasants and workers from

1930 to 1940 indicates that they grew steadily during the period, reaching a peak in the final year mainly in the Central Luzon provinces of Pampanga and Nueva Ecija plus Manila.[50]

Organizationally the activity of urban workers culminated in the formation of the Collective Labor Movement (CLM) in 1938, a radical coalition of 76 affiliates that joined liberal and conservative federations in 1939 to form the National Commission of Labor. Despite these gains official labor policy was far from liberal, placing restrictions aimed at the radicals and communists on the qualifications for "registered" union status and requiring management consent before a dispute could be submitted for arbitration.[51] Nevertheless, the movement grew between 1930 and 1940 from 122 registered unions with 70,000 members to 391 embracing nearly 97,000 workers, while the number of registered disputes in the same period grew from 35 to 158.[52] The radical CLM was the strongest element in the movement, estimated by 1939 to have more members in its unregistered unions that the 97,000 in its official affiliates, since it drew heavily on the estimated 190,000 members of proscribed groups.[53]

To summarize, the prewar years witnessed a general organization and mobilization of workers, significant increases in labor unrest, and militant protest, and all of this based on a broad coalition of rural agricultural and urban industrial workers:

The labor movement in the Philippines was not strictly a movement of industrial workers. Rather it was composed of a mixture of industrial workers and peasants . . . the political level of the Philippine labor movement rose, for organized labor was not only demanding higher wages and other concessions but was beginning to challenge the whole system of landlordism and free enterprise.[54]

Three streams fed this rising tide of militant reformism. First, as we have seen, dramatic changes in agrarian social organization were generated in response to large increases in industrialized sugar production for the quota race. Peasant immiseration increased with the alienation of land, deteriorating conditions of tenancy, and coerced wage labor. Second, in the Philippines context this was part of the labor problem, but bona fide industrial workers also experienced unfavorable conditions owing to low wages, limited job opportunities, paternalism and arbitrary conditions of employment or dismissal, and strong resistance to independent labor organization. Third, political elites, engaged in their own factional struggle, responded to mass protests of the Sakdal party and Popular Front with reforms of the Social Justice program that opened the door to popular movements and legitimated their initial efforts.

Naturally, this incipient revolutionary situation was arrested, or redirected, with the Japanese invasion in December of 1941. The Hukbalahap resistance movement was formed in March 1942, drawing its cadre and organizational base directly from preexisting confederations of peasants and labor such as the KPMP, PKM, AMT, and CLM, as well as the Socialist and Communist parties. Although predominantly, and of tactical necessity, a rural-based movement, the Hukbalahap recruited beyond the peasantry. Many labor leaders joined the movement, including the supreme commander of the Huks, Luis Taruc, a twenty-six-year-old leader of Pampanga's sugar workers and a member of the National Commission of Labor. Manila groups including the Communist party carried out communications, intelligence, and support activities. The Hukbalahap enjoyed overwhelming support among the peasantry because it was viewed as continuous with their earlier resistance to landlords and rural police (PC), successfully protected civilians from the invaders with guerrilla tactics, and provided a shadow government and local peacekeeping force through the infiltration of Japanese-created neighborhood associations.

Beyond their role as protectors, the stature of the Huks increased because many other Filipinos chose collaboration with the Japanese, including most absentee or self-exiled landlords and key political figures. Their perceived cowardice contrasted sharply to the esteemed warriors of resistance. Moreover, in the absence of exploiting landlords and through the fortune of bountiful harvests, the economic situation of the peasants actually improved.[55] An important legacy was produced by the war: "The Huks fought the Japanese while at the same time righting some of the economic inequities of the past. While attacking the enemy, the Huks also put together the rudiments of a new social organization with its own leadership, customs, and institutions based on a rough form of socialist democracy."[56]

It was, therefore, with renewed confidence and ambition that nationalist forces looked to the future after MacArthur's return and liberation early in 1945. Yet, within a year and one-half the country would be plunged into violent revolt. What happened in this final critical period? What were the proximate causes of revolution?

Four interrelated circumstances help explain these developments. First, the Huk freedom fighters were subject to a series of abuses and indignities by U.S. forces of occupation and the other national groups the United States chose to support. During the liberation fight in 1945, American troops turned against the Huks, and government forces began arresting members of the resistance. Almost as though they had been the enemy, Huks were asked to turn over their weapons and lists of their personnel, a request met with reluctance by some, who were later justified when these were used against them. Minor but nettlesome was the issue of back pay given to the USAFFE (United States Armed Forces in the Far East)—whose guerrilla bands had provided more opposition to the Huks than to the Japanese—but denied to the few Huks who requested it, despite the fact that they were equally entitled under the program. The explanation for all this lies in the fact that the U.S. liberation forces made common cause with reactionary elements they believed to be "the people"—namely, the USAFFE, landlords, and political elites, who, as historical enemies and rivals, managed to convince them that the Huks were a threat to peace.

Of course, the Huks were a threat to those groups and their hopes for a return of the status quo ante. Perhaps the greatest affront was the elevation of known or suspected collaborationists to important positions in the new government. General Douglas MacArthur appointed many Filipinos to government posts under occupation, persons whom he had encountered in prewar official circles. Among the Huks many of these had pro-Japanese reputations or were prominent in USAFFE. Despite their major responsibility for keeping the resistance alive and subsequently helping to rout the Japanese, no Huks were included in the postwar government. Moreover, it was MacArthur's "selective absolution" that branded some as leading collaborators and others, with very similar Japanese connections, patriots—such as Manuel Roxas, later backed by the United States as the first president under independence.[57]

Second was the resurgence and ultimate repression of popular democratic forces. Immediately after the war the same forces that had constituted the Popular Front of the late 1930s regrouped in new organizations with a determined purpose. As the Huk leader Luis Taruc noted, "It was extremely easy to organize among the people after the work of the Hukbalahap."[58] In the countryside the PKM inherited the followers of the disbanded Hukbalahap and grew to include a half-million people, twice the size of the various prewar peasant organizations combined. In the labor movement a Congress of Labor Organizations (CLO) was formed in 1945 and, following the radical tradition of the CLM, became the dominant labor federation of the early postwar period, including though not dominated by, Philippine Communist party (PKP) members. The CLO combined numerical strength with activism in pressing labor demands.

In anticipation of the crucial election of 1946 that would empanel the first fully independent national government, popular forces from the PKM, CLO, PKP, Hukbalahap's Veterans League, a variety of independent unions, and many others combined to form the Democratic Alliance. "The DA represented another attempt to converge two streams in Philippine politics—the peasant movement in Central Luzon and the predominantly urban left . . . a possible third tributary . . . was the labor union movement, particularly a new federation called the Congress of Labor Organizations."[59]

The Democratic Alliance put forward twenty-three candidates for the House of Representatives in various parts of the country and reluctantly endorsed Osmeña, the Nacionalista party candidate for President, mostly out of fierce opposition to Roxas, who represented the new splinter Liberal party. Although failing to block Roxas, the Democratic Alliance won an unprecedented victory in the election of six of its congressmen, all representing Central Luzon, and made respectable showings in other regions, including Manila. However, in an undisguised act of repression by the Roxas government-elect, the Democratic Alliance was prevented from taking its seats for rather transparent reasons associated with the following point.

Third was the imposition of a set of neocolonial policies that served to deepen and exacerbate historical conflicts. The centerpiece of neocolonialism was the Philippine Trade Act of 1946 (or the Bell Trade Act), signed by President Truman immediately after the election of Roxas and sent along to the Philippine Congress, where its adoption required an amendment to the constitution. Two key provisions of the act called for a twenty-eight-year extension of free trade relations and "parity" for U.S. investors along with nationals. In effect, the first provision meant that the Philippines would continue to be a completely open, duty-free market for U.S. products. The original ten-year free trade period (though later extended) would be followed by imposition of graduated duties, while the United States enjoyed the unilateral right of setting quotas on Philippine exports destined for the home market (again, to satisfy U.S. farmers).

This arrangement, backed by Filipino landlords and *compradores* tied to the U.S. market, especially the sugar bloc, perpetuated the old colonial relationship for the crucial first 28 years of the suppposedly independent nation. It ruled out industrialization as effectively as in the colonial period, it kept the Philippines in a backward agricultural state, and it prevented the needed diversification of international trade and of domestic production. Politically, it served to keep in power the reactionary landlord *comprador* groups allied to U.S. interests.[60]

Similarly, the "parity" arrangement gave U.S. investors the same rights as Filipinos in the national economy, including 100 percent ownership of corporations, nullifying an amendment to the Commonwealth Constitution limiting foreign participation to 40 percent ownership of national corporations.

The euphemistically named "parity" provision virtually prohibited the development of independent Filipino industries by placing them on the same footing with U.S. multinationals and preventing any form of protection necessary for infant industries (as, for example, in the earlier development of the United States). Parity preserved the dominant position of U.S. investment in the Philippine economy and gave it a decided advantage over other potential foreign investors.

Included in the Trade Act's terms of neocolonialism were important military arrangements, particularly retention of ninety-nine-year leases for twenty-three U.S. military bases, including the huge Subic Bay naval complex (home of the U.S. Seventh Fleet) and the 136,000 acres of fertile agricultural land in Central Luzon turned over to Clark Air Base. The Philippines not only provided a garrison outpost for U.S. military operations in the Far East, but domestic armed forces were provisioned and controlled by a Joint U.S. Military Advisory Group (JUSMAG), all at the expense of the Philippine government and people.

The Bell Trade Act had a profound impact on national politics. Its passage by Congress required a two-thirds majority, which Roxas calculated would not be forthcoming if the Democratic Alliance representatives were seated. Since the receipt of large amounts of postwar reconstruction aid from the United States was contingent upon passage of the act, Roxas denied the seating on trumped-up charges that the Democratic Alliance had employed terror and intimidation to win their elections. Subsequently the Bell Act passed by a single vote.

Fourth, as in the particular case of the Democratic Alliance, the new government resorted to a wholesale campaign of political and police repression. Huk and peasant organizations were declared illegal, and their presumed members or sympathizers were harassed, raided, jailed, and even massacred by military police seeking pacification in the form of a reimposition of landlordism. The symbolic failure of pacification and peasant recourse to self-defense was marked by the murder of a revered resistance leader in August of 1946. Landlords resisted earlier reforms (e.g., a sixty–forty crop-sharing program), which, in the midst of general political and economic chaos, led to a rapid deterioration in material conditions of the peasantry— particularly by contrast to the relatively prosperous years of the Japanese occupation. In addition to the Democratic Alliance affair, leftist political figures at the provincial and local levels were purged. Similar repression was visited upon organized labor and the Communist party.

Thus, in August of 1946 the HMB, or People's Liberation Army, was formed out of essentially the same constituents as the Hukbalahap and predominantly for defensive reasons by reluctant rebels. It arose in the face of government repression imposed on a grid of longstanding and accelerating economic grievance and political frustration: as one participant observed, "Our very lives were at stake. What do you do? We had no choice but to go underground."[61]

The protracted and bloody events of the Huk Rebellion will not concern us here, having been amply described by the revolutionaries, their opponents, and observers of varying degrees of objectivity between.[62] Rather, analytic interest centers on participants in the revolt, its organizational bases, and the manner in which it was ultimately quelled.

As with most movements of national liberation, the conventional Western interpretation is that the Huk Rebellion was communist led or inspired or dominated.[63] Similarly, members of the Philippine Communist party (PKP) are happy to take credit for so broad and formidable a national movement.[64] Both positions are ideologically myopic. In a more disinterested vein, Kerkvliet argues persuasively that, although the PKP was intimately involved in the revolt, it never provided effective leadership or coordination.[65] Some of the Huk leaders, such as Luis Taruc, were members of the Socialist party and became de facto PKP members when the two parties merged, but they later split formally with the communists precisely over the strategy and aims of the liberation movement. The rank-and-file peasant– worker Huks, of course, had little conception or use of party politics by contrast to their own concrete grievances. The PKP was one among several formal associations that lent active support to the movement. But the social movement itself grew directly out of historical conditions, political groups, and popular leadership of longer pedigree.

Although Kerkvliet's recent study is easily the best work on the Huks and includes a wealth of original material, it falls into another trap of exclusive interpretation signaled in its subtitle, "A Study of Peasant Revolt in the Philippines." On that score Pomeroy's studied appraisal and demur is convincing in light of the historical record reviewed here. His most succinct criticism is that the study, based on a typical rural community in Central Luzon, "failed to comprehend the national characteristics of the Huk Revolt or the national scope of the struggle of which the peasants in San Ricardo comprised but a segment."[66] In a masterful summary of historical influence and detailed events of the revolt he shows the critical role of the working class and trade unions allied with the peasants and the HMB's activities in "the phase of the armed struggle that occurred in Manila."[67]

Moreover, the revolt went beyond peasant–worker alliances to become a national movement resting on a broad base of class mobilization. Various class segments participated out of motives as complex and differentiated as the penetration of neocolonialism itself.

Besides the working-class link other class groupings supported or participated in the HMB. From the peasantry itself tenant farmers or their children were but a portion of HMB recruits; agricultural laborers, fishermen, sugar mill workers, or peasants who had left the land for various jobs in the towns made up a large percentage of those in the armed struggle. In the regions where mass support for the movement existed or was developed, town dwellers—shop-keepers, laborers, rural professionals and intellectuals, teachers—contributed money, supplies, intelligence information, or gave safekeeping to wanted members. In Manila in the late 1940s and early 1950s, as a national crisis and growing HMB strength were plain, a considerable number of petty-bourgeois people came into the movement—journalists, university professors, cinema actors and directors, students. Businessmen both large and small contributed funds, food, medicines, shoes, clothing, and equipment to the HMB. All of this took place not as aid to a "peasant revolt," but as support for a national liberation struggle.[68]

Ultimately, of course, the Huk rebellion was put down in 1953. The single most important explanation for its defeat was the superior military force and counterinsurgency methods lent to the Philippine Ministry of Defense by the United States. On one hand, massive numerical forces, materiel, and combat advisors were thrown against an ill-equipped, resistance-trained popular army cut off from its community support bases and hunted down in strategic redoubts. On the other, huge U.S. aid expenditures offered the carrot of rural development to noncombatants.

The victory of force, however, should not detract from other contributors to the arrested conflict. An important factor was the sheer weariness of the people after a dozen years of struggle against superior force. In this context the Huks and their flagging sympathizers looked hopefully to announced government programs for land reform and industrial peace. The programs were closely associated with the person of Ramon Magsaysay, who served as Secretary of Defense from 1950 to 1953 and President from 1953 to 1957. Magsaysay's provincial and lower-class origins, Filipino appearance and surname, war record, and expressed concern for the common person all encouraged those who hoped for a peaceful solution.

As Secretary of Defense, Magsaysay's policy toward the Huks was summarized in the adage "all-out force and friendship." The army was increased to unprecedented size, but reformed in the process. The much despised Philippine Constabulary was absorbed into the army, officer assignments were shifted from their home areas, and a civil affairs corps was created to live and work among local community folk. The intent was to eliminate flagrant personal abuses, peasant intimidation, and corruption of military personnel and to sever their former close connection with the landlords. The army was to be cast in the role of friend and advisor to the people. Community development programs were awarded to zones of unrest such as Luis Taruc's hometown. This new role was exemplified in the army-directed Economic Development Corps (EDCOR) responsible for the major policy approach to agrarian problems, namely, resettlement of Luzon farmers in the open spaces of Mindanao. Clearly, the hope of this program was for a no-cost solution to tenant overcrowding *and* commercial agriculture, with the potential added advantage of self-exile by Huk sympathizers and the disappearance of unrest.

The history of attempted agrarian reform in the Philippines dates at least from the beginnings of American rule and the purchase and redistribution of friar estates.[69] Yet effective land reform has always been successfully opposed by the political power of the landed upper class. Magsaysay's unquestioned good intentions met the same fate.[70] The legislation he proposed for improvements in the conditions of agricultural tenancy and for land reform were gutted in the Congress dominated by large landowners. The land reform programs depended on voluntary compliance with no right of public expropriation. Higher taxes on large holdings were summarily rejected. No public funds were provided for the purchase and redistributive sale of private lands. Large-holders were encouraged to sell off pieces to solvent tenants, but they were provided no incentives to do so—and, no doubt, were discouraged about the prospects of industrial investment of their potential profits in an economy dominated by multinational corporations or closed circles of investors (including the powerful Chinese merchant class). Resettlement was the only program that "worked," and it appealed only to a small segment of the overabundant Luzon tenants and wage workers willing to leave their home lands. Neither Magsaysay nor his successors were able to alter the basic political fact that ensures rural poverty and underdevelopment.

The landed interests are still represented in Congress, and Congress is reluctant to force them to sell their lands or to make expropriation a simple matter. At the same time however, Congress has not been able to provide the landlords with sufficient incentives to sell their lands and to divert their capital elsewhere. Thus, there is a stalemate, and Congress avoids the subject of land reform as often and as well as it can.[71]

Consistent with the broad sources of unrest behind the Huk rebellion, efforts were made to respond to worker demands with the Industrial Peace Act or "Magna Carta of Labor" in 1953. The changes in labor relations involved two areas, greater freedom of union organization and collective bargaining. With the qualifications for registered union status greatly liberalized, their numbers increased dramatically in the mid-1950s. Similarly, compulsory arbitration was ended, and the frequency of both strikes and collective bargaining agreements increased. Although labor reforms were far from complete by worker's standards (e.g., wages in Manila, where the unions were strongest, rose more slowly after the act than before),[72] the relative ease of reform in this area by contrast to agrarian conditions calls for some explanation.

In fact, the explanation is as straightforward as it is critical to an understanding of postrevolutionary society. Two circumstances combined to produce the change. American influence was firmly behind the changes modeled on the (U.S.) Taft–Hartley law, probably because U.S. advisors and businesspeople felt the reform represented an advance that they could live and prosper under. The multinationals required a trained and dependable labor force, and Philippine wage rates were already very low by U.S. standards. Moreover,

foreign managers saw a certain advantage in collective bargaining. Aside from the fact that Americans were familiar with this particular technique of labor relations, as a spirit of nationalism increases, the disadvantages involved in a foreign employer appearing against a Filipino union before a Filipino judge increase also. Therefore, pressures may have been exerted on MSA [the Mutual Security Agency, Labor Division] by the American business community in Manila to pay particular attention to collective bargaining. . . . They knew that few of the unions with which they had to deal were strong enough to pose a serious bargaining threat.[73]

The second key circumstance accounting for labor reform was the fact that it faced no real opposition of the kind that blocked land reform: "The political elite, instead of being united, was fragmented by the appearance of new competing interests."[74] Indeed, the powerful land and sugar interests that were closely allied with the American business community may have seen some advantages in the reform. "The landed elite were either passive in this struggle between the forces of arbitration and collective bargaining or tacitly supported a measure which they thought might weaken the power base of the new entrepreneurial elite."[75]

Yet the new entrepreneurial elite, or national bourgeoisie, is not to be discounted as a force shaping the state and society that emerged from revolt. Since the early rebellions against Spain, nationalism has been a mercurial ingredient in Philippine politics. Modern bourgeois nationalism dictates that no state policy or administration become too closely identified with United States or other foreign interest. While dealing with the realities of economic power (e.g., trade and the sugar interests), aspiring leaders under the commonwealth had to maintain a posture of nonsubservience and independent bargaining in relations with the United States.

The clearest contemporary example of this attitude was the "Filipinos First" program of the García administration, which followed Magsaysay's popular appeal and identification with the condition of the peasantry and working class. Filipinos First was a slogan that appealed to another important segment of the polity and a mood characteristic in Southeast Asia and the Pacific (e.g., Malaysia and Indonesia) in the late 1950s. The program promised needed political mileage. Purportedly, the policy involved giving Filipinos a greater advantage in trade, commerce, and industry as a means toward a more self-reliant and independent nation. In fact, the program had more to do with executing the terms of the Retail Trade Nationalization Act (passed under Magsaysay in 1954) by forcing the Chinese (both alien and native) merchants out of their estimated 70–80 percent control of retail trade.[76] For concrete, rather than symbolic, purposes the program was never very successful, which was probably a good thing since the flight or secreting of the large sums represented by Chinese capital and normally spent on purchases within the country (unlike repatriated multinational capital) could be traced to local recessions. The larger importance of the Filipinos First policy was that it rallied nationalistic sentiment behind a political elite, obscuring the facts of dependency at the expense of a small and vulnerable ethnic minority.[77] As we shall see later, very similar measures were adopted in Kenya after independence with respect to East Indian merchants.

The most recent manifestation of economic nationalism appeared in the late 1960s and played an important role in the imposition of martial law in 1972. Once again international influences were at work, with the United States mired in Vietnam and indicating a desire to shift the combat role to Vietnamese national forces—to abandon a Southeast Asian ally, as indeed happened a few years later.

The wave of economic nationalism which swept the country in the late sixties and early seventies appeared to threaten U.S. economic interests. . . . Pushed by mounting nationalist pressure from the media, intellectuals, students, and certain sectors of Philippine business, the Philippine Congress adopted the "Principles and Objectives of Economic Nationalism" and began to pass restrictions on the behavior of foreign investors. The same mass pressures led the Supreme Court to decree several controversial rulings, including one which declared that all private lands that had been purchased by U.S. citizens after 1945 had essentially been acquired illegally (the famous "Quasha Decision"). On the eve of the declaration of martial law in September 1972 the Philippine Constitutional Convention was concluding the drafting of a new constitution whose economic provisions would have radically curtailed the entry and operations of multinational corporations in the country.[78]

It would be impossible to weigh the contribution of this circumstance along with others in the decision of President Marcos to declare martial law or to determine the actual influence exerted by the United States and its multinational subsidiaries. It is true that the first constitution since commonwealth was being drafted at the time by a group of national leaders generally opposed to the Marcos government and including persons of the democratic left strongly advocating an end to neocolonialism.[79] But the government was under other pressures. Inflation had risen steeply, and the peso was devalued twice in 1962 and 1970, when it was floated on the international market at the urging of the International Monetary Fund. Foreign debt and payments deficits had mounted—the economy was in trouble. A third generation of Huks was active publicly in the Federation of Free Farmers (FFF) and the Free Farmers Union (MASAKA) and unofficially in the New People's Army (NPA). Violence had erupted in Mindanao in the form of a Moslem separatist movement and with attacks on the Liberal party and the president's wife in Manila.

Whatever the assortment of immediate causes that led to martial law, they reflect the conditions of poverty among landless and rural wage earners, paternalistically managed urban workers, and the factional strife between the national bourgeoisie and *"comprador"* interests associated with foreign trade and multinational enterprise. Under martial law the state outlawed political competition, banned strikes, censored the press, abandoned agrarian reform, and liberalized further the incentives to foreign investors. These policies earned the growing support of the World Bank and International Monetary Fund, perhaps because some of the policies originated there. Apparently judging the regime on the proper road to economic development, the World Bank increased their loans to the Philippines elevenfold between 1973 and 1976, elevating it from number thirty to eighth on the list of eighty-two recipient countries.[80] Recently the government sponsored a sham reelection of Marcos in the hope that his "normalization" program would rekindle the confidence of international lenders, who virtually support the regime. The high rate of abstention (despite legal penalty) and renewed activity of the NPA and Moro Liberation Front may have had the opposite effect.

It would be a long and obviously unwarranted step to imply that the present authoritarian state was somehow a result of the military defeat of the Huk rebellion. This overview of recent changes in Philippine society is intended, rather, to indicate in historical relief the important tendencies set in motion by the political crisis and national revolt of the 1950s. Closer specification of these requires that we ask, first, what the Huk rebellion accomplished.

Among the most tangible consequences of the revolt are the reforms in agrarian and labor relations that were intensified in the mid-1950s. Although no genuine land reform took place on a measurable scale, the peasant condition was ameliorated by rent reductions and more respect for the laws on tenant crop-shares. Landlords were rudely awakened to the sanctions that accompany violation of peasant rights. These changes, in turn, signaled the arrival of greater class consciousness and more clearly drawn class lines that came to replace the patron–client relations of traditional rural society. The same wave of reforms attempted to promote industrial peace by allowing workers to organize more effectively in legally recognized unions, both in the industrial setting and among wage workers in rural agribusiness. Courts of Industrial and Agrarian Relations were established and came to function more effectively as an avenue of redressing peasant and worker claims. Lower classes throughout the society made small, if hard-won, gains in legal and organizational power. A more enduring result, perhaps, was the sense of pride and efficacy engendered by the Huks. Speaking for themselves some of the rebels reflected, "Even if we got nothing, that's not important. What's important is that we *had* to fight back. And we fought so well that the big people and the government will never forget us again. . . . No strike, no demonstration, no rebellion fails. Protest against injustice always succeeds."[81]

From the standpoint of the state, however, the consequences were less hopeful. The revolt brought into the open the major interests and cleavages that characterize contemporary Philippine society. The landed, agribusiness elite consolidated its political strength and economic privilege. From abroad, the U.S. government, business interests, military, and closely allied international financial institutions raised a single voice heard above all others in developmental policy making. National politicians were governed principally by the interests of these two power blocs, with autonomy given to institute reforms only insofar as they complemented powerful interests or concerned peripheral issues. Under these conditions a wedge was driven deeply between the national and internationally dependent bourgeoisies. Attempts to placate the former included campaigns of ethnic persecution but stopped short of even mild forms of economic nationalism. Peasants and workers earned only a reprieve from economic inequality and subsequently were forced to seek relief in the harsh world of urban society and the informal economy.

The Huk rebellion was precipitated in a political crisis that pitted expectant and mobilized popular organizations against an ambitious, if weak, state obedient in major policy matters to the military and economic dictates of its former colonial patron. At some point the interests of foreign investors and agribusiness were fundamentally antagonistic to those of peasants, rural wage earners, urban workers, and petty entrepreneurs. Once that point was reached, the state lacked the resources, skill, or inclination to meet the crisis in any way save a repressive response materially supported by, and in the long-term interest of, the metropolitan power. In the short run, the rebels paid heavily for the attempt to better their lives or simply to defend themselves. Yet, through the suppression of their ambitions in a Faustian pact of economic and political dependency, virtually the entire society paid dearly in the long run. And, for all that, a revolutionary situation continues.

Notes

1. Wuthnow, "On Suffering, Rebellion, and the Moral Order."
2. Kerkvliet, *Huk Rebellion,* p. 210.

3. Hartendrop, *History*, p. 368.
4. Wickberg, *Chinese in Philippine Life.*
5. Graff, *American Imperialism;* Miller, "Our Mylai of 1900"; Pomeroy, *American Neo-Colonialism.*
6. Phelan, *Hispanization of the Philippines.*
7. Schurz, *Manila Galleon.*
8. *Ibid.*, p. 54.
9. Constantino, *History*, p. 47.
10. Murray, "Land Reform," p. 153; McLennan, "Land and Tenancy."
11. Constantino, *History*, pp. 57, 83–108, and ch. 6.
12. Phelan, *Hispanization*, ch. 10; Crippen, "Philippine Agrarian Unrest"; Zaide, *The Philippines Since Pre-Spanish Times;* Constantino, *History*, pp. 83–108.
13. Sweet, "Proto-Political Peasant Movement."
14. Constantino, *History*, p. 132.
15. *Ibid.*, p. 119.
16. Mahajani, *Philippine Nationalism*, p. 50.
17. Constantino, *History*, pp. 159–60.
18. Mahajani, *Philippine Nationalism*, p. 64.
19. Constantino, *History*, p. 161.
20. The two views are argued, respectively, in Constantino, *History*, pp. 172–97, and Mahajani, *Philippine Nationalism*, pp. 70–79.
21. Graff, *American Imperialism*, pp. 1–35.
22. Mahajani, *Philippine Nationalism*, p. 89.
23. Friend, *Between Two Empires.*
24. Sturtevant, "Sakdalism."
25. Constantino, *History*, pp. 246–80.
26. Kerkvliet, "Peasant Society," p. 174; Guerrero, "Colorum Uprisings," p. 66.
27. Guerrero, "Colorum Uprisings," p. 69.
28. Sturtevant, "Sakdalism," p. 201.
29. Hayden, *The Philippines*, p. 387.
30. Sturtevant, "Sakdalism," pp. 202–3.
31. *Ibid.*, p. 203.
32. *Ibid.*, p. 208.
33. *Ibid.*, p. 211.
34. Crippen, "Philippine Agrarian Unrest"; Kurihara, *Labor.*
35. Crippen, "Philippine Agrarian Unrest," p. 191.
36. Jacoby, *Agrarian Unrest*, p. 192.
37. Golay, *The Philippines*, p. 47.
38. *Ibid.*, p. 45, figures for 1937–1940.
39. Friend, "Philippine Sugar Industry," p. 184.
40. Weinstedt and Spencer, *Philippine Island World*, ch. 10.
41. Larkin, *Pampangans*, pp. 293–94.
42. Jacoby, *Agrarian Unrest*, pp. 199–209; Kerkvliet, *Huk Rebellion*, ch. 1; Larkin, *Pampangans*, pp. 295–97, 309.
43. Sayer quoted in Friend, "Philippine Sugar Industry," p. 192.
44. For example, Kerkvliet, *Huk Rebellion.*
45. Friend, "Philippine Sugar Industry."
46. Kurihara, *Labor*, p. 256.
47. Crippen, "Philippine Agrarian Unrest," p. 347.
48. Wurfel, "Trade Union Development," pp. 584–85.
49. *Ibid.*, p. 586.
50. Kerkvliet, "Peasant Society," p. 210.
51. Carroll, "Philippine Labor Unions."
52. Wurfel, "Trade Union Development," pp. 587–88.
53. Kurihara, *Labor*, p. 70.
54. *Ibid.*, p. 83.

55. Kerkvliet, *Huk Rebellion*, pp. 75–77.
56. Larkin, *Pampangans*, p. 311.
57. Friend, *Between Two Empires*, pp. 249–50, 261.
58. Taruc, *Born of the People*, p. 218.
59. Kerkvliet, *Huk Rebellion*, p. 138.
60. Pomeroy, *American Made Tragedy*, p. 20.
61. Quoted in Kerkvliet, *Huk Rebellion*, p. 168.
62. Taruc, *Born of the People* and *He Who Rides the Tiger;* Pomeroy, *Forest;* Baclagón, *Lessons;* Lansdale, *In the Midst of Wars;* Kerkvliet, *Huk Rebellion;* Lachia, *Huk.*
63. Scaff, *Philippine Answer to Communism.*
64. Pomeroy, *Forest* and *American Made Tragedy.*
65. Kerkvliet, *Huk Rebellion*, pp. 264–66.
66. Pomeroy, "Philippine Peasantry," p. 498.
67. *Ibid.*, pp. 510–11.
68. *Ibid.*, p. 511.
69. Murray, "Land Reform."
70. Wurfel, "Philippine Agrarian Reform"; Starner, *Magsaysay.*
71. Murray, "Land Reform," p. 164.
72. Wurfel, "Trade Union Development," p. 600.
73. *Ibid.*
74. *Ibid.*, p. 595.
75. *Ibid.*, p. 600.
76. Appleton, "Overseas Chinese"; Agpalo, *Political Process.*
77. Lichauco, "Lichauco Paper"; Hamilton, "Pariah Capitalism."
78. Bello, "Marcos."
79. Lichauco, "Lichauco Paper."
80. Bello, "Marcos."
81. Quoted in Kerkvliet, *Huk Rebellion*, p. 269.

REPUBLIC OF COLOMBIA

CHAPTER THREE

La Violencia

ONCE AGAIN, a useful introduction to the analysis of national revolt begins with some reflection on the implications of the nomenclature used in standard accounts. Theories are embedded in words, and much that should be taken as problematic is too often assumed in uncritical use of linguistic convention. In official inquiries and scholarly autopsies the events that convulsed Colombia in and around the 1950s are typically referred to simple as "the violence," connoting a bloodthirsty, primitive, and chaotic conflict lacking purpose, direction, or a definable set of antagonists. This is also the imagery behind received analyses of La Violencia that eschew any notion of revolutionary significance in favor of an admixture of civil war and fratricidal peasant struggle, blending traditional vendettas with modern political party loyalties.[1] The events are presented replete with themes of elemental passion, irrationality, barbaric attack on conventional social organization, and, above all, melancholy chaos—the sad fate of a sad country's history. Violence, unlike revolution, has no protagonists.

This portrait arouses skepticism. For one thing, the chronicles that advance it were written by the elites that survived the conflict and by their academic retainers. For another, "run amok" interpretations of popular psychohistory commonly dissolve under the analytic gaze of social historians who discover the causal relevance of economic and political circumstance in major social disturbances.

La Violencia occupied the years 1946–1958, although protracted incidents of guerrilla warfare and banditry continued well into the 1960s. The revolution is estimated to have cost 200,000 lives, massive dislocation in property loss and forced migration, and a climate of fear from which the nation and its political arrangements have never completely recovered: "It represents what is probably the greatest armed mobilization of peasants (as guerrillas, brigands, or self-defense groups) in the recent history of the western hemisphere, with the possible exception of some periods during the Mexican revolution."[2] The twelve-year period included the return of Conservative party domination after twenty-six years of liberal reformism and modernization, a short-lived (1953–1957) dictatorship resorted to unsuccessfully to stop the fighting, and a National Front government coalition begun in 1958 as a transitional return to normal party politics in 1974. The National Front ended the Violencia as a movement and continues to define much of the framework of Colombian politics, although it has recently been superseded in a cautious return to open electoral procedures.

The violence was an undeniably complex movement whose assorted events divide reflective interpretations based on civil war and social revolution.[3] Yet all of these identify similar historical roots and structural causes, including the conditions of Colombia's incorporation into the global economy, economic modernization, upper-class conflict, and popular resistance. Among the events themselves it is generally recognized that the explosive beginning of the revolt came with the assassination in April 1948 of the charismatic Liberal party leader Jorge Eliécer Gaitán. The elections of 1946 returned the Conservative party to power after a long absence and were followed by sporadic incidents of rural violence that helped mobilize the opposition. More than 100,000 Liberal opponents of the new regime demonstrated in the central plaza of Bogotá a few days before the assassination. Gaitán's murder provoked the massive Bogotazo riot that raged for three days—looting and killing in the capital joined by government troops and police and spreading rapidly to other cities such as Cali, where Liberal insurgents seized the local government. The urban origins of the conflict and its subsequent rural concentration, as well as the influence of the political parties and their associated constituencies, begin to introduce some of the complexities that must be followed through in their historical development.

Until the end of the nineteenth century Colombia was (and in

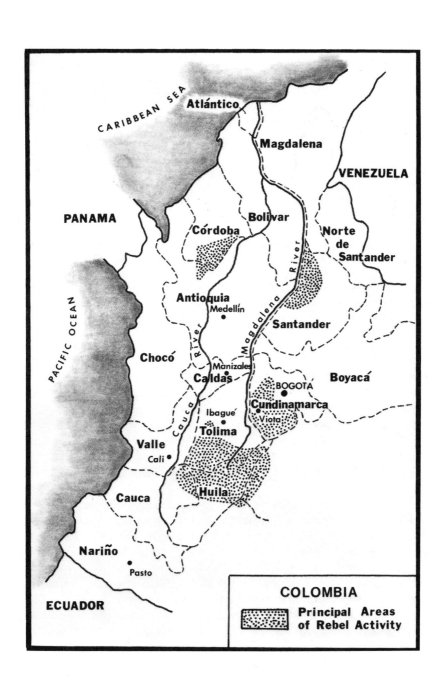

CARIBBEAN SEA

Atlántico

Magdalena

VENEZUELA

PANAMA

Córdoba

Bolívar

Norte
de
Santander

Antioquia

Medellín

Santander

PACIFIC OCEAN

Chocó

Manizales

Caldas

Boyacá

BOGOTÁ

Cundinamarca

Ibagué

Viota

Tolima

Valle

Cali

Huila

Cauca

Nariño

Pasto

ECUADOR

COLOMBIA

Principal Areas
of Rebel Activity

some respects remains) a highly traditional republic in the Spanish colonial mold. Despite the political achievements of independence, the prosperity stemming from gold mining and coffee, and early attempts to create a technical elite, Colombia entered the twentieth century with a castelike social system.[4] The rigid hierarchy rested on a landed oligarchy divided internally by custom and geography owing to the fact that different "nations" of Spaniards (Andalusians, Catalans, Basques) had settled regions of the colony geographically divided by rugged terrain. After independence in 1810 regional overlords, or *caudillos,* dominated fiefdoms, and their armies fought a protracted series of civil wars culminating in the 1899–1902 War of a Thousand Days.[5]

In the colonial period Hispanic upper-class control over a subservient labor population and a virtual upper-class monopoly of land and other economic resources created an economic structure that discouraged interest in technical development. Upper-class control of land and labor made it possible to hold down wages. Low payment meant that local markets lacked a broad base and were rather anemic.[6]

Colombian society of the nineteenth and early twentieth centuries was highly localized except when visited by destructive forces from the outside, such as the civil wars between liberals and conservatives or the labor struggles on the banana plantations of North American companies. In the magnificent novel *One Hundred Years of Solitude,* Gabriel García Márquez recalls this tragic history from the vantage of a town in the Caribbean coastal region whose liberal heroes had little sense of the purpose of the wars and whose community fell into ruin with the departure of the banana companies in the face of violent strikes.

As elsewhere in Latin America, the Spanish conquerors came mainly in search of precious metals and only secondarily to establish dominions and trade. In most parts of Nueva Granada where the promise of mineral riches was denied, they settled down on extensive royal land grants in agricultural production employing a commandeered native labor force under the *encomienda* system. The native population was either effectively enslaved as peons on the haciendas, or driven from the good valley land up the Andean slopes to cultivate small plots intensively. Black slaves were imported to work for the mines, riverboats, and plantations. Extensive and inefficient production characterized colonial agriculture devoted to cattle ranches and sugar plantations. Although more advanced, the Cauca Valley presented a situation approximated in many regions:

The amount of land and the number of serfs on it were becoming the measure of wealth in the economic vacuum of the colony. The growth of the estates and the diminution in the size of subsistence plots resulted in the expansion of pastoralism over food crops and the increased pressure of the landlords on the serfs.[7]

Colonialism everywhere encountered the problem of labor supply, and the manner in which this problem was solved contributed heavily to the ensuing pattern of social organization. In Spanish America the initial practice of enslaving Indians quickly proved disastrous; many of those who resisted were killed, and others who acquiesced still perished in large numbers from European diseases and overwork. In response to this problem and to the Crown's insistence on more humane treatment of the Indians, slaves were imported more generously, areas were reserved for Indian agriculture, and the *encomienda* fostered reproduction of the labor it exploited. These arrangements did not prevent repeated rebellions such as the rising of Indians in Popayán in 1553 and the rebellion of the slaves who worked the Antioqueño mines in 1598.

In the social order a pattern of ethnic stratification evolved bearing some similarities to the Philippine case, save for the inclusion of Negroes at the bottom of the ladder rather Chinese in the middle. At the top the same division existed between Spanish *peninsulares* and American-born *criollos*. Next came the Spanish–Indian mestizos, mulattoes, and *zambos* of Negro–Indian parentage. What is special about Latin America, however, is that a more drastic reduction of the native population necessarily led to a more rapid and complete "mestizoization" (actually a triangular racial intermixing).[8]

Naturally, the peninsular Spanish dominated the divided society of Nueva Granada, but the political innovations of Charles III at home combined with incipient conflicts in the colony to produce the metamorphic Comunero rebellion of 1781. Spain's new policy endeavored to rationalize the colonial economy and to create "a unitary state in which all the resources of Spain's diverse and far-flung dominions could be mobilized to defend the monarchy."[9] In the Philippines this policy was reflected in an effort to revive the galleon trade under liberalized terms of trade, but it came too late to stem British and Chinese competition. In Nueva Granada it included similar attempts to stimulate commerce, increase taxes, limit the amount of land and labor consumed by the Indian reserves, and manage more efficiently the Crown's monopolies. The direct effects of competition in the evolving world system had yet to reach Nueva Granada, although they were not far off. Increased taxes and tighter control from state corporations, such as the tobacco monopoly, which tried to restrict cultivation by private growers, led the local population to begin forming their own *comunes* with elected officials who protested Crown policy. The *criollo* oligarchy was caught between sides, favoring the tax revolt and economic autonomy pressed by the *comuneros* but recognizing their own dependence upon colonial administration. The Comunero revolt began when a main force of 20,000 marched on Bogotá, stopping at the expropriated Indian salt mines of nearby Zipaquirá, while a second column moved into the Magdalena River valley, attacking Spanish garrisons on the way and liberating slaves. Under the onslaught the archbishop entered negotiations with the *comuneros,* buying time for the return of royal reinforcements. The substantial Capitulaciones de Zipaquirá made to the *comuneros* included cancelation of the new taxes, abolition of the tobacco monopoly, an end to the destruction of Indian reserves, and the return of their salt mine. Although the capitulations were nullified with the return of Spanish troops, it would be mistaken to infer that the rebellion failed.

> **Those who have interpreted the Comunero Revolution as the first chapter of political emancipation or as a frustrated social revolution have concluded that the movement was a dismal failure. Viewed in the context of 1781 . . . the Comuneros achieved a solid success. Although the authorities soon repudiated the capitulations of Zipaquirá . . . after reestablishing royal authority [they] set about making significant concessions to the very sources of discontent that had precipitated the protest. . . . The lesson that the comuneros taught Charles III and his ministers was that they could not violate with impunity the deeply rooted political traditions of Nueva Granada. Paradoxically . . . [this] built the bridge connecting the colony with independence.[10]**

The independence that came to all of Latin America in the 1820s was occasioned by the continuing eclipse of Spain as a world power and its consequences for the *criollo* oligarchy. The dominant local interests had no objection in principle to a trading economy under Spanish sovereignty. However, because Spain failed to industrialize, it was unable to supply the colonies and became an expensive intermediary with the rising European economies, particularly England.[11] The lively trade in contraband proved not only that the Spaniards were being undersold but also that they had lost control of the seas off South America. England became the dominant commercial power in the region and banned the slave trade, less as a humanitarian act than as a blow to the last lucrative enterprise of Spain.[12] The *criollo* oligarchy, whose economic power rested on export from the mines and agriculture and import of manufactures, led the protracted struggle for independence.

The victorious Independence War was fought between liberal *criollos* and the Spanish, who had their local sympathizers among the plantation and slave-owning landlords. In the Republic of Gran Colombia established in 1821, this split grew as it shaded into new issues of state power. The division was between nineteenth-century liberals and conservatives, although the two factions did not organize as political parties until the 1840s. The liberals, of course, were the dominant merchant class that favored free trade, decentralization, and the new constitution. The conservatives drew support from landowners and the clergy wedded to the Spanish tradition of state centralism. The complex history of Colombia's first 100 years tells a story of almost continuous civil war, violent political struggles between the Liberal and Conservative parties, themselves increasingly based on divided social class bases, the grudging progress of liberal reforms in ecclesiastic and economic affairs, and the consequent perpetuation of a weak state.[13]

The trials of the new nation were experienced differently in the distinctive regions defined by Colombia's rugged geography and intricate patterns of settlement. Gold was found in the isolated northwestern province of Antioquia, whose mines became the best known in Latin America. They flourished initially using primitive methods of surface collection (including burial site robbery) by large gangs of Negro slaves and Indians. This prosperity was short-lived as the surface ore was exhausted, the slaves rebelled, and disease and the short supply of food crippled the labor force.

Provincial administrators responded to this challenge with unprecedented progressivism in a series of reform laws beginning in 1775 that embraced a comprehensive plan of development. Small-scale placer mining was still profitable, but the key problem for the isolated region was food supply. The reforms attacked this problem through creation of new towns in which families were granted town lots and farm land, everyone not engaged in mining was required to raise a certain amount of corn, town commissions provided for administration and compliance with the new laws, production quotas were established with bonuses for cultivation of new crops, trade schools were built, and welfare measures were adopted for the indigent. All of this gave rise to the heralded movement of Antioqueño colonization that brought some 400,000 people to the region between 1808 and 1870. Colonization under this enlightened program produced fundamental economic and political changes. Transportation routes were established linking towns in former backwash areas. Mining and agriculture prospered on a humble scale based on free-holding, which in turn sustained active regional commerce. The region exhibited a unique autonomy and did not suffer the debilitating effects of incorporation in the colonial economy characteristic of so much of the rest of Colombia and Latin America.[14]

> **To sum up, the extreme parcelization of the lands of recent Antio-queño settlement must be interpreted chiefly in the light of the recency of their occupation. Only the old granitic massif of the Rione-gro–Madellín–Santa Rosa heartland was effectively incorporated into the colonial structure and even here the strong emphasis on mining and the scattered nature of the deposits did not favor the development of the deeply rooted feudal traditions which sprang from the agricultural and livestock haciendas in other parts of New Granada. . . . The concept of wealth, then, was not tied either to subject peoples or to the soil as much as to hard work and initiative. On the new volcanic lands to the south and west the extremely broken nature of the country, together with the coffee planters' proud, free, and independent spirit of self-determination combined to produce this anomaly of a democratic society of small holders on a continent dominated by traditional Latin latifundism.[15]**

Curiously, Colombia was a latecomer to the production of coffee for which it is now famed. There were, of course, reasons for this that need not be explored here, such as ill-fated national government efforts to promote tobacco plantations, export monoculture, and a generally complacent attitude toward development among the landed elites that controlled most of the country and indulged in the continuous civil wars. However, around 1860 coffee was brought from Venezuela and Costa Rica to Antioquia, where the natural conditions (mountainous volcanic soils) and social ecology (of small-holders) were especially conducive to cash cropping. The initiative in coffee cultivation was taken by liberals excluded from other opportunities by the conservative "regeneration" government of the late nineteenth century.[16]

> **In contrast to the organizational structure of coffee growing in Brazil or Central American countries a large share of total coffee production as well as a large number of producing farms were small-holder peasant operations. . . . This difference in the organizational structure of coffee production is a major explanation for the favorable impact of coffee growing on Colombian development. . . . From the point of view of economic and social change, the most important fea-**

ture of the introduction of coffee as an export product was that it drew significant numbers of the population directly into the market. The older hacienda operations introduced only a small portion of the population into a money economy. Coffee production introduced a shifting over from non-market orientations for thousands of peasant families. Small-holders dealt directly with urban buyers of coffee and sellers of consumer goods. [17]

By 1880 the country as a whole began to recover from a protracted economic slump under the drive of the coffee boom. But production of the berry, so much in demand in North America, also brought new dangers. The lucrative export market encouraged consolidation of some lands and crop conversion on others for coffee plantations.

At the turn of the century, as the United States was acquiring the Philippines, it was also active next door in Panama, which had been Colombian territory until 1903, when Teddy Roosevelt and the U.S. Navy bought and engineered the transparent Panama revolt. Panama's secession from Colombia led to the creation of a new country more agreeable to American designs for a canal and enhanced Colombia's attractiveness as an ally, trading partner, and aid recipient.

With these events, the final termination of the nineteenth-century civil wars, and the beginning of a long reign of the Conservative party, the country experienced a period of phenomenal prosperity. At bottom the boom relied on coffee export, but it flourished on industrialization (e.g., of textiles in Antioquia), the rapid growth of foreign exchange earnings that were devoted to huge domestic capital investments (e.g., the coffee railways), and a flood of foreign investments and loans (British in the railways and mines, American in plantation agriculture). [18]

According to Fluharty, "three major influences cooperated to shake Colombia out of her somnolent colonialism": the growing importance of new (mostly coffee) markets and participation in the world trade with World War I; new norms created by the spread of proletarian doctrines after the Russian Revolution (especially the growth of militant labor unionism); and the "great influx of foreign capital in the twenties [that] brought vast changes to the social and economic structure, and forced upon government the necessity of adapting to these revolutionary mutations" [19]—in other words, major changes attendant to Colombia's incorporation into the world economy and the penetration of new material and ideological influences.

In the late nineteenth century (c.1880–1905) the average annual value of Colombian foreign trade was about 23 million pesos deriving from a reasonable balance of commodities, although the share of coffee in total exports rose from 13 percent in 1878 to 40 percent in 1905.[20] However, from 1912 until 1929 and the worldwide depression, these figures escalated dramatically. In 1913 exports were valued at 61 million pesos (a nearly threefold increase in just eight years), rising to 155 million by 1920 and 227 million by 1929—or more than a tenfold increase in the first two decades of this century.[21] Similarly, the contribution of coffee exports to the total value of trade rose from 40 to nearly 80 percent in the mid-1920s.[22] Even more spectacular was the associated increase in U.S. investment in Colombia, estimated at 2–4 million pesos in 1913, increasing to 30 million in 1920 and 280 million by 1929. The intersection of these trends in the principle that "trade follows investment" is found in the proportion of Colombian imports originating from the United States, which rose from 27 to 48 percent between 1913 and 1926, and the increased purchase of Colombian exports by the United States from 44 percent in 1913 to 86 percent in 1926.[23] This export boom and shift in the preponderance of reciprocal trade toward the United States followed the same pattern observed in the Philippines.

The "dance of the millions" aptly describes the prosperity enjoyed by foreign investors and certain sectors of the domestic economy during these halcyon days.[24] Colombia came into the twentieth century and the global economy with expansive confidence. The burgeoning export market stimulated agricultural production from the coffee and fruit plantations down to the ambitious sharecropper. Massive public works provided an important new source of nonagricultural employment, and urban industrialization attracted a wave of migration. Labor shortages developed, and the real wages of agricultural workers rose temporarily.[25] The gross domestic product was increasing at an average annual rate of 7.3 percent (in 1925–1929), and, not to be forgotten, the country's population grew from 5 million to almost 8 million between 1912 and 1929.[26]

Yet the benefits of this prosperity were far from equally distributed. Perhaps the most serious problem and characteristic feature of the dance of the millions was rampant inflation induced by the flood of foreign investment, rapidly rising export commodity prices, and huge public works expenditures—themselves heavily supported by U.S. development loans. Commenting on the late 1920s Rippy notes, "The cost of living has risen so rapidly during the last few years that the country has become one of the most expensive regions of the world."[27] The *overall* result was that workers suffered a decline in real wages between 1922 and 1929, while the upper classes prospered enormously.

In summary, this early experience of unbridled, uneven capitalist development introduced grave inequities that would later be the object of modernizing reforms.

In proportion as the dollars flooded tumultuously into the internal market, the migratory currents from the country to the city, to the roads and railroads and mines, grew. In 1926 and 1927 the fields of Boyocá were depopulated by the system of labor recruiting, to supply with cheap common labor the public works on divers fronts. Inflation began to operate like an endless screw: as the inflow of dollars increased, the programs of public works multiplied; and as these programs multiplied, more hands were drawn away from the fields and the demand for articles of consumption increased without the State undertaking any policy whatever for the bettering of techniques of food production to the end, at least, of maintaining old levels of productivity. And as these demands shot up, and the demographic potency of the cities swelled, the production of the countryside and the fields diminished.[28]

It was in this situation of falling real wages and oligarchic prosperity that "the Colombian proletariat shook itself awake," particularly with the formation of unions and strike committees initially among dock and rail workers. Once the strike wave spread to artisans and textile workers, a National Workers Confederation was formed in 1925.[29] Between 1918 and 1920 there were at least ten important strikes resulting in riots and clashes with the police.[30] The most celebrated labor protests were aimed at U.S. companies. The Tropical Oil Company, owned largely by Standard of New Jersey, was struck three times between October 1924 and January 1927, as workers demanded wage increases of 25 percent, no dismissal without just cause, an eight-hour day and Sundays off, and better food and sanitary conditions. Although these strikes were attended by violence, massive worker dismissals, and suppression by the army under martial law, the workers won significant concessions in wages and working conditions.[31]

The infamous strike of banana workers against the United Fruit Company in 1928 did much to dramatize labor unrest, promote a leftist political organization, and contribute to the subsequent fall of the Conservative government. Again, workers petitioned United Fruit for wage increases, regular wages rather than piece work, a day off each week, insurance and accident compensation, elimination of scrip payment and company stores, and medical facilities. And again, the

Colombian army was sent to keep order. As a result of *agents prov-ocateurs* or blunders by the strikers (reports mention both), troops fired on the workers and casualties resulted—somewhere between 40 and 1,500 killed, depending on the reporter.[32] The incident was sub-sequently investigated by the rising young politician, Jorge Gaitán, and a national scandal created by an official report that depicted the Colombian army in the service of U.S. imperialism slaughtering hon-est peasants. "Colombians of both parties awoke with a start, as it became clear that Colombian bayonets had helped support the banana empire when challenged by poor peasants. During the congressional debates, the government was completely discredited."[33] This com-plemented anti-Yankee sentiment still festering over the Panama in-cident and its delayed monetary compensation.

Peasant unrest paralleled and interacted with labor militance: "In 1918 the first peasant organizations appeared, and the first peasant demonstrations related to urban disturbances occurred."[34] Strikes in that year broke out simultaneously on the coffee and banana planta-tions. With the coffee boom, commercial production and the hacien-das had expanded, often encroaching on the peasantry. Increasingly, two general systems of agricultural production, plantation–hacienda and small-holder–tenant, grew and came into conflict. In the Cundi-namarca region west of Bogotá, the only area of the country "where most of the coffee lands were held in large plantations . . . conflicts became particularly numerous and often violent."[35]

Again, parallels with the situation in the Philippines are strong. Two systems of agricultural production existed side by side under antagonistic social relations. Small-holders and tenants struggled for survival under increasingly disadvantageous terms. On one hand, the large-holders wanted to consolidate more land and rid themselves of anachronistic tenant obligations. On the other, they needed their la-bor.

The coffee boom simultaneously provided strong incentives for the expansion of the haciendas, for the eviction of tenants with com-mercialization, *and* for cash-cropping by tenants and new settlers. The Colombian peasant was drawn into the world market. On the plantations,

conflicts arose in the twenties over the seemingly trivial demands of these peons to be allowed to plant coffee trees. . . . This demand was strongly opposed by the plantation owners who sensed that once the peasants owned coffee trees they would cease to be peons. With a cash income of their own they might turn into a less reliable labor force.[36]

Adjacent to the plantations, squatters moved on to public lands and private ones where titles were unclear or cultivation infrequent. The "availability" of land in various shades of use or rightful possession combined with the dependable export market that could support small, free farmers to produce the circumstances of constant conflict over land and labor control.

In the earlier period of extensive colonization in Antioquia, which established the small-holder system dominating most of Colombia's coffee production, conflicts over land tenure were much less frequent and usually solved amicably since land was more available and coffee a less lucrative business at the time.[37] The 1920s witnessed not only the great expansion of coffee production but also a significant regional shift in the areas of its cultivation from the eastern and northern regions of Cundinamarca and Norte de Santander to Antioquia, Caldas, Tolima, and Valle—later the major centers of the Violencia.[38] As a result, *latifundistas* and peasants came increasingly into face-to-face conflict.

During the twenties and early thirties direct action to dislodge settlers became more frequent, probably because the lands then being occupied were closer to the "core" of the haciendas over which the owners maintained effective control. Evictions also took place for a variety of reasons: because the tenants had planted coffee trees against the owners' will; because tenants gave signs of becoming disaffected, unionized, or otherwise subversive; and simply, as President López was to put it in one of his eloquent speeches, "because they felt like it" (*les viene en gana*); because they wanted to reaffirm their "supreme and feudal rights" to do as they pleased on their property.[39]

In the late 1920s the dance of the millions came to an end with Colombia in the throes of sometimes violent socioeconomic conflict and the world immersed in a depression. The depression was more severe in Colombia than in many Latin American countries, given its new-found and extensive ties to the United States. Foreign trade and its tax income came to a virtual halt. Between 1929 and 1931 government income fell from 75 million to 35 million pesos at the same time it was struck with U.S. loan payments for its public works projects. Banks foreclosed on businesses and agricultural enterprises, leading to new concentrations of capital and land—inequalities deepened.[40]

The depression came as a culmination of lessons in inequality drawn from unbridled capitalist development under foreign sponsorship and ushered in a period of reform. The crisis required a rejuvenated, stronger state capable of direct intervention in the economy and redistribution of its product. Having been on the sidelines for Colombia's spectacular entry into the twentieth century, in 1930 the Liberals returned to power amid calamity. Agrarian conflicts were most visible, but the nation found itself burdened with international loans, dependent upon volatile trade balances for income and financing of public works, and confronted with the birth pangs of industrialization and trade unionism. Beginning tentatively with the coalitional administration of Enrique Olaya Herrera, and then more decisively with the Colombian New Deal of Alfonso López in 1934, a series of reforms were initiated under the banner of Revolución en Marcha: "The state was strengthened to accommodate Colombian society to capitalist socioeconomic structures, to accelerate integration into the world capitalist system, and to compensate for the decline of traditional mechanisms of social control."[41]

Concretely, military force was augmented and given greater responsibility for controlling domestic conflict. State-subsidized gremial associations were introduced, initially with the National Coffee Grower's Association and subsequently through the incorporation of workers (CTC), industrialists (ANDI), and merchants (FENALCO) into the national planning effort. The state became the principal actor in the economy, meaning that all social classes and private interests became more dependent upon state patronage. "What had changed was the importance of the newly interventionist state and the increase in the potential impact of exclusivistic, hegemonic politics."[42]

Foremost among the reform targets was the problem of the landed oligarchy, large unproductive estates, and absentee ownership. The Land Law of 1936 (Law 200) recognized squatters' rights and provided for confiscation of private land not in productive use. In the field of labor, the rights to organize unions and to strike were granted, and the Confederation of Colombian Workers (CTC) was formed with 900 locals and 100,000 members. More efficient and egalitarian tax reforms were initiated. A liberal philosophy of the interventionist state was adopted giving the state the means to protect domestic industry, regulate customs, and provide credit through new public institutions. Public education was nationalized and made obligatory, while efforts were begun to limit the power of the church in education and politics. Although no attempt was made to nationalize foreign property or restrict investment, the reforms were nationalistic in tone, affirming a policy of "Colombia first for the Colombians." In what was potentially or theoretically the most important change, property itself was deemed no longer an absolute right but was to serve a social function. In its broader outlines the Revolución en Marcha represented a basic transformation of the state—its assumption of the modern role of the state as agent and guarantor of liberal capitalist modernization. Control of the state shifted partially from the landed aristocracy to the new political forces of export production, commerce, and industrialization.

Doubtless the reforms accomplished few of their "intended" effects and were mild in the implementation, accomplishing at best indirect results. But that accounting of presumably intended effects misses their central, political meaning. What López sought, and in many ways achieved, was the creation of a new political coalition, primarily urban and backed by the new nationalist industrialists and implacably opposed to the "feudal" oligarchs. That coalition depended upon the support of the newly aroused forces of labor and the peasantry. Concerning López's appeal to the latter group, Gilhodes observes perceptively:

> He was not as the popular imagination had made him. His aim was the development of capitalism in Colombia, not at all a popular revolution. In order to carry out his objectives and, in particular, in order to politically and economically weaken the land-holding class, he built himself a base of support in the peasantry; yet by no means did he mean to share power with the peasants.[43]

Power was shared with, indeed relied on, organizing urban labor and the new industrialists insofar as the Liberals were able to wed their interests to the party through economic growth.

Naturally, the lines that separated this modernizing elite coalition from the old landed aristocracy were often blurred. Some of the new industrialists (e.g., agribusiness in the Cauca Valley) had their roots in the latifundia, and many of the settlers and small-holders in the coffee regions were becoming a new agrarian bourgeoisie.[44] Nevertheless, the coalition for reform and liberal capitalist development had definite outlines and embraced broad segments from moderate to radical political leanings.

López's revolution was interrupted from 1938 to 1942 by the moderate regime of Eduardo Santos, and the former President's return in 1942–1945 was marked by a disappointing retreat from his reformist goals. But Liberal modernization had a profound effect in the twin senses of encouraging the popular movement led by Gaitán and forging the resolve of the Conservatives to fight back under the direction of Laureano Gómez.

Historically, and even under reform, the two major parties were elitist and sometimes only subtly divided ideologically. The Conservatives tended to include the landowners and defenders of the church, while the Liberals attracted merchants, exporters, industrialists, and intellectuals. Yet regional and divided economic loyalties (e.g., in export agriculture) and intraclass conflicts complicated this picture. The political directorates of the parties shared an upper-class world in common, but the reform coalition was strained at the top. Conversely, for the first time the liberal reforms had begun to enfranchise popular elements that tended toward the reformist party but were more at home as an independent populist crusade. There were strains at the bottom, exacerbated by the indifferent performance of the second reformist administration.

Under these circumstances, the Liberal party began to split between advocates of "bourgeois revolution" and progressive forces that supported Gaitán's UNIR (the National Leftist Revolutionary Union, formed in 1933).[45] In light of the implications of that split and a deteriorating political situation marked by factional strife and scandal, the elite associations of industrialists and merchants (ANDI and FENALCO) veered toward Gómez on the right.[46] But more important than all the in-fighting, the Revolución en Marcha was destroyed, and the counterrevolution advanced by the domestic consequences of World War II.

Once again, war brought maldistributed prosperity, particularly through the export sector. Coffee exports skyrocketed, and national industry prospered in the absence of foreign imports. The net effect was a huge accumulation of foreign exchange and pent-up demand. This led to a new and more serious round of inflation producing unemployment, precipitate declines in real income, and speculative capital ventures in land and urban real estate. Based on 1905 as an index year (= 100), the wages of urban workers, which had risen to 170 in 1941, fell by more than half at the end of the war to 82 in 1944. Similarly, if less drastically, real agricultural wages in the coffee zones fell from the 100-base years of 1935–1937 to between 68 and 93 in 1945–1949.[47] Citing contemporary reports, Fluharty indicates:

The cost of living index for Bogotá was 171.7 at the end of 1944, in comparison with 142.4 at the end of the previous year. In other cities the range was about the same. Industrial wages rose at a slower rate than the cost of living, and real wages had declined steadily since 1941. . . . In November of 1946, the cost of living of a (Colombian) workingman's family reached 229 (1937 as 100). . . . During 1947, living cost indices in Bogotá rose to 253.2. These rises continued in 1948. During the single month of March, 1948, the cost of living index for an average workingman's family rose by 17.3 points, to a new high of 283.8.[48]

Meanwhile, spectacular profits were earned by coffee producers (including some small-holders) and export merchants benefiting from wartime trade, and by local industrialists temporarily "protected" by the cessation of metropolitan imports.[49] By the end of the war, imports and luxury commodities continued to be restricted, leaving upper-class Colombians with large unexpended balances of speculative capital. The results of this situation were predictable: "Investment in real estate zoomed upward, raising rents for the poor, to add another burden to rising food costs."[50] Similarly, rural landownership became more concentrated since the majority of small-holders (i.e., the estimated 87 percent with farms smaller than three hectares) also depended upon declining wages.[51] A new wave of uneven development swept over the postwar landscape carrying mass poverty along with great speculative profit.

These cold, bare figures display the other side of the picture: That of mass misery, of hunger, of wages lagging behind living costs, of food becoming dearer daily, and of unemployment spreading. The violence in the provinces, the arming of the Liberals, the repressive measures of the Political Police and the counteractions, all of these are understandable only in terms of want and economic hardship. The people were distressed and hungry. In 1948 the violence was accompanied by looting—a sure indicator of danger ahead.[52]

Following sixteen years of Liberal rule and the misfired Revolución en Marcha, the Conservative "counterrevolution" succeeded in 1946 with a valuable assist from Liberal factionalism. In the presidential election of that year Gaitán chose to do battle with Conservatives and Liberal moderates, ultimately running third and splitting the Liberal majority of votes cast. Yet the numerical strength of Gaitán's showing (about 26 percent of the electorate against the victorious Conservatives' 41 percent) was impressive, all the more so given its predominantly urban mass base, which was expanding rapidly. Political observers were agreed that Gaitán and the maverick Liberals stood a good chance of gaining the presidency in the next election in 1950. Moreover, the rising force of *gaitanismo* was a clear and present threat to the established interests of both Conservatives and Liberals, whose differences had more to do with the appropriate methods of capitalist development than with its elitist management and bourgeois goals. *Gaitanismo* was very significant for what followed:

This trend in Colombian politics undermined the entire basis of the two-party oligarchy, for it threatened to *turn the parties into social movements* and, what is more, to transform the Liberal party, with its appeal to the poor, into the permanent and overwhelming major-

ity party. This development can be regarded as the root cause of the civil wars of 1949–53. Faced with virtual long-term eclipse, the Conservatives had to fight back, and, after the insurrection of 1948 had shown them the full danger of their position, they did so by means of a systematic attack on the Liberal regions of the country, combined with a *deliberate conversion of the State apparatus*, notably the police and army, into a *Conservative vested interest*. [53]

In some respects these developments parallel the Philippine case, where electoral gains by a popular movement (e.g., the Democratic Alliance) led to a closing of elite ranks, new coalitions, and reactionary politics.

Faced with this threat not only to their own survival but to that of the Colombian tradition of oligarchic political domination, the Conservatives launched a counterrevolution against Liberal populism and all of the institutional reforms of the 1930s. Naturally, the Conservatives needed powerful allies for the counterrevolutionary coalition and, in the face of the growing popular movement, they found them among the same groups that had supported Liberal governments. Under the political circumstances, this rotation of bedfellows was not surprising.

National industry and commerce (particularly the export–import trade) were the basic pillars of these governments. But, whereas during the period of Liberal rule these forces attempted to promote capitalist development of Colombia on the basis of an unequal alliance with the people, in the period of Conservative hegemony they joined with the latifundistas against the people. The new policy of alliances (which was really a capitulation) grew out of the ruling group's fear of increasing conflicts in the cities (which were not true labor struggles), and in the countryside, particularly after the impact of *Gaitan-ismo*. [54]

The Conservative government, backed by this new coalition, attacked the threat at its sources by crushing the CTC labor federation, repealing labor and social legislation, tightening the reins of executive power and press censorship, and initiating military actions (e.g., tenant evictions and land possessions) against Liberal peasants, thus producing the actual beginnings of violence prior to 1948 and the Bogotazo.

Beginning with sporadic rural violence of this new character in 1946, the dramatic onset of La Violencia came on April 9, 1948, with Gaitán's assassination (whose plotters were never discovered). Although the rioting and looting of the Bogotazo spread from the capital, it was at this time an exclusively urban insurrection, which the peasants did not join and heard about vaguely only later.[55] Many of the political maneuvers and armed conflicts of the Violencia took place in, or were linked with, the cities.[56] Nevertheless, the tactical front soon shifted to the countryside, where political partisans were clearly divided by perennial issues and territorial lines.

The Conservative government instigated armed attacks on Liberal strongholds in the rural areas because these zones combined the terrain suitable for military campaigns against spatial concentrations of the opposition (as contrasted with the legislative campaigns against labor) and the interests of the most stalwart Conservatives, the large land-owners. The army and police were flung against regions, towns, and farms of Liberal sympathy. Initially in self-defense, guerrilla forces were organized predominantly by Liberals in the face of attacks by Conservative vigilantes, although later they resorted to the offensive. In this "first wave" (1948–1952) of violence the fighting spread from the traditionally volatile western coffee-producing zones through most of the country, including the eastern plains. In the "second wave" (1953–1957) it concentrated once again at its point of origin in the western departments that contributed to the high correlation between the production of coffee and casualties.

Common themes in the thousands of violent incidents in the rural areas included: possession of land by force; extortion and eviction of the possessors; floods of homeless migrants and refugees; pitched battles between typically Liberal settlers and tenants and Conservative army forces; Liberal counterattacks that shifted to like aggression; butchery and "pointless sadism"[57]—all with the encouragement and participation of the highest levels of government and the political parties.

The epicenter of the Violencia was in the western departments of Tolima, Valle, Antioquia, and Caldas—along with the interesting and somewhat divergent case of the eastern Llanos, where Liberal ranchers were a force the government sought to capture.[58] Casualties concentrated overwhelmingly in these departments: Tolima, 35,294; Valle, 10,700; Antioquia, 10,000; Caldas, 9,500; and Llanos Orientales, 9,000; followed at some distance by Cundinamarca, 3,500.[59] These areas were not only devoted predominantly to coffee production, but were also the "frontier" zones of colonization, tenancy, squatters, and small-holdings. Areas with settled coffee plantations were scarcely touched by the fighting, while "the zones affected by political violence coincide exactly with the fronts of modern colonizations."[60]

These were the areas in which the world economy had reached

the peasantry, where fortunes were tied to the export economy, land titles were in dispute, speculation and aggrandizement took root, and the Liberal peasants lived in close proximity to the Conservative landlords. Accordingly, it was here that material interests took political form in the imposed violence and reactive counter violence. This interpretation is consistent with the checkerboard pattern of peaceful and violent areas within a single region that some have mistaken for the absence of structural or economic correlates.[61] Moreover, it accords with descriptive accounts of the conflict involving land and crop seizures, extorted and devalued property sales, land invasions, attacks on villages and tenants' haciendas, and so forth.

The most recent and best study of the Violencia by Oquist correctly emphasizes its regionalized character and warns against a singular economic interpretation or partisan politics explanation. Among the five types of violence he identifies and locates geographically, "coffee crop violence" most resembles the foregoing description and has, perhaps, the strongest economic undercurrents, while "guerrilla civil war" corresponds more to violence instigated by the political parties for control of national territory. Beyond these, however, there were contagious "traditional rivalries between villages" and struggles for "control of local power structures" and for "control of land" (an occasion for dispossession of small-holders and longstanding Indian–*latifundista* conflict). Oquist's impressive and generally successful theoretical effort provides the kind of theory necessary to incorporate all of these complex types in a unified explanation. The core of his analysis is the conjunction of an expanding, interventionist state and a political elite deeply divided by partisanship and intraclass economic interest. Policy issues that were increasingly important to the survival and prosperity of various social classes were at the same time more the fulcrum of partisan rivalries, acrimony, and potential violence. The result of this unstable situation was a "partial collapse of the state," a deterioration of institutional mechanisms for regulating competing interests, an inability to hold back the enhanced military, which took sides, and the flight of any national authority. The main types of violence, in my judgment (based on the locations of casualties and the most sustained conflict), had economic and political bases, but others, more consistent with Oquist, flared from traditional struggles because the state was now physically absent to restrain them or because armed factions of the state joined the vendetta.[62]

From the events of the Bogotazo to the political struggles that fed the Violencia, urban groups and interests were continuously involved. This is clear from careful examination of the standard analyses that make "the curious assertion that La Violencia was confined to rural areas while recounting many examples of urban violence,"[63] or focus only on the more overt struggles in the countryside[64] and fail "to explore systematically the process that linked rural violence to national politics."[65] The fact that much of the violence was perpetrated by peasants upon one another should not lead to the erroneous conclusion of a fratricidal rural conflict. The larger social context (including the urban origins of certain key events) and the political responsibility for initiating the violence, if not always carrying it to the end, suggest a different interpretation. Barrington Moore might have had the Violencia in mind when he wrote:

> In any violent conflict the social composition of the victims will not *by itself* reveal much about the social and political character of the struggle. Let us suppose that a revolution breaks out in some Latin American country where the government is under the control of wealthy landlords and a few rich businessmen. Let us suppose further that the army is made up mostly of peasant conscripts and that one section of the army breaks off and joins the rebels who are seeking to overthrow the government and establish a communist regime. After a few pitched battles, the statistician would no doubt find that the casualties on both sides were mainly peasants. To conclude that the main split in this case was a vertical one, to deny that class conflict was the key to the political struggles would be patently absurd. . . . In a word, it is not only who fights but what the fight is about that matters.[66]

At times even Oquist's superior analysis falls into this habit by emphasizing very real intraclass party factionalism in lieu of searching for parallel class interests that may also animate traditional rivalries and local power struggles.

The Violencia was fundamentally a fight about who would control the state, what kind of a state it would be, and how the costs and benefits of its development would be distributed. Set in one liberal capitalist direction in the 1930s, the state was recaptured in the late 1940s by a new Conservative coalition of landed, commercial, and industrial elites closely linked with the export economy and metropolitan centers of the world system.[67] This new direction was opposed by some Liberals and their working-class and peasant allies.[68] The revolt itself was a purposive struggle in this sense of control of the state, although the elite partisans clearly lost direction over the violent actions of those they hoped would win the struggle for them. The distinguishing feature of the Violencia is found not in its internecine peasant battles or in question-begging "traditional political rivalries," which can only be understood as intervening variables, but in the encouragement and service into which they were put by national elite power struggles over control of the state and modernization.

The fact that instrumental violence got out of control is another circumstance that has obscured the character of the revolt, yet it can be analytically illuminating in its own right when viewed as political impotence and stalemate (indeed, "partial collapse") rather than irrational chaos. On this view, the following conditions were essential. Although the Conservative government received initial support after it launched military strikes against rural zones, possibly in the hope of a rapid reconsolidation of order after the Bogotazo, its coalitional and military supporters soon began to break ranks (including wholesale defections of military units). In the short time since their narrow electoral victory the Conservatives had not established a strong base, and much of their reluctant support derived from a "dreaded alternative" (*gaitanismo*) that paled against the violence. For their part the Liberals were divided among those who continued to play by parliamentary rules and those who organized defensively in guerrilla armies or, more aggressively, joined in direct military confrontations with government forces for the control of regional enclaves. There were genuine revolutionaries in the rural and urban struggle drawn from the left of UNIR, the CTC, and small Colombian Communist party (PCC), and the peasantry, but they had little success at creating an attempted National Conference of Guerrillas. On the national and, especially, provincial levels rural combatants received support and parallel action from urban groups pursuing labor issues, but none of this approached a coordinated national movement. The prototypical regional alternative was the establishment of (or revitalization of pre-violence) "independent republics" and guerrilla bands with their own territorial claims and political subsystems. Apropos of multiple sovereignty, some of these (e.g., in Cundinamarca, Tolima, and the Llanos) became virtually autonomous principalities whose borders were not violated by government forces. The Violencia was as fragmented as Colombian geography and postwar politics.

But this fact does not degrade the purposive struggle of the rebels to irrational, fanatic, or kindred residual portraits. From weak and isolated bases they were fighting (sometimes among themselves after official violence had begun a chain of vendetta) for their land, freedom from agrarian and industrial paternalism, an adequate income, and a channel of political expression. The fact that the constituted authorities were nearly as weak and, having unleashed the violence could not carry it through, should not obscure with suggestions of civil war the nature of this inefficiently prosecuted class and political war. The weaknesses of the revolt were also the weaknesses of the society.

Before passing to the series of political strategies that tried to bring the Violencia under control, some interpretive comment on its causes is necessary. I am arguing, of course, that the Violencia is best construed as a national revolt (a protracted, violent, and nonlocal struggle of mobilized classes and status groups that claim national sovereignty and attempt to transform the state), rather than a civil war or loosely connected ensemble of traditional, economic, and localized power struggles. The argument rests, so far, on changes in state policies for development and their expression in the political struggle of social classes to control the state in the face of fundamental economic change stemming from the world system. On several particular points this interpretation differs with the conceptual thrust of Oquist's outstanding monograph, which does not attempt to locate the Violencia in the purview of revolutionary theory. In the first place, Oquist's useful and well-documented notion of a "partial collapse of the state" may downplay purposive efforts to control the floundering state, but more important it begs the further question—Why did the state partially collapse? Oquist's answer dwells mainly on the intraclass, partisan conflict without delving far enough to discover the economic bases of the class struggle for control of the state that also took place, interacting with, even determining, the party struggle. The fact that class differences did not always separate the political parties does not imply that they were absent among parties to the violence.[69] Without this emphasis Oquist's explanation, like Skocpol's "structurally given" potential for peasant unrest, sometimes becomes residual—here in the dress of "traditional rivalries" that are simply unleashed by the physical absence of a state once able to keep the lid on. This is not always the case in Oquist's analysis, but it seems to enter with his leanings toward an exclusively political explanation (albeit of a new and fertile kind) based more on ready intraclass differences than on the economic roots of coalitional class politics. This, obviously, is a matter of emphasis since both inter- and intraclass struggles were prominent. The real problem with Oquist's preference for the latter is the complication it introduces by requiring separate explanations of a nonresidual character for all the "unleashed" violence. If that was not class-based, but simply thrived on party loyalties in the absence of state-imposed order, what was it about? What was the tangible content of party and traditional rivalry?

Between 1948 and 1953 the violence spread from the western departments to virtually the entire country as the political struggle was generalized and acquired a certain autonomy. National politics continued to function, but with no pretense of coalitional accord. The Conservatives retained power, moving further in the reactionary direction when Laureano Gómez, long the force behind the party officials, assumed the presidency in 1950. Political squabbling was continuous and labyrinthian with the Liberals compromised so many times that their influence was nearly eclipsed. Yet Gómez fared no better in renewed military measures to end the violence. The flagging enthusiasm of his supporters was turned to veiled opposition by officially condoned attacks on the Bogotá homes of leading Liberals (including the former and future Presidents López and Lleras Restrepo): "Such actions broke the tacit rules of the game that the violence was not to strike directly at members of the elite and was to be principally confined to areas outside the major population centers."[70] The question of a supposed "gentlemen's agreement" limiting the areas of violence raises another about the extent of urban violence. In fact there was no such agreement, and fatal conflicts erupted in the cities from the Bogotazo to the "small and medium-sized cities of the coffee region. . . . [T]hese political and economic assassinations reached the point of systematic terrorism. . . . [U]rban Colombia was perhaps most massively affected by violence when the phenomenon began to decline in the countryside."[71] The sense in which an agreement was involved in these events more visible and shocking to the political elites was only that they created greater pressure for a political solution—a formal truce such as the one that followed the Bogotazo that also "genuinely affected the interests of the dominant groups of both parties."[72]

But finally, it was the defection of a disillusioned army that brought Conservative rule and the first wave of the Violencia to an end. At close range the army became convinced of the futility of ending the civil conflict with increasingly repulsive military methods. In a surprsingly peaceful coup, no doubt aided by dissension in the party, the Conservatives were replaced by the military government of Lieutenant General Gustavo Rojas Pinilla in June 1953. Rojas was welcomed with enthusiastic relief and marked cessation of the violence. Espousing reforms such as rural credit and development projects, Rojas's most telling appeal was in promised amnesty and bipartisan government. But the honeymoon was brief. The military administration was staffed mainly by civilian Conservatives. Liberals and other citizens were tolerated, but the order of privilege persisted as before. Moreover, Rojas reacted poorly to criticism. In June 1954 police and army units opened fire on student demonstrators in Bogotá, and in August 1955 the country's leading newspaper was closed for an alleged insult to the "Supreme Chief." Increasingly the administration took on the trappings of dictatorship conveyed by Rojas's embarrassingly transparent attempts to imitate Argentine President Juan Perón in executive manner and populist style. Rojas grew unaware of much of the political reality that surrounded him, including corruption, and his general incompetence verged on buffoonery. Worse, as new abuses arose, the violence returned in a second wave, albeit confined once again to the western provinces.

Among the important effects of the Rojas regime (including an elevated mass awareness of the oligarchic privilege he railed against) was, finally, a truce between the surviving and wiser factions of the two parties. In extensive negotiations of party leaders, an agreement was reached for establishment (by plebiscite) of a bipartisan National Front government. In the "days of May" 1957, with the army defecting again from the government's side, Rojas went into exile. As an indication of new-found harmony in the aftermath of revolt,

the "days of May" were not engineered by the same urban lower classes and refugees from rural violence who had assaulted the bastions of political authority on April 9, 1948 [in the Bogotazo]. The clubs, the Church hierarchy, the business associations, and the leadership of the two parties were its principal authors. When it came to street demonstrations in Bogotá students from Jesuit university were prominent among the leaders, not just those of the more "radical" universities. On the morning of May 10 those who poured into the streets of the capital came in the first instance from the northern districts of the city, not from the south where resides the *"chusma"* (riff-raff). Nor did the guerrillas "come over the mountains" as some euphoric souls believed they would. The small Communist party, which had combatted Rojas for several years, was hardly even the tail of the revolutionary kite. All these facts helped to determine both the nature of the revolution and the identity of those who would be its inheritors.[73]

What finally brought peace and bipartisan cooperation was less the carnage and dehumanization of the common people than the contamination of upper-class urban life—the humiliation and abused aristocratic sensibilities suffered by the privileged classes at the hands of a gauche Rojas engaged in unseemly displays of populism. Perhaps the sharp contrast between the Rojas government and the grand illusions of Colombian democratic urbanity brought people to their senses in a way that the suffering of the lower classes could not.

At all events, a decade of generalized violence began to abate in 1957 as preparations for the National Front were made. Violence had not, and has not to this date, ended completely. Small guerrilla forces persisted in new ways of life that included autonomous regional armies or politicized police forces, revolutionary guerrilla *focos,* and banditry.[74] But the National Front continued some of the saner policies of the dictatorship, including amnesty, relief and rehabilitation teams, agricultural loans, and employment-generating public works programs. The revolt was over.

Harking back to a number of experiments with bipartisanship dating from the nineteenth century, the National Front was based on the scheduled rotation of Liberal and Conservative national administrations (in four-year terms from 1958 to 1974) with elected and appointed positions within any administration divided equally among the parties. The same principle was carried to the department and municipal levels. Elections were held that ranked individual aspirants on party slates drawn upon to fill the available quotas of bipartisan positions. Parity among the parties and representation of their internal factions were observed in the staffing of all public posts. After overwhelming approval of this "Pact of Stiges" (named for the town in Spain where it was negotiated with the exiled Gómez) in December of 1957, the Liberals led off with the first administration of Alberto Lleras Camargo (1958–1962) and so on for the specified sixteen years. Political peace, at least by standards of the Violencia, prevailed even in the post-1974 period of *"desmonte"* as gradually more open elections tended to follow party rotation. The pact, of course, came from above—power was shared, but not very broadly. What the National Front provided was an "instrumentality for retaining real power in elite hands *while at the same time* carrying forward Colombia's economic development, and instituting those changes in the social order that would both advance elite material interests and ward off social revolution."[75] And, in that sense, it worked.

When we reflect on what the Violencia accomplished and the long-run outcomes of the revolt, the fundamental fact is that the National Front was the direct result of the conflict and the economic and political issues that were its roots. Through the agreement to share power and to get on with economic modernization, the National Front, in effect, accomplished what the Revolución en Marcha had attempted in the 1930s before it was stopped by the counterrevolution. The difference was that where the reforms of the 1930s required Liberal hegemony, the National Front effected a genuine coalition owing (beyond the stimulus of tragedy) to the fact that the elements to be coalesced were different. The unalloyed landed elite was less substantial after the violence, and many of its numbers could accept Liberal modernization policies, including export and agro-industry. Similarly, the violence had moved the church toward the center. The modernizing coalition that called itself "revolutionary" in the 1930s was now developmentally orthodox.

The National Front, accordingly, took steps to redress rebel grievances. Land reform headed the agenda, and while the Colombians pushed the easy solution of colonization (not totally unrealistic given the amount of open land, particularly in the eastern plains) so popular in the Philippines, they went a good deal further. After long and intricate negotiation the Social-Agrarian Reform (Law 135) was passed in 1961 and provided, in Hirschman's approving phrase, "revolution by stealth."[76] Although the law was far from drastic in its provisions (e.g. with no expropriation of large productive holdings), it ensured that a good deal of unused or inadequately cultivated land could be acquired by modest peasants through long-term, low-interest public bonds. The threat, rather than the actual use, of expropriation was there as an incentive to more productive exploitation of large holdings. The Colombian Institute of Agrarian Reform (INCORA) was established and became a major government agency managing acquisitions but also pursing a variety of other programs such as land reclamation and technical assistance. Since 1961 the landed and agribusiness interests have fought INCORA bitterly and, from the standpoint of their inviolable property rights, successfully.[77] At the same time, the *latifundista* is on the defensive, and many thousands of peasants have acquired land.

The Violencia also produced a measure of independence and autonomous self-government in certain portions of the Colombian countryside. In official portraits the "red republics" have been painted as *caudillo* fiefdoms, and doubtless there is truth in that. But given the historical fact of landlord fiefdoms, self-governing ones may be considered an advance. "Through the Violencia these persons achieved new ways of governing or of controlling their own destinies, impossible in traditional society. Displaying an impressive amount of resolution some of them were even able to establish 'independent republics.' "[78] On the eastern plains, particularly, "[the] guerrillas increased the quality of their control as they progressively consolidated alternative authority and power structures. Guerrilla legal codes, courts, and taxes replaced those of the national government."[79] If power was not shared on the national level, it was occasionally taken regionally.

Urban labor confederations supported the National Front ending the Conservative policy of attempting to undermine one independent group (CTC) through sponsorship of another quasi-official union (UTC). Labor reforms of the 1930s were restored. Labor became better organized and more militant in urging on the National Front policies of price control, housing, employment, and welfare.

Although the National Front may be fairly characterized as elitist, upper-class, bourgeois at the heart of its development policies, and cozy with the plethora of multinational corporations operating in the country, there are some things it was not. It was not a regime heavily influenced by the army or foreign military entanglements. Historically, and in the dark hours of transition from counterrevolutionary and dictatorial rule, the army decisively took the way out. Indeed, the army appeared more conscience-struck by the violence than did the politician instigators.

Similarly, although Colombia has willingly accepted political and economic dependence upon the United States (including military aid and CIA expertise in rooting out guerrilla revolutionaries), in other ways it has stood for its national interests against metropolitan pressure. Ironically, an envious Filipino nationalist has written accurately that "when the IMF insisted in 1966 that the government of Colombia devalue the currency and dismantle controls, the Colombian president, Carlos Lleras Restrepo, defied the conditions and refused to devalue. Instead, he banned all nonessential imports, collected more taxes, and imposed price controls."[80] It was the same, admittedly exemplary, Lleras administration that imposed controls on the flight of national capital and began to trade with the Eastern European countries in a multilateral strategy that succeeded in improving the terms of trade.

Contemporary Colombia, in many respects, continues to live in the somber mood of García Márquez's *One Hundred Years of Solitude*. The Violencia was the abyss, and another hundred years may be required to erase its tragic impact. But some lessons were drawn from the experience. Bipartisan class rule has allowed militant labor organization and land reform. Democratic political traditions are alive, if often in the fight for their very preservation. The Violencia produced permanent changes in the organization of the state and society. By contrast to the contemporary prevalence of authoritarian regimes

in Latin America, Colombia resembles more those republics that claim
a successful revolution.

Notes

1. Guzmán, Fals, and Umaña, *La Violencia;* Fals, "Violence."
2. Hobsbawm, "Anatomy," p. 16.
3. *Ibid.;* Fluharty, *Dance.*
4. Henao and Arrubla, *History of Colombia;* McGreevey, *Economic History;* Safford, *Ideal.*
5. Fals, "Violence."
6. Safford, *Ideal*, p. 8.
7. Crist, *Cauca Valley.*
8. Phelan, "Free Versus Compulsory Labor."
9. Phelan, *The People and the King*, p. 3.
10. *Ibid.*, p. xix.
11. Wallerstein, *The Modern World-System,* ch. 4.
12. Hobsbawm, *Age of Revolution*, p. 135.
13. Oquist, *Violence*, pp. 42–78.
14. McGreevey, *Economic History;* López Toro, *Migración;* Walton, *Elites.*
15. Parsons, *Antioqueño Colonization*, p. 101.
16. Ospina, *Industria y protección*, p. 245.
17. McGreevey, *Economic History,* pp. 196–97.
18. *Ibid.*
19. Fluharty, *Dance,* p. 28.
20. Rippy, *Capitalists*, p. 152; DeRoux, "Social Basis," p. 269.
21. Rippy, *Capitalists.*
22. DeRoux, "Social Basis," p. 236.
23. Rippy, *Capitalists,* pp. 152–53.
24. *Ibid.*, ch. 8; Fluharty, *Dance.*
25. Oquist, *Violence,* p. 94.
26. Dix, *Colombia,* pp. 79–80.
27. Rippy, *Capitalists,* p. 192.
28. García, *Gaitán,* p. 242.
29 Fluharty, *Dance,* p. 34; Oquist, *Violence,* p. 100.
30. DeRoux, "Social Basis," p. 234.
31. *Ibid.;* Rippy, *Capitalists,* pp. 188–89.
32. DeRoux, "Social Basis," pp. 182–88.
33. Fluharty, *Dance,* p. 38.
34. Gilhodes, "Agrarian Struggles," pp. 411–12.
35. Hirschman, *Journeys,* p. 142.
36. *Ibid.*
37. Parsons, *Antioqueño Colonization;* McGreevey, *Economic History;* López Toro, *Migración.*
38. McGreevey, "Tabaco y café," p. 210.
39. Hirschman, *Journeys,* p. 146.
40. Fluharty, *Dance,* p. 44.
41. Oquist, *Violence,* p. 157.
42. *Ibid.*, p. 167.
43. Gilhodes, "Agrarian Struggles," p. 422.
44. Walton, *Elites;* Havens, *Támesis;* Ocampo, *Dominio.*
45. Sharpless, *Gaitán of Colombia.*
46. Martz, *Colombia.*

47. DeRoux, "Social Basis," pp. 246–83.
48. Fluharty, *Dance*, pp. 91–93.
49. Frank, *Capitalism and Underdevelopment*.
50. Fluharty, *Dance*, p. 91.
51. DeRoux, "Social Basis," pp. 280–81; Currie, *Bases de un programa*, p. 10.
52. Fluharty, *Dance*, p. 92.
53. Hobsbawm, "Revolutionary Situation," p. 250, emphasis added.
54. Gilhodes, "Agrarian Struggles," p. 427.
55. *Ibid.*, p. 425.
56. Guzmán, Fals, and Umaña, *La Violencia*, 1:131; Bailey, "La Violencia"; Agudelo and Montoya, *Guerrilleros intelectuales;* Le Grand, "Perspectives."
57. Hobsbawm, "Anatomy," p. 18.
58. Franco Isaza, *Guerrillas;* Maullin, *Soldiers, Guerrillas, and Politics*.
59. Guzmán, Fals, and Umaña, *La Violencia*, 1:291.
60. Duque, quoted in Dix, *Colombia*, p. 368.
61. Fals, "Violence."
62. Oquist, *Violence*, especially chs. 5 and 6.
63. Guzmán, Fals, and Umaña, *La Violencia;* Bailey, "La Violencia," p. 570.
64. Williamson, "Theory"; Weinert, "Violence in Pre-Modern Societies."
65. Pollock, "Violence, Politics and Elite Performance," p. 24.
66. Moore, *Social Origins*, p. 518.
67. Posada, *Colombia*.
68. Torres, "Social Change."
69. Oquist, *Violence*, p. 165.
70. Dix, *Colombia*, p. 113.
71. Oquist, *Violence*, p. 233.
72. *Ibid.*, p. 174.
73. Dix, *Colombia*, pp. 120–21.
74. Torres, "Social Change"; Maullin, "Private War"; Gott, *Guerrilla Movements*.
75. Dix, *Colombia*, p. 131.
76. Hirschman, *Journeys*, p. 209.
77. Walton, *Elites*.
78. Fals, "Violence," p. 199.
79. Oquist, *Violence*, p. 209.
80. Lichauco, "Lichauco Paper," p. 55.

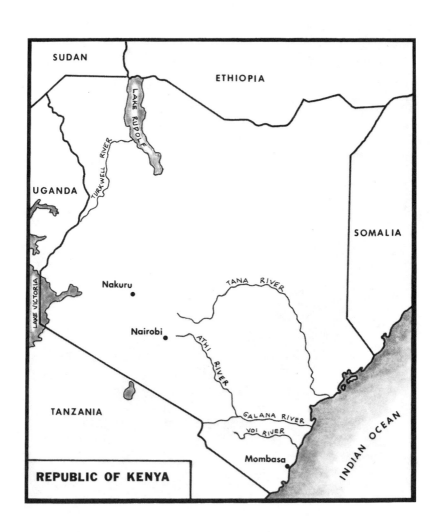

SUDAN

ETHIOPIA

LAKE RUDOLF

TURKWELL RIVER

UGANDA

SOMALIA

LAKE VICTORIA

Nakuru

TANA RIVER

Nairobi

ATHI RIVER

TANZANIA

GALANA RIVER

VOI RIVER

Mombasa

INDIAN OCEAN

REPUBLIC OF KENYA

CHAPTER FOUR

The Mau Mau Revolt

ONE OF THE more curious sidelights of the national revolt that convulsed Britain's Kenya Colony in the 1950s is the mysterious origin of the term *Mau Mau*. The words have no meaning in any known African language and, initially, were entirely foreign to the national liberation movement born in the 1920s. Mau Mau was a name coined by the colonialists to designate what they imagined was an organized secret society intent on their destruction. The Africans knew of no such organization apart from the general nationalist cause that was carried forth by several widely recognized associations. The fact that Mau Mau is now a commonplace in history books and chic lexicon testifies that the colonialists not only succeeded in imposing their own definition of reality on the liberation struggle, but also managed to give it a menacing name that conjured primeval sentiments.

Among other things, this circumstance has given rise to the etymological pastime of trying to determine the origins of the term.[1] Included among the various accounts are the possibilities that the Kikuyu word *uma,* meaning "get out," was transposed as a slogan or, more likely, that the colonialists simply mispronounced African words (as they had in reference to Mount Kenya and the subsequent name of the colony) that they heard warning people off from clandestine meetings of political organizations banned by the govern-

ment. Among Africans there never was an organization calling itself
Mau Mau, despite the fact that the colonial regime tried, convicted,
and imprisoned for nine years Jomo Kenyatta as the leader of that
alleged secret society. The liberation movement as a whole "did not
have any special name; the world knows it by a title of abuse and
ridicule with which it was described by one of its bitterest
opponents"[2]—although later rural guerrilla groups did sometimes refer to their activities within the movement as the Land Freedom Army.
Africans considered Mau Mau simply the European name for their
movement, and indeed, it served the useful fiction of suggesting that
responsibility lay with a small criminal cadre whose radical peasant
members could be imprisoned and, perhaps, "rehabilitated." It is
with good reason that the major work on the movement is entitled
The Myth of "Mau Mau." [3]

Strictly speaking the Mau Mau revolt dated from October 20,
1952, when the colonial government declared a state of emergency
and called in British troops, to October of 1956, when the last of the
guerrilla "generals" was apprehended—although the emergency was
not officially lifted until 1960. According to a parliamentary inquiry
by the British Colonial Office (the Corfield Report), the revolt claimed
the lives of 11,503 "terrorists," 1,819 African civilians, 63 Europeans in security forces, and 32 civilians, plus a few Asians and additional numbers of wounded. Some 80,000 Africans were placed in
detention camps, and the estimated cost of the campaign to Britain
was £55 million.[4]

The revolt was precipitated by a growing wave of unrest in the
cities and on the "native reserves" where the African population had
been increasingly concentrated in conditions of dire poverty since European occupation of the land began shortly after the turn of the century. Following the years of prosperous export during World War II,
economic grievances intensified with the steady maturation of the nationalist movement. Indeed, the constitutionalist methods of the Kenya
African Union (KAU) were being challenged by radical factions based
in the swelling cities and trade unions. The British system of indirect
rule through the pliable tribal "chiefs" they selected was breaking
down. The urban radicals were suspected of assassinating a prominent loyalist and giving cause to the declaration of an emergency.
Others believe that the new colonial governor, Sir Evelyn Baring,
who arrived in early October, was "set up" to act rashly by pressure
from the Kenyan settler community. Whatever his reasoning, Baring's declaration of emergency was implemented with draconian thoroughness. British troops were brought from abroad, loyalist and set-

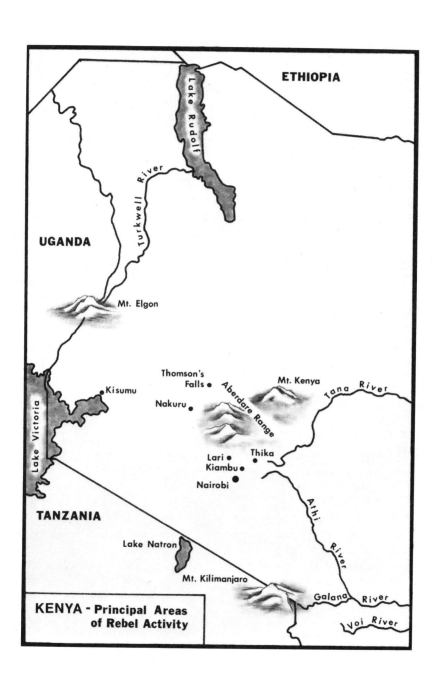

ETHIOPIA

Lake Rudolf

Turkwell River

UGANDA

Mt. Elgon

Thomson's Falls ●

Mt. Kenya

Tana River

Kisumu ●

Nakuru ●

Aberdare Range

Lake Victoria

Lari ●

Thika ●

Kiambu ●

Nairobi ●

TANZANIA

Athi River

Lake Natron

Mt. Kilimanjaro

Galana River

Voi River

KENYA - Principal Areas of Rebel Activity

tler forces mobilized, and the declaration followed immediately by the arrest of KAU president Jomo Kenyatta, five members of the organization's central committee, and eighty-one activists in the nationalist movement.

The declaration of war against the KAU effectively decapitated the movement of its leadership cadre and forced the fighting into strategic redoubts in the Aberdare Mountains and Mount Kenya vicinity. During the first nine months of the armed conflict the forest fighters held the initiative, with dramatic victories such as the raid on the Narivasha police headquarters. In 1954 the government's Operation Anvil swept Nairobi, arresting some 27,000 and eliminating the movement's urban partisans and support. In the countryside Operation Hammer followed in 1956, systematically picking off the isolated and directionless rural units. Kenyan settlers organized their own brigades to secure farms and launch forays on the mountains. Thus, much of the actual fighting involved a series of guerilla encounters with settlers and skirmishes with the army at police headquarters and loyalist settlements, followed by search-and-destroy missions by the settlers and official forces, all giving the misleading impression of a peasant revolt. As the following account will show, in fact this was only the culmination of officially initiated violence aimed at a predominantly urban-based, politically oriented, nationalist independence movement that had passed from the phase of "primary resistance"[5] to organizational politics in the 1920s.

The early exploration of East Africa by the British, Germans, and Belgians was soon monopolized by the Imperial British East Africa Company, chartered in 1888. In 1890 an Anglo–German agreement was signed designating their respective spheres of influence, with present-day Tanzania falling to Germany and the Kenya–Uganda region up to the frontiers of the Belgian Congo set aside for British exploration. In the interests of reconnaissance and the ivory trade, Lord Lugard headed the British expedition to the interior, where he made treaties with African representatives of various tribes exchanging the company's "protection" for recognition of its suzerainty.[6] Although Lugard regarded these arrangements as liaisons with "chiefs" commanding large territories, the tribes themselves were not centrally organized. Initially, colonial objectives were confined to promoting the ivory trade and securing the territory against encroachment by other Europeans. Yet Lugard and a few other visionaries were quick to see the commercial potential and strategic advantages of a colony located at the headwaters of the Nile and the eastern approach to Suez. As the British became conscious of the growing importance of Africa in world affairs they declared a protectorate over Uganda in 1893 and took control of the area between Uganda and the coast in 1895, when the Imperial British East African Company failed. As a critical part of the design for turning the colony into a commercial asset the Uganda Railroad was begun in 1896 at the port of Mombasa.

Almost from the beginning the benign visage of British colonialism turned to a grim policy of military conquest and suppression of indigenous authority and resistance. The most extensive early punitive expeditions were conducted against the Nandi peoples, whose grazing land stood in the way of the railroad that reached (or better, led to the European creation of) Nairobi in 1899 and Lake Victoria in December 1901. The "pacification" of tribal groups by violent means throughout the colony continued from 1895–1920, including a defensive revolt in the Giriama coastal region in 1914, when the British "first tried to collect tax there in the hope that in order to pay, the Giriama would have to enter the labor market."[7]

Within the broad compass of mercantile colonialism the railroad itself figured importantly in the direction of development. Estimated initially at a price tag of £3 million, the Uganda Railway ended up costing the waning empire nearly £8 million: "The new factor which made the economic development of the Protectorate imperative was the construction of the Uganda Railway. . . . For it was the need to make such an expensive investment pay its way that precipitated the economic exploitation of East Africa."[8] Settler colonialism was the strategy selected for this objective for a variety of circumstances, including: British opinion that only Europeans could develop successful commercial agriculture in the colony; the alleged efficiency of the West African plantation system was not yet proven; and settler colonialism was method for keeping down colonial administrative costs.[9]

From the standpoint of the global economy, it is useful to recall that Britain at the time (ca. 1914) was in retreat as a world power: "As a result the British colonial system tended to operate from a position of weakness . . . and this conditioned many of the attitudes which dominated policy-making."[10] Policy was based on actively attracting European settlers, since in 1902 there were estimated a mere twelve Europeans actually cultivating the soil and "so small a proportion of the East African Protectorate appeared to be occupied by Africans that there seemed little danger of injustice if settlers were allowed into the country."[11] The principal means of attracting settlers were land grants, and so began the long, complicated, painful, and, for present purposes, important history of the alienation of African lands.

Between 1893, with the establishment of the protectorate, and Kenya's becoming an official colony in 1920, the fundamental structures of settler colonialism were created in closely interrelated institutions governing land, labor, and indirect rule of Africans. To attract settlers the protectorate offered large tracts of land for lease or purchase, which resulted in European claims to over a million acres by 1905. These included such huge grants as 100,000 acres in the fertile Rift Valley awarded to the stalwart colonist Lord Delamere for an annual rent of less than £200 [12] and properties ceded to commercial concerns such as the East African Syndicate, Grogan Forest Concessions, and Uplands of East Africa Syndicate, ranging from 200,000 to 350,000 acres. [13] Naturally, this was prime crop and grazing land located in the mountain valleys mainly north and northwest of Nairobi, the attractive core of European settlement that was soon designated the White Highlands.

The value of this land had not escaped the Africans. The highlands area was the historical province of the Kikuyu, a group of settled agriculturalists who, together with closely related tribal entities (e.g., the Embu, Meru) constituted the largest indigenous society, with about 36 percent of all peoples. As the previous reference to sparse occupation and the small danger of any injustice from European settlement suggests, there was an important misunderstanding between African and colonial custom. Although some of the area was for a time sparsely populated, by customary African law it was regarded as Kikuyu land and played a critical role in their tribal social organization.

During the later years of the nineteenth century population in the highland regions of Kenya was drastically reduced by a combination of disease and warfare. Thus when the railway first came to be built across this land much of it appeared to be unoccupied—no one stopped to establish the fact that existing tribes still claimed rights of ownership over much of it, which they regarded as a natural outlet for increases in population. [14]

As the eminent archaeologist and scholar of the Kikuyu tribe L. S. B. Leakey has shown, the land was rightfully theirs. [15] Moreover, land was "the key to the people's life," the basis not only of subsistence but also of individual and family status, lineage, political organization, and the gamut of social practices from marriage to communal rites. Other tribal groups, such as the more nomadic and pastoral Masai, despite forced moves, adapted better to the European invasion, avoiding some of the pains of colonial settlement. The Kikuyu, however, were infected from their material to their spiritual being. Jomo Kenyatta's description of Kikuyu social organization in *Facing Mt. Kenya* (a book that gained scholarly and political notoriety), shows how expandable landholdings were crucial to the system of family clans and village to regional governments. Having reached the age of majority and passed through circumcision rituals, with their first marriage young Kikuyu warriors were awarded an existing or new plot of family land. Possession of land confirmed the warrior and his wives as full citizens of the family clan and village. Propertied males later could become village elders in the councils that were organized in a decentralized democratic hierarchy reaching the regional and tribal level. Moreover, the fruits of the land were essential to ceremonial customs such as the bridal gift or "purchase" awarded to her family. Contrary to European interpretation, communal or tribal ownership of land was uncommon. Certain areas were used as public places and common pasturage, but most of the land was privately held by family units. "It is of these lands that the European travelers reported that they had seen huge lands 'undeveloped' and 'unoccupied.' To them it may have seemed so, but to the Gikuyu every inch of their territory was useful in some way or another."[16] When the colonialists began occupying Kikuyu land they simultaneously (perhaps unwittingly at first) began to destroy the foundations of that society.

The alienation of land and regulation of expropriated groups was effected by a series of colonial ordinances. Fundamental were the Crown Land Ordinances of 1902 and 1915, which, initially, empowered the protectorate to grant leases on all land not in the (undefined) "actual occupation of natives" and, later, "for all intents and purposes completely nullified the Africans' legal rights to the land."[17] The system of governance for indigenous groups through indirect rule began with the Native Courts Regulations of 1897, which provided British oversight of customary legal ministrations by chiefs and elders. When this arrangement proved ineffective, owing to the fact that the authority of local chiefs was not "recognized over a sufficiently wide area to make them competent to administer the country under a minimum of supervision," the Village Headman Ordinance of 1902 was promulgated. This allowed direct intervention through the appointment of "official headmen in charge of a number of villages who were paid a small salary from a rate levied on the inhabitants of the Villages. The headmen's duties consisted in delivering criminals to justice, in helping with the collection of the hut tax and in supplying labour for public works."[18]

Although efforts to promote indirect rule and preserve indigenous patterns of social organization were, in theory, advanced by a series of colonial dictates including the Native Authority Ordinance of 1912, the system worked poorly in practice for two general reasons. First, it was incompatible with traditional tribal governance, particularly among the decentralized and democratic Kikuyu.[19] Second, it was conceived and dedicated to European domination of agriculture "because the development of settlement required the net transfer of resources from the African to the expatriate sector and hence very repressive economic policies."[20]

Instances of the latter included, of course, land alienation and the early appearance of reserves. Although designation of reserve land set aside for Africans was officially resisted at first in the hope that European and native settlements could be intermixed, military conquest in the 1890s had already begun segregation in some areas. In 1906 two Kikuyu reserves were officially "gazetted," although not thereby protected from subsequent alienation. The Crown Lands Ordinance of 1915 provided for the first time legal protection, and therefore the creation, of reserves by setting aside designated areas for Africans on land that could not be sold, leased, or otherwise transferred. The system, begun as plain segregation without great economic disparities, became pernicious with the arrival of new settlers, competition for land, the need of agricultural labor, and steady encroachments on the land. By 1917 a government pamphlet indicated that the highlands were already divided into black and white areas and should be maintained that way.[21]

The policy of attracting settlers through generous concessions of land and economic assistance began to produce results. First came a number of "Boer irreconcilables" from South Africa around 1906, followed by a large contingent of "soldier settlers" after World War I. Wall posters in London advertised the prosperity and salubrious living offered by "Britain's new Kenya colony." By the end of World War I the British economy was experiencing major dislocations in its industrial export and agrarian sectors. Metropolitan interest in colonial settlement was encouraged by the fact that the once powerful commercial farmer was now too small for optimum efficiency, but too large and steeped in the gentry way of life to join in new cooperative arrangements. The landed classes that had no additional source of income were losing any national importance, and many "disappeared from sight; as often as not to Kenya and Rhodesia where the colour of the lower orders' faces guaranteed another two generations of undisturbed gentlemanly life.''[22] But Kenya had to compete for settlers with a variety of desirable places such as the established dominions of Australia, New Zealand, and Canada, or the United States.

> To have any success in this market Kenya had therefore to offer something which a significant number of people would regard as preferable to anything available to them in the rest of the English-speaking world. Kenya could offer an attractive climate, open space and plenty of lions and elephants to shoot. All this appealed directly to a species of Englishmen, of which Lord Delamere was a good example, brought up on the writing of Kipling and Haggard, and too undisciplined to find much satisfaction in the mainstream of English society. But a settlement had to be built on more than the romantic dreams of aristocratic misfits: it had to provide something substantial for ordinary people.[23]

The rationale for attracting white settlers, of course, was to turn the protectorate into a profitable enterprise within the empire—and inter alia to pay for the heavy investment in the railroad and other infrastructure such as port facilities—through commercial agriculture and export. Although the Europeans helped themselves to large parcels of land, the indispensible ingredient of commercial success was local labor. But the Africans who had lived comfortably (except during natural disasters) for centuries in a nonmonetized economy that combined agriculture with trading and petty commodity production[24] had no incentive to become wage laborers for the colonial usurpers. On the contrary, they had good reason to avoid that in preference for their own autonomy and customary way of life. For settler colonialism to succeed, therefore, stern measures were required in labor recruitment and "primitive accumulation" in general. Africans, in the settlers' appraisal, had to be compelled to work.[25] In March of 1908 a Labour Inquiry Board looked into this problem:

> The recommendations were similar in character to those put forward by the settlers with the added proposals that a tax rebate should be granted to Africans who worked for Europeans and that land set aside for native reserves should be limited to the existing requirements of the African population since larger reserves would reduce the labour supply available to the settlers. Two months later the Governor did concede that the introduction of a poll tax, supplementing the already existing hut tax, might be desirable to tap the supply of young, unmarried men who, in his opinion, would provide an adequate supply of labour if they could be induced to leave the reserves.[26]

It is difficult to overestimate the importance of the diverse methods of labor recruitment and control. Initially they were a by-product of land alienation and the reserves as the better land was occupied and some Africans were kept on as tenants and "squatters." Subsequently the imposition of monetary taxes required Africans to engage, at least seasonally, in wage labor. Policy concerning the reserves was designed to ensure that they would not be economically viable (e.g., in plot sizes), meaning Africans had to supplement their income by working on white farms. Later, when these methods were not always successful at proletarianizing the small farmer-trader, crop restrictions were introduced preventing African cultivation of export cash crops such as coffee. The competitive advantages of European agriculture were further enhanced through a variety of state infrastructure supports. As Leys observes, "Of all the ways in which capitalism wrought transformations in the pre-existing modes of production in Kenya the employment of wage labor stands out as the most far-reaching . . . in some areas—notably in Kikuyu country but also in parts of western Kenya—most adult men were regularly engaged in wage labour as early as the 1920s."[27]

In addition to these "indirect" means by which wage labor was encouraged, openly coercive measures were also adopted in the Resident Natives Ordinance, which effectively obligated squatters to perform paid services. The Registration Ordinance of 1921 required Africans to carry identification and was used mainly as a method of tracking down those who had broken their labor contracts. An early version of pass laws, this *kipande* system later became a major source of dissatisfaction serving various political ends. Finally, adding to these sources of discontent, the White Highlands were greedily enlarged and increasing numbers of Africans became concentrated on the reserves at the same time that much of the European land went uncultivated. The poetic memoir *Out of Africa* by Isak Dinesen, who managed a highland farm from 1914 to 1931, testifies "I had six thousand acres of land, and had thus got much spare land besides the [600 acre] coffee plantation. Part of the farm was native forest, and about one thousand acres were squatters' land, what they called their *shambas*."[28] In the mid-1920s more than 4 million acres had been alienated, of which only 6–8 percent was under cultivation.[29]

Before tracing the consequences of these events to Kenyan nationalist politics, it must be recalled that the changes were closely related to vicissitudes of the global political economy. "British attitudes to colonial development were decisively conditioned by her needs as a major manufacturing and capital exporting country."[30]

Yet, since the late nineteenth century the British role in the world economy had been dwindling. Traditional export industries such as textiles and steel were in a state of continuous decline and underemployment. Export markets had been lost to other European countries and the United States. Accordingly, Britain turned increasingly to solutions to her economic problems within the empire.[31] A stimulant to British exports was required, and that, in turn, meant the enhancement of production and purchasing power in the colonies.

At the colonial end this system required that each territory find one or more primary products in demand on world markets. . . . At the British end it required export-oriented industry capable of taking advantage of the opportunities created by new colonial markets. . . . The problem was one of creating demand by expanding colonial primary production.[32]

Settler colonialism in Kenya could advance these ends through the development of export agriculture, particularly as this, on one hand, relied on expanded public works projects such as the railroad built with British steel and, on another, provided cotton and wool imports for the textile industry. British policy, as codified in the Colonial Development Act of 1929, reflected this strategy linking high levels of unemployment at home with export production in the empire—a policy that harmonized with the ideology of the colonial service seeking to recreate in Kenya an idealized version of England's rural past.[33] However, this developmental strategy required an active interventionist state capable of controlling land and labor policies that exploited indigenous groups and simultaneously promoted the productivity of the typically ill-equipped settlers.

The extent of state intervention and the weight of suppression of indigenous enterprise can be appreciated in light of recent work on the native economy from 1920 to 1940.[34] By contrast to the settler notion that the British brought prosperity to a primitive subsistence economy, it has been shown that Kenyan peasants actively developed commodity production and interregional trade. Colonial agriculture was divided between thoroughly commercial plantations and the more typical "mixed farms" of the White Highlands that combined export production with provision for local needs (e.g., vegetable crops, dairy). Settler mythology notwithstanding, it now appears that the mixed farms were inefficient by contrast to native agriculture, even despite the enormous concessions the Europeans received in financial assistance from the state, crop restrictions that gave them a monopoly on export commodities such as coffee, road and rail transportation built to their convenience and marketing advantage, and coerced cheap labor.[35] The final irony was that the whole system was supported, the Europeans subsidized, by a tax system in which the Africans contributed the lion's share.[36]

In this light, and beyond all the gratuitous racism, one is struck by a sense of pathos in the Robert Ruark novels *Something of Value* and *Uhuru* that portray the white Kenyan farmer as a heroic pioneer responsible for prosperity and the civilizing arts. Indeed, if Ruark accurately describes the dominant mentality of paternalism and African incompetence among the settlers and colonial service (an attitude that had its critics in people like Leakey the scholar, and Norman Leys, a colonial medical officer and later member of Parliament), the angry nationalistic response is readily understood.

The early 1920s witnessed the beginnings of modern Kenyan nationalism primarily in Nairobi. The capital city had grown rapidly and provided an intersection of many of the forces under discussion. It was close to the White Highlands and Kikuyu country, attracting dispossessed cultivators and others seeking nonagricultural employment in a growing urban labor market of commerce and services. World War I had mobilized large numbers of Africans for British operations against the Germans in Tanganyika—an estimated 46,000 having lost their lives mostly as a result of disease—many of whom stayed on in Nairobi after their discharge. Segregated into their own districts, the African communities in Nairobi served as a link between urban and rural grievances, as well as between multitribal interests, which evidently were harmonized to some extent in this communal setting.

In 1921 the intertribal East African Association (EAA) was formed in Nairobi by Harry Thuku, a Treasury employee of the colonial government and product of missionary school, who was to become "the first undisputed hero of the politically conscious Kikuyu."[37] Close to the same time the rural Kikuyu Association (KA) was established, and "both associations articulated a number of grievances that arose from the administration's policies of land alienation and labor recruitment, and each fiercely regarded itself as the only legitimate channel for the expression of such grievances."[38] Evidently, Thuku's organization took an early lead in protesting threatened wage reductions in 1921, hut and poll taxes, and the Kipande registration system—enough so that, following mass meetings and press-released resolutions, Thuku was arrested and deported in March 1922. In response, leaders of the EAA called a general strike in Nairobi that turned out 7,000–8,000 demonstrators and culminated in 56 African deaths when police and settlers opened fire on the crowd. Thereafter the East African Association went into rapid decline.

In response to the same current of discontent the Kikuyu Central Association (KCA) was formed in 1924. Beginning as a rural organization more militant than the KA, by 1927 it had set up headquarters in Nairobi enjoying the leadership and vitality of young Jomo Kenyatta, who became its general secretary in 1928. While continuing to protest policies of land, labor, and taxation, the KCA added a new dimension of cultural nationalism to the struggle, particularly as it was expressed in the "female circumcision" controversy. Colonial opposition to clitoridectomy, in isolation a humanitarian position, was part of a broad set of interferences with African custom and social organization collectively aimed at converting the indigenous population to the status of servants of an alien political economy. Circumcision was practiced among the Kikuyu as part of the rite of passage in which boys and girls became eligible for marriage and landownership. Accordingly, the attempted ban in the case of females struck at the core of tribal custom and provided one of the most virulent issues of cultural nationalism.[39] Another was the drive for public education separate from the missionary schools, leading to the subsequent foundation of the Kikuyu Independent Schools Association.

By 1930 the KCA had branches in central Kenya and parts of the western Rift Valley. It gained prestige from Kenyatta's 1929 trip to London to express before colonial authorities various KCA demands: the security of tribal lands; educational facilities; abolition of the hut tax for women; and elected African representatives to the colonial Legislative Council that oversaw the territory along with the governor and Whitehall. The return of Harry Thuku from nine years' exile in 1931 was greeted by initial enthusiasm and, as the acknowledged leader of the KCA, his election as its president in 1932. But conflicts with the Kenyatta and other factions led to a split and Thuku's formation of the Kikuyu Provincial Association (KPA), leaving the KCA leaderless while "Kenyatta, as ambassador at large of the Kikuyu in London, was safely isolated from the factional strife of Nairobi and Kikuyu politics. His strength and stature in the tribe were rising rapidly."[40]

Throughout the 1930s the tide of political organization and protest rose. Although the land question dominated the KCA, the Kisumu Native Chamber of Commerce (KNCC) in the western Luo region protested restrictions on their enterprise, particularly the prohibition on coffee growing by Africans and the discouragement of cotton planting. The Kamba area organized an Ukamba Members Association (UMA), closely allied with the KCA, to protest government destocking programs for purposes of reconditioning the land destroyed by erosion—"the Commissioners failing to recognize the paradox in reducing the cattle stock in supposedly economic and self-sufficient reserves."[41] In organized opposition to these programs, 2,000 Kamba set up a "protest camp" in Nairobi in July 1938 that resulted in a compromise with the government on the number of animals that could be kept and in strengthened ties between the Kamba and KCA.

The principal target of demands from the nationalist movement was, of course, the colonial government, whose role as an intermediary between the Africans and European settlers was ambivalent and shifting. The Colonial Service was charged with two contradictory responsibilities: to make the colony economically self-sufficient, and to provide for the welfare of the African population. In the early days the latter was taken seriously. Members of the Colonial Service were a special breed of liberal, university-educated civil servants who saw theirs as a civilizing mission. They resented the settler demands for more land and what they reported (in ministerial memos) as a growing tendency to deny African rights. They condemned South African precedents in racial affairs, blaming many abuses in Kenya on South African migrants and crediting improvements to English gentlemen— although the district and provincial commissioners had a detailed knowledge of the rule and its many exceptions.[42] Administratively the control structure was headed by the Secretary of State (and later a separate colonial secretary) in London, followed by the local governor and Secretariate, under whom the district and provincial commissioners served having responsibility for direct dealings with the settlers and village headmen or "chiefs" (many of whom were nominated by the commissioners themselves through advisory native councils). As the colony grew, this structure was complemented by specialized services with their own departments and field officers (e.g., for agriculture, health, public works). The settler community was represented by legislative councils at the local level and in Nairobi in which the various interest groups (agriculture, commerce, and the missions) convened with the heads of government departments.[43] Unofficial members of the legislative councils (mainly Europeans and a few Asians) were elected according to a practice the settlers hoped would evolve into self-government—a prospect the Colonial Service could never accept, judging that it would exclude Africans and destroy the humanitarian aims of their own mission. From the earliest settlement until independence sharp policy differences separated the colonial governors and settlers—a gulf rivaled only by their mutual distance from the African population.

Effective political power was very unevenly distributed. The nationalist movement was hostilely regarded by the settlers and considered by the Colonial Service an illegitimate, regressive alternative to the tutelary native councils. The colonial governor monopolized power, translating general directives from London into concrete policy according to the objectives of the Service, the settlers, and a smattering of African interest that was imperfectly conveyed through village headmen. At one time the district commissioners represented a critical voice in policy matters since they had an intimate, often sympathetic, understanding of the African mood, which they articulated in the ideology of the Service. However, as the colonial government grew and concentrated in Nairobi, and as economic demands on the colony intensified, the once-decentralized system faded and with it the commissioners who best symbolized the civilizing ideal and reflected African interests. The doctrine that "white interests must be paramount" became harsher in its application.

Up to this point agrarian issues had dominated and led to protest organization, the introduction of modern political methods, and the formation of regional-nationalist associations (e.g., the Taita Hills Association) that allied with the KCA. However, an important new development in the summer of 1939 was the organization of labor in a general strike of 6,000 protestors led by municipal, rail, and dock workers in Mombasa. Centering largely on urban problems such as housing and rents, treatment of migrant labor, wages, and the conditions of health and safety, the general strike proved a qualified success owing, in part, to the support it received from Nairobi's Labour Trade Union of East Africa (LTUEA).[44]

These promising beginnings of the nationalist movement were temporarily halted with World War II. A ban was imposed on all African associations considered (in particular reference to the KCA) subversive, despite their declarations of loyalty, by a government concerned with the prospect of an Italian invasion from Ethiopia. Kenya, like the Philippines and Colombia, enjoyed a period of mounting prosperity during the war since here, too, primary products were in brisk demand while metropolitan intervention abated. Indeed, the prosperity, economic transformations, and attendant inequalities that took root during the war laid the foundation for revolution.

During the second World War two crucial processes of change began to accelerate in Kenya. First, with the war the settler-dominated

monetary economy began a process of rapid and sustained growth that lasted for almost two decades. The growth of this sector had been moderate during the interwar decades and had suffered serious set-backs during the depressions of the early 1920s and the 1930s. Between 1940 and 1960, however, the available evidence indicates an average growth rate of 6 percent per annum, with a staggering rate of 13 percent per year in the period 1947–54. . . . Second, even as they were unaware of this rapid growth, colonial authorities in the colonies and various interested individuals and groups in Britain, made a commitment to the active promotion of the social and economic development of the colonies.[45]

The essential features and transformative consequences of this boom are suggested in the following facts. Economic development was rapid and premised on colonial strategies of capitalist production for export, i.e., the production of primary products for foreign consumption based on a "free" labor force once other opportunities for subsistence had been closed to them. In the years prior to the revolt in 1952, the income differential between Europeans and Africans grew much wider. The value of exports increased sevenfold between 1938 and 1952 from £3.8 to £25.8 million. At the same time the African labor force doubled in size reaching 438,702 in 1952 out of a population of 5.5 million. African dependency on wage income rose dramatically to become the rule: "In 1951, 32.5 percent of African real income was earned outside the African economy. . . . About two-thirds of Kenyan African earnings were derived from wages."[46]

Nowhere were the consequences of this uneven development more keenly felt than in the relation between rural and urban society. Generally, the countryside experienced a qualitative change with further commercialization for agricultural export, as the local economy declined and the reserves became overcrowded on lands of decreasing potential. Although wage labor was the major alternative to this plight, the conditions and rewards of labor were simultaneously deteriorating. Urban migration was increasing as an alternative, resulting in new forms of overcrowding and transplanted poverty. On the crest of these developments, nationalist politics gained in momentum and frustration. Economic hardship was most acute in Kikuyu country, where European settlement and export production continued to encroach on African lands and lives. In the Kikuyu Land Unit conditions were verging on starvation as a result of the increasing numbers of people confined in a fixed space, with the consequent depletion and erosion of the land from overcropping. In reference to the Kikuyu reserves, a Kenya Land Commission report noted with alarm in

1933 that the density of people per square mile had reached 283, implying an average plot size below the requirements of subsistence.[47] A survey of the same general area in 1944–1945 showed that the population density had risen to 542 per square mile and that, despite an increase in land under cultivation, "there had been a fall in yields and in the amount of traditional crop surpluses sold outside the reserve . . . the position was rapidly approaching where insufficient food would be available for subsistence, let alone to enable the Kikuyu to earn a satisfactory cash income."[48]

The fortunes of rural Africans outside the reserves (as "squatters," tenants, and wage laborers) were equally precarious. With the intensification of land use by European farmers, squatters were now denied the advantages of grazing their own livestock or cultivating small truck gardens. Moreover,

The systematic reduction in squatter's land and stock was not compensated for by an increase in wages. In 1950, the average rate for squatters was eleven shillings per month. It is worth noting that in 1946 the Labour Commission for Kenya estimated that squatters would need twelve shillings per month just to exist. Four years later, with a considerable rise in prices, the fall of real wages of squatters was clearly drastic. One government official estimated that in real terms the wages of farm labourers had fallen below the level that existed at the beginning of European settlement.[49]

Yet under these dire and worsening conditions the government was prepared to take no action, not even something as simple as lifting the ban on coffee growing (which was postponed until 1951), and certainly not the provision of more land in the White Highlands despite its very low density by contrast to the reserves. Wage labor was construed as the general solution, but the government had no concrete plans for how that could be promoted.

To the extent that rural Africans on the reserves found any solution, it lay in migration on one of three general patterns.[50] First, there were those who left the reserves for agricultural labor on the European farms and plantations. As just noted, this group met with declining wages and squatter privileges, a condition that led some of them to refuse to sign labor contracts. In 1947, there was widespread unrest among ex-squatters, who marched on the Government House in the Rift Valley, and the 1948 annual report for Nakuru District made the first official reference to the "Maumau association" presumably responsible for agitation on several farms.

Second, there were the Kikuyu who migrated to other African

reserves, where they encountered conditions that, if not as desperate, were at least inhospitable to additional numbers. In these circumstances the government attempted resettlement schemes, the best known of which occurred at Olenguruone on land purchased from the Masai on the Mau plateau (and thus, inevitably, another theory of the origins of *Mau Mau*). Olenguruone was officially "settled" by 4,000 Kikuyu who had already squatted there or were transferred from the Masai reserve. A number of problems arose with relocation: at 8,000 feet traditional Kikuyu crops fared poorly, assigned plots were too small, and erosion wasted the steep hillsides. A serious conflict developed when the government attempted to force (largely female) labor on a terracing project to prevent erosion under the "rules of occupation" to which the Kikuyu refused agreement. As the only apparent effort on the part of government to deal with the land problem, the case attracted the attentions of the new Kenya African Union and Kenyatta. When positions hardened and settlers still refused to sign occupation permits, the government undertook Operation Eviction. Police moved in, confiscating crops and livestock, huts were burned, and the settlers were moved to Kiambu or to a detention camp.

The Olenguruone episode was another symptom of the growing conflict between the Kikuyu and government. Moreover, the abrupt termination of the settlement and the return of some settlers to Kiambu did not make for good relations in Kiambu. Dr. L. S. B. Leakey, who visited Olenguruone with the Chief Native Commissioner in 1943, said that the settlers had originally left Kiambu to settle in Masai country because of quarrels with their relatives; the sending of some of the settlers back to Kiambu was likely to re-open old sores. The Olenguruone settlers, like the resident labourers in the Rift Valley, may well have been connected with the early development of Mau Mau before they arrived at Kiambu, the first centre of the movement in the reserve.[51]

The third alternative was urban migration, principally to Nairobi. By 1948, there were 29,000 (predominantly male) Kikuyu residents, who comprised 45 percent of the city's African population. Nairobi's total African population was estimated to have nearly doubled from 1938 to 1947, reaching 77,000 in the latter year and rising to 95,000 by 1952.[52] Although the few Africans educated in missionary schools were able to find minor posts in the colonial administration (much earlier Kenyatta had worked for Nairobi's City Water Department), the great majority were absorbed in private commerce and services or underemployed in the informal economy. One description of the 50,000 Nairobi Africans in 1941 estimates that 10,000 worked for the colonial government, railroad, and city; 22,000 in private employ, including 8,000 domestics; 1,500 petty traders and craftsmen; 3,000 unemployed; 2,000 daily traders; and 11,000 dependents.[53] Urban wages were low, and although they increased significantly from 1939 to 1952, they only managed to keep pace with the steeply rising cost of living resulting in a stationary value of real wages from 1946 to 1952.[54]

In the postwar years, as since the 1920s, Nairobi was the indisputable center of nationalist politics. Its growing proletariat was residentially concentrated in designated African quarters served by a rapidly growing nationalist press published in Swahili, English, and the vernacular languages. In the urban milieu, patterns of tribal isolation, actively promoted by the British, were

beginning to give way to broader groupings of an African national character . . . a growing number of Africans were entering economic, political, and other associations where tribal identification was overriden by racial, occupational, and residential criteria [and on another dimension] as the urban African population was comprised largely of migrant workers with one foot in the city and the other in their respective rural areas, the multitude of associations in the city, and especially the fast-growing African nationalist and trade union movements, tended to cross-link the many rural peasant aggregates.[55]

Closely related to these developments was the rapid rise of African trade unionism and the East African Trades Union Congress (EATUC, an outgrowth and federated extension of the Labour Trade Union of East Africa, or LTUEA). Founded in the 1930s and active in the 1939 Mombasa general strike, it was now attracting a new breed of worker-politician.[56] The EATUC headquartered in Nairobi participated in another general strike in Mombasa in 1947 involving 15,000 workers and a general strike from May through August 1950 in Nairobi.[57] The EATUC collaborated with leading political associations as the conditions of urban labor took an important place, along with the land question, in the forefront of the nationalist movement. "This collaboration was hardly surprising; to the Kikuyu participants, trade unionism and political activity were part and parcel of the general struggle for independence; and both were to some extent by-products of the social and economic conditions in the towns and in the Kikuyu Land Unit."[58]

By far the most important force, indeed the synonym of the postwar nationalist movement, was the Kenya African Union (KAU).

Following the war the government refused to lift the ban on the KCA. Naturally, most of the same issues and persons were around in 1944 with a renewed interest in gaining a voice in the colony's direction. To that end Oxford-educated Eliud Mathu was nominated to the historically all-European colonial Legislative Council: "To support Mathu in his new task and to provide a transtribal organization for the advancement of African interests, thirty-three Africans, reflecting in part a new educated leadership from various tribal backgrounds, met in Nairobi on October 1, 1944, and formed the Kenya African Union (KAU)."[59] A month later under government pressure the name was changed to the Kenya African Study Union, but reverted back to KAU in February 1946. Harry Thuku was the first chairman, reflecting its KCA origins, but lasted only a few months as his nationalist credentials were now suspect. In September 1946, Jomo Kenyatta returned to Kenya after a sixteen-year absence, mostly in England, and assumed the presidency of KAU in June 1947. Thus he took the commanding role in Kenyan nationalism that was lost only with his death thirty-one years later.

From its inception the KAU was an eminently political (as opposed to revolutionary) organization that drew its leadership from the newly educated African elite. Its leaders and constituents were principally, though by no means exclusively, Kikuyu, and its social bases were primarily urban.

The union drew most of its Kikuyu leadership from the urban elite and most of its mass support from the urban unemployed, the ex-squatters, and the resident farm labourers. At the same time it had much passive support in the reserve from junior clerks, school teachers (particularly in the independent schools) and the general mass of poor peasants.[60]

With a clear commitment to constitutional means, the KAU program emphasized achieving equality of Africans and Europeans, that is, self-government of elected Africans by enfranchised Africans; to that end, more African seats on the Legislative Council; a solution to the land problem through the calling of a new land commission that would restore African territories "stolen" by the settlers and colonial government; and generally, a series of concrete measures that would eliminate repression and second-class citizenship (the *kipande* labor registration, racial restrictions of movement and residence, puppet leaders in the Native Councils, etc.) and provide essential services (especially public African education and housing). In 1950 the KAU boasted a membership of 100,000.

In pursuit of its program the KAU encountered repeated frustrations and patronizing responses from the colonial administration. A few African representatives were nominated to the Legislative Council (Leg Co), mostly on the advice of the native councils, but as these were added the body was expanded to include more Europeans, and, now, Asians diluting any power the African demands might have won. "African appeals for elected Leg Co representatives and for a seat on the Governor's Executive Council were turned down on the grounds that they had not had the experience or demonstrated the ability to exercise so important a 'public trust.' "[61] On the land question the government argued that original settlement had occurred on uninhabited land, and, at all events, claims had been fairly adjudicated in the "comprehensive and final" solution of the Kenya (Carter) Land Commission of 1934. In all matters the government viewed the KAU as a group of amateurs and opportunistic malefactors. They were not taken seriously.

The predictable outcome of this frustrating encounter with constitutional politics was a growing restiveness within the ranks of the KAU and in the nationalist movement as a whole: "Those African leaders who believed that it was possible to achieve political development by a steady and rapid increase of the representation of African interests began to lose influence, giving way to men who were prepared to employ direct action and violence."[62] These men, and a good many women, were the urban radicals associated with the labor movement. They were predominantly Kikuyu and could demand independence now and press working-class issues without the restraints imposed by the KAU's efforts to build a transtribal, rural–urban movement. Indeed, on several key issues such as the timing of independence and the Nairobi general strike of 1950 the EATUC and KAU parted company.

The urban radicals were loosely organized in the "Anake a 40," or "40 group," which derived its name from the Kikuyu practice of age grouping at the time of circumcision (here in 1940) and included young men who were typically in the labor movement and had seen action in the World War II campaigns in Ethiopia, Burma, Madagascar, and India. The 40 Group included among its first members

the unemployed, petty traders, thieves, prostitutes, and others of the lumpen proletariat of Nairobi. Many of the leaders were ex-soldiers and traders who felt that within the colonial system there was little scope for their skills and ambitions. Many of the leaders saw the 40 Age Group as the Vanguard of the African Nationalist movement. According to one of its leaders . . . "We felt that KAU was going

too slow and that the only way to change things was through violence." [63]

The 40 Group was widely believed responsible for the assassination of loyalist chief Waruhiu (and of Nairobi City Councilor Tom
Mbotela), which helped to precipitate the declaration of emergency
and played a central role in the activities that came to be called Mau
Mau. Although it is extreme to conclude that "the 40 Group, and
other movements associated with it, represent the most successful
populist political initiative in Kenya's history to this day," [64] there is
no doubt the group, and the related EATUC, helped to exert a radi-
calizing influence on the KAU. And once the leadership of the KAU
was detained in the Emergency, the urban militants provided what
little leadership the nationalist struggle by then enjoyed.

By mid-year of 1951 events seemed to be on a collision course
as the KAU continued meeting official intransigence interspersed with
repressive action and "the urban militants consolidated their hold on
power in Nairobi and began to extend their influence in the national
movement on a country-wide basis." [65] The best evidence of the
spread of aggressive nationalism was in the mounting pace of public
oathing ceremonies, a traditional African practice to bind the individual on pain of death to tribal objectives, now turned to good (if publicly risky) use in the mobilization of a modern political movement.
The use of mass oathing in the nationalist cause is believed to have
begun with the Olenguruone affair. [66] Frightening to the colonialists,
the mysterious oaths helped sustain interpretations of Mau Mau as an
atavistic uprising. [67] These proper Englishmen had forgotten the important contribution of secret oathing as it helped unify working-class
consciousness in their own history slightly more than a century before. [68] In fact, the oaths symbolized a new and perhaps decisive stage
in the development of political consciousness and mass-based organization. For its part the government failed to see any connection
between the rising tide of unrest reflected in the oathing ceremonies
and political-economic issues, reasoning circularly that agitation was
the cause of dissatisfaction. Consequently, repressive measures were
instituted to get at the "cause," including police efforts in Nairobi to
clear the city of the unemployed and the detention of squatters such
as at Olenguruone.

These actions, of course, helped engender the very circumstances they were designed to eliminate, reinforcing the colonial
reading of nationalist politics as irrational and primeval. A celebrated
example during the Emergency was the Lari massacre of March 1953.

In this savage affair, ninety-seven loyalist villagers were killed in a raid on their homesteads. On the surface a senseless and barbaric act, the cause was later found in the government's forcible resettlement of Olenguruone squatters in a hostile and economically precarious setting.[69] That is, among all those natives dispossessed from the highlands, one group (concretely identified for the first time as Mau Mau raiders) had been victimized by the government's resettlement of another in their impoverished midst, and they reacted by attacking the "invaders." Nevertheless, the superficial reading of Lari came to symbolize the essence of Mau Mau in the colonial mind and to confirm the lurid use of the term. Berman summarizes the immediate causes of the Emergency:

> **The inability of the Kenya African Union to effect meaningful changes in policy or resolve specific grievances in the face of the aloofness and rigidity of the Secretariate and the overt hostility and harassment of the Provincial Administration led to a shift in the political initiative towards more militant elements. The conviction among field officers that violent anti-European conspiracy lay behind the facade of the KAU and other Kikuyu associations became a self-fulfilling prophecy.[70]**

The declaration of emergency and the Mau Mau Revolt that followed is to be understood as a "crisis of modernization," though in a more exacting sense than that phrase is sometimes bandied. Essentially it was a crisis of the class state created by settler colonialism. The state found itself in a position of having to respond to the conflicting demands of the settlers—who were frequently at odds with London and the colonial administrations over policies that might inhibit (or fail to subsidize to the fullest) their commercial and export production activities—and the impoverished peasantry and misused urban labor force that were historical products of the political economy. Caught between these forces, and guided only by the anachronistic ideology of "Catonism"[71] (a belief that all interests could be harmoniously served in the creation of an organic community), the colonial administrators were ill equipped to develop the kind of modern state apparatus necessary to coopt competing interests. As a result their response was a regressive attempt to restore an older order.

> **The collective violence of the Kenya Emergency cannot be adequately explained as originating in armed rebellion by a portion of the African population of the colony [since they had not prepared for it].**
> **. . . The Emergency, in reality, was a pre-emptive attack carried out by the incumbent colonial authorities against a significant segment of**

the African political leadership of Kenya and its supporters. **So it was understood by the administrative officers in the field who had demanded it and by the Kikuyu who believed "the intent of the white man was to eliminate the whole Kikuyu tribe."** [72]

The state in some senses reflected a balance of political forces heavily weighted on the settler side. But it also reflected a certain autonomy in meeting the crisis with a limited repertoire of methods inherent in the scant resources London provided and in the world view of the Colonial Service. In that sense it was a weak state, encouraged only vaguely by London to maintain peace and gradual political evolution, yet confronted by economic contradictions and social divisions beyond its means to solve. The bankruptcy of the solution chosen signaled the imminent demise of the colonial state in Kenya.

The strategy or intentionality in the nationalist movement has been viewed from distinct perspectives. On one hand, "it is submitted that Mau Mau was an act of desperation; a rather spontaneous movement on the part of an economically, socially, and politically frustrated people." [73] On the other, "the radical leaders of KAU and the trade unions had their objective fulfilled—namely to produce a situation of social discontent and a climate of endemic hostility that would bring the conditions under which Kenya Africans lived directly to the attention of the overseas colonial authority." [74] These, of course, are not incompatible since they refer to different segments of the movement, the "people" and the radical leaders. Nevertheless, the revolution probably failed to satisfy either group.

The divisions and chaos created by the Emergency were not confined to sympathizers with the nationalist movement, as Graham Greene who covered the revolt for London's *Sunday Times* saw with the novelist's eye for irony and insanity. People on all sides seemed to have reconcilable views, which the government negated by pitting the most reactionary settler position against the nationalists. Among those caught between,

the Kikuyu were perhaps too close to ourselves. They were naturally a democracy (it was the government which had forcibly substituted chiefs for the council of elders), they believed in God, even their discontent had European parallels . . . [and] the liberal settler was common . . . the young man who recognized that the White Highlands could not remain white forever and that unused land would one day have to be sequestered; the old veteran who said, "Those who don't love Africa had better get out of here. It's not the country for them." . . . Sometimes one felt surprised that the Kikuyu tribe

had not all taken to the forest, for the man who was called a loyal Kikuyu too often gained no friend, while if he became a Mau Mau he had one enemy less.[75]

The state of emergency declared in October 1952 lasted for seven years, although the colonial war was effectively suppressed within the first four. Hours after the emergency declaration Kenyatta and the top KAU leaders were arrested in a maneuver that the authorities calculated would quickly snuff out the revolt—or so their analysis of its causes suggested. In the same "Jock Scott Operation," British troops were flown in from the Egyptian canal zone to restore order and, unavoidably, to demonstrate that the government was unable to suppress the conflict. That fact was painfully obvious. Apart from the repressive resettlement schemes and token appointments to Leg Co, the colonial administration had made no meaningful concessions to the nationalist movement and was bereft of resourcefulness under the dogged insistence of the settlers that their world stay the same. As a result, the impulsive effort to smash the opposition only served to inflame resistance. Detention of the KAU political elite angered and mobilized the radical nationalists, reinforcing their defection from Kenyatta's relative moderation and, of course, belying the colonial interpretation of the revolt.

By contrast to the Violencia and Huk rebellion, the violence of Mau Mau was less continuous with the past than a product of the Emergency itself. Ironically, in the early months neither the government (hoping the show of force would end matters) nor the rebels really knew what to do next: "The kind of panic that led to the declaration of a State of Emergency and the lack of any real preparation for military action on either side gave an unreal, improvised air to the early operations."[76] The Lari massacre changed all that as British troops began implementing tried methods of detention, containment of noncombatant supporters, and a "Mau Mau manhunt" for the rest. Most of the hostilities involving large numbers of combatants and casualties took place on the reserves and, like Lari, pitted African rebels and loyalists against one another.

Accordingly, the initial tactic of the British was to pacify the reserves and protect loyalist settlements by their sheer presence. Next, the "passive wing" of Mau Mau sympathizers and suppliers was detained in a series of camps that effectively imprisoned 80,000 people. These were the major operations that left the rebel forest fighters with about 15,000 recruits isolated in small and uncoordinated bands in the strategic redoubts of Mount Kenya and the Aberdare mountains. Occasionally the rebel bands attacked loyalist villages or district police headquarters, but increasingly theirs was a defensive struggle for survival against the elements and well-provisioned mopping-up operations by British soldiers trained in other (Asian) guerrilla wars. Successively the principal bands of Waruhiu Itote (''General China'') and Karari Njama were subdued, and the manhunt concentrated on the heroic figure of Dedan Kimathi, who was captured on October 21, 1956, four years to the day after Kenyatta's arrest.

The rebels themselves were a mixed assortment of dispossessed cultivators, impoverished squatters, refugees from the overcrowded reserves, lesser political activists who escaped the early arrests, and urban wage workers who fled Nairobi, where all the Kikuyu and unemployed were threatened with detention. They were both the residual of the nationalist movement after the core of KAU leaders had been subtracted and a new radical populist leadership that pursued the same ideals (of land, independence, native tradition, and African education) with methods they understood. These, certainly, did not include the parliamentary machinations that had absorbed the futile efforts of the KAU elite. Once the fighting was over, these two wings of the nationalist movement were even further divided by strategy and sacrifice. That fact has led to an ambiguous reading of the significance of the Mau Mau revolt in African history and postcolonial politics.

Fundamentally, the consequence of the revolt was to hasten independence in Kenya and other areas of the continent. Obviously, additional factors were at work, including the increasing drain of the colonies on England's meager resources. Yet liberation movements with more equivocal results have been celebrated as victorious revolutions (e.g., in Southeast Asia and Portuguese Africa). What was different about the revolution in Kenya?

Possibly Mau Mau was the most crucial movement to take place in colonial Africa during the years following the Second World War: it forced the pace of nationalism and ensured that British East Africa as a whole achieved independence much sooner than otherwise might have been the case, with additional repercussions upon decolonization farther south. Even so, the leaders of Kenya since independence, and especially Jomo Kenyatta, have gone out of their way to play down the share of nationalist success that Mau Mau could claim in the achievement of freedom, implying by this attitude that Mau Mau was incidental to the nationalist cause rather than central to it. Nowhere else in Africa has so successful a part of the nationalist movement met subsequently with so scant a recognition.[77]

As implied, the reason for this construction of events lay in the divisions within the nationalist movement—the fact that Kenyatta and the KAU had not orchestrated the revolt, could not take credit for it among the militants who, nevertheless, were needed for support in the transition to independence. The postrevolutionary leadership had to heal, first, the division among loyalist and militant Kikuyu, and subsequently construct a transtribal political base that would reassure the white and Asian populace of a peaceful dawn of independence. For accomplishing these ends "forgetting Mau Mau was vital."[78] Historical appreciation of these political exigencies reveals simultaneously the direction reforms would take and the arbitrariness of revolutionary nomenclature. The revolutionary character of the transfer of state power that followed needed to be obscured for its very success—and apart from the fact that the result was fully as consequential as others realized under circumstances where the revolution could be beneficially announced to the pleasure of uncritical historians.

The consequences of the revolt were felt before it was over and long before the political prisoners were released with the formal termination of the Emergency in 1960. In retreat, the colonial government played an important role in establishing the contours of independence politics. The Lyttleton Constitution of 1954 provided Africans direct representation in a multiracial government, along with Europeans and Asians, although it withheld majority rule, which was gradually won in the newly constituted Legislative Council. The Lyttleton plan and the first direct elections held in March 1957 (with African political associations and parties still restricted) were designed to ensure moderation by breaking the power of the militant nationalists and Kikuyu through regional representation. Democratization under these circumstances played heavily on tribalism, magnifying these distinctions, and the local issues they embodied, to a prominence they had not previously held.[79] With the KAU chieftains still in detention, non-Kikuyu politicians rose in stature. Prominent among them were the Luo trade unionist Tom Mboya and regional leader Oginga Odinga, who, nevertheless, had been active in the KAU. The important point is that regionalism *cum* tribalism was encouraged along with the militant–loyalist split as a way of neutralizing the nationalist movement.

In addition to promoting regionalism as a basis of postcolonial politics, the government endeavored to fortify incipient political associations outside the mainstream of the nationalist movement by intimating that they could vault into a strategic position. In 1960, when the Emergency was officially ended and national political parties legalized, these divisions were symbolized in the formation of the Kenya African National Union (KANU, the successor to KAU and all the previous associations of the nationalist movement) and the Kenya African Democratic Union (KADU, which incorporated many of the politicized non-Kikuyu elites). Yet the KANU–KADU differences were mainly instrumental with the non-Kikuyu leaders bargaining for leverage in the government of independence that Kenyatta's party would surely dominate (especially after decisive electoral victories in 1963). The real political struggle took place along a different axis separating those who suffered most under and those who had an interest in maintaining the essential structure of the colonial economy—the radicals and elites within KANU.

Although formal independence was not granted until December 12, 1963, it had been assured in 1960 with British government acceptance of the principle of majority rule. The transitional years were devoted to consolidating the base of an independent state that, under Kenyatta, would pursue two overarching ambitions: rapid economic development and political unification behind KANU. Far from solving the problems of underdevelopment, Mau Mau had only made a dire situation worse. During the Emergency the economy had come to a standstill, due in large part to the fact that African labor had either been interned or had withdrawn from the settler environment of mutual distrust. When added to the persistent prerevolutionary conditions of landlessness, overcrowding, and unemployment, this constituted an unqualified emergency.

Yet the political and economic reconstruction had to proceed in tandem. The farms and factories would scarcely run again, much less develop rapidly, until the various classes and ethnic segments were provided a place in the new order. Whatever may have been the range of possible alternatives at this critical juncture, the KANU brand of nationalism, which had always reflected the interests of the African elite, elected to follow a path of reconciliation with the powerful forces of colonial society. In the interests of rapid economic development a new coalition was fashioned that included European capital and external assistance, the emergent African bourgeoisie, the new classes of labor and the bureaucracy, with marginal participation by peasants and urban workers, in the creation of a neocolonial state.

An understanding of the nature of these developments begins, again, with recognition of the fact that Kenyatta neither controlled nor identified with the radical wing of the nationalist movement. Like the Europeans, Asians, and other tribal groups, they were an element to be accommodated, although their principled militance deriving from the revolutionary struggle made that increasingly unlikely within the compass of Kenyatta's reforms. The radicals advocated a populist and redistributive brand of socialism, charging the KANU leadership with complete capitulation to foreign capital, while Kenyatta and his elite allies called their "African socialism" the pragmatic and harmonious route to development that was being obstructed by subversive and tribal perversity. After 1964, when KADU was absorbed into KANU, the radicals were steadily purged from party posts. Once that exclusion was made official policy, the opposition regrouped in the Kenya People's Union (KPU), which, despite a strong regional following, was harassed out of existence through legislative gambits (the "Little General Election" of May 1966) and, ultimately, the tactics of arrest and proscription once used so effectively against the nationalist cause.

The legacy of reforms that followed Mau Mau and the transfer of state power focused on land, labor, national capital, and the role of foreign capital. Among these the land question had historical precedence and the manner of its resolution provided the centerpiece of developmental policy under independence. Prior to 1963, the colonial government began reforming rural society through policies of land consolidation and "villagization" designed to render communities more viable economically by eliminating the mini-farms—an otherwise difficult task made easier by the reduction of rural population through casualties, internment, and migration to escape the violence. At this stage land reform was accomplished through consolidation of marginal holdings into larger units conducive to production for export. The important change was that African agriculturalists were finally given a place in the export economy.

Following independence the more ambitious "Million Acre Scheme" was launched providing the "linch-pin of the transition from colonial rule" through agrarian reform of the former White Highlands.[80] By 1970 this program resulted in the settlement of a half-million Africans on more than two-thirds of the land that had previously been devoted exclusively to the "mixed farms" of the European settlers. In this area a large number of settlers either sold out voluntarily or were expropriated under generous terms of compensation. Some repaired to Nairobi or England to reinvest their profits, while others stayed on as resident managers of Arican-owned farms. African purchase of the land was financed through government loans, heavily supported in turn by developmental assistance from England. Importantly, government loans for land purchases under reform required individual ownership for collateral. This provision effectively eliminated surviving traditions of family and clan ownership and thoroughly converted land to a commodity in this expanded system of capitalist agriculture and export production.

Beside the individualization of land tenure, another key mechanism in the land reform was differential provision of credit. Credit policy favored the significant few, prosperous African farmers and those with customary titles on the reserves, rather than "the landless in the overcrowded parts of the former reserves who found themselves worse off . . . to the extent that the new individual title-holders might be less inclined to afford them customary rights to cultivate small subsistence plots." [81] Moreover, since the agrarian reform program was begun under the withdrawing colonial administration and subsequently implemented by former settlers who stayed on to join KANU and the new government, "In no other sphere was the transition from colonial political control to one of pervasive metropolitan influence—based on advice, technical assistance and credit—so clearly visible." [82]

Some figures on the scope and distributional impact of the reform provide useful clues to the nature of the transformation of state and society. First, that portion of the White Highlands (covering at the time about 3 million hectares) actually reformed was the settler, mixed farm area, comprising about 1.4 million hectares. For reasons of their productivity, the remaining 1.6 devoted to plantations and ranches were not considered primary targets of reform. Second, of the mixed farm area reformed, only 40 percent was given over to settlers, while 60 percent became African-owned large farms—thus fortifying the incipient African rural bourgeoisie. [83] So, we can appreciate Leys's studied choice of words when he noted that by 1970 "the edge had thus been taken off the land hunger of the fifties, with a minimum of disturbance to the colonial agricultural economy." [84] Nevertheless, in the context of neocolonialism this was a fundamental transformation. In the process of reducing land hunger the agrarian reform fostered "an intermediate stratum of larger peasant producers, and above them a stratum of potential capitalist farmers." [85] In the process subsistence opportunities were broadened. At the same time, the new economic franchise integrated rural society more closely with the urban sector dominated by foreign capital.

Reform of the conditions of urban labor was typified by the Tripartite Agreement adopted in early 1964. Essentially, the agreement between the new labor federation (Kenya Federation of Labour), employers (Federation of Kenya Employers), and government traded jobs for labor restraint. The formula called for increases in the size of the labor force by 10 percent in the private sector and 15 percent in government, with a one-year wage freeze and a ban on strikes. This agreement, which was renewed in 1970, simultaneously invested the government with considerable powers of regulation and intervention in the trade unions and ensured a special relationship with employers. Along the lines of the corporatist state, the unions became quasi-public bodies losing the independent political role they had exercised so effectively in the nationalist period. In exchange for expanded sources of employment, wages were kept low as a stimulant to industrial and foreign investment.

As suggested previously, Kenya's policy toward national capital bore many similarities to that of the Philippines. Economic nationalism and the African bourgeoisie were to be encouraged as solutions to indigenous problems of unemployment and productivity, but not to the point of exposing contradictions with foreign investors who dominated the most lucrative fields of the local economy. One "solution," of course, lay in the potential openings in commerce and services that might be created by forcing out the Asian population that had traditionally monopolized these enterprises. To promote the competitive advantage of Africans in this area, "The only alternative was to give them special protection. This was politically attractive in that in several fields it could be done at the expense of local Asian businessmen and not at the expense of foreign-based investors."[86] Accordingly, the Trade Licensing Act of 1967 prohibited noncitizens from trading with rural areas and in the central areas of towns and from dealing in a growing list of commodities. Yet the Philippine experience was repeated here: ambiguities arose about the meaning of noncitizen (since literally the category did not include many long-time Asian residents), partnerships and kindred evasions were commonplace, African entrepreneurs lacked the capital and specialized knowledge to successfully operate the enterprises, and the attempted exclusion produced bottlenecks and inefficiencies.[87] Nevertheless, where government policy failed to eliminate the Asian entrepreneur, it succeeded in fostering a protected, small-scale African commercial class that joined the ranks of their rural counterparts and public employees in the new national bourgeoisie.

Finally, the strongest link in the state coalition was forged with foreign investors and national aid donors. Where it was Britain's desire to extricate itself from the financial and political burdens of empire, it wisely sought to maintain close neocolonial ties of trade. Generous to a fault, the British had provided the capital to underwrite agrarian reform. Kenya, in turn, welcomed new investment from

Britain in the industrial sector as the natural source of rapid development. At the time of independence foreign capital already dominated banking, finance, tourism, and the largest agricultural enterprises (e.g., plantations). Subsequent emphasis on industrialization brought in many of the world's cast of multinational corporate characters (e.g., Unilever, Union Carbide, General Motors, Schweppes, Firestone, Coca Cola, Del Monte, Singer, Esso, Mitsui). As the new industry grew to rival the sources of the colonial economy, foreign control assumed an ever-increasing magnitude.[88]

But the relationship between foreign and domestic capital is not one of simple domination. The national bourgeoisie is not a mere intermediary for foreign capital.

The indigenous bourgeoisie in Kenya have used the state to support their investment, first in large-scale agriculture and then in manufacturing. The post-colonial state has also acted to ensure the conditions of capital reproduction in general by ensuring civil order and repressing the labour movement, which has obviously been to the advantage of both local and foreign capitalists. . . . Capital accumulation in Kenya has exhibited two contradictory trends in the post-colonial period: *nationalism and internationalism*. Since 1970 there has been a trend of government investment in all the major sectors of the economy and this has been accompanied by the expansion of domestic capital into manufacturing. Industrial development has taken place during the 1970s through the *partnership* form of joint ventures between local and foreign capital. . . . Where domestic and foreign capital compete, the state will invariably (as in the case of tea) act in support of national capital . . . by the mid-1970s the development of an "economic nationalist" ideology was quite advanced within Kenyan bureaucracy and this was reflected in the high-level political struggles over the conditions of foreign investment.[89]

Economic nationalism was more aggressive in Kenya than what we have seen in Colombia and the Philippines. In 1965 a system of exchange controls was created to limit the rate of profit repatriation and the extent to which foreign firms were capitalized locally. Both practices, the Kenyans had learned, were typical of multinational corporations operating in countries such as Colombia and the Philippines and meant that foreign companies contributed very little to their hosts by risking local capital for their own exaggerated expatriate profit.[90] The Kenyan government also made concerted attempts to Africanize the multinational labor force, management, and equity. Within limits, these policies were successful. The problem, of course, was that the limits were fairly narrow (e.g., exchange controls cannot regulate "transfer pricing" as a means of smuggling profit, and broader equity does not transfer control). The important point is that the Kenyan government achieved what it sought, namely a close, flexible, and effective alliance with foreign capital.

Assessing the general impact of developmental policies that followed in the wake of national revolt, Leys concludes,

> The neo-colonial system was consolidated in the years after 1963 by a combination of policies which had a common thread running through them: on the one hand, the adaptation of the "peasant" modes of production to the capitalist mode in new ways, and on the other, the establishment of the new African petty-bourgeois strata within sectors of the economy formerly reserved for foreign capital.[91]

Without disputing the analytic cogency of that evaluation, it is also true that the Mau Mau revolt was directly responsible for the very achievement of political independence (although this fact was intentionally veiled in the interests of reconciliation), the end of the white settler economy, an agrarian reform that brought some relief to the landless and impoverished squatter (and real prosperity to the larger-holders), and jobs for the unemployed. The fact that all these came in train with new forms of dependency on international capital was neither the intention nor the complete responsibility of the nationalist movement. In the wake of Mau Mau the new leaders sought to redress a desperate situation of poverty and economic stagnation with policies that would simultaneously consolidate their political base, mobilize necessary resources, and strengthen their capacity to execute reforms. In the early 1960s few could foresee the new forms of inequality and underdevelopment embedded in the alliance with metropolitan capital that appeared to the pragmatic elites as developmental orthodoxy. Indeed, in neighboring countries of East Africa such as Tanzania, where more socialistic and autarkic policies were pursued in the face of fewer colonial obstacles (and fewer resources), some of the same new forms of bureaucratic and class privilege emerged.[92]

Mau Mau was a tragedy in the twin sense of its destructiveness and its desperate futility—a war fought by uncertain defenders of settler mythology, mercenary soldiers, and reluctant advocates of the right merely to subsist with customary dignity. Yet it paved the way for the ultimate victory of those others who carried the banner of nationalism for more than forty years—a revolutionary victory whose final irony was the denial of its insurgents. The novel *Petals of Blood* by Ngugi Wa Thiong'O reflects a good deal about the new order, poetically in the degradation of freedom fighters and common folk at the hands of elite arrogance and politically in the author's subsequent imprisonment. Under the African elite leadership of KANU a new coalition was created linking metropolitan capital and the auxiliary bourgeoisie of politicians, higher civil servants, large farm owners, middle peasants, export traders, protected merchants, employers, and the aristocracy of labor. Although plural in its social bases, this ruling alliance was capable of repression when challenged by the egalitarian nationalism of the left (i.e., the KPU). This was not the broad result sought after by the mass supporters of the KCA and KAU, the urban radicals or the Mau Mau forest fighters. But after the events of the Emergency, the new KANU party was the only political force able to maintain wide allegiance and the center of the nationalist movement by virtue of its continuity and astute leadership. From the center it could orchestrate the needs of the impoverished, the aspirations of militant nationalists, and the changing character of the metropolitan system. Between these forces it negotiated the kind of transformation that best suited its pragmatic political and material interests.

Notes

1. Barnett and Njama, *Mau Mau*, pp. 53–55; Kushner, "African Revitalization Movement," pp. 765–66; Singh, "Mau Mau," pp. 10–11.
2. Kariuki, *"Mau Mau" Detainee*, p. 24.
3. Rosberg and Nottingham, *Myth*.
4. Corfield, *Historical Survey*.
5. Ranger, "Connexions."
6. Ingham, *History*, p. 170.
7. Brantlay, *Giriama;* Rosberg and Nottingham, *Myth*, p. 11.
8. Ingham, *History*, pp. 209–10.
9. Good, "Settler Colonialism."
10. Hobsbawm, *Industry;* Brett, *Colonialism*, p. 53.
11. Ingham, *History*, p. 212.
12. *Ibid.*, p. 213; Rosberg and Nottingham, *Myth*, p. 21.
13. Kilson, "Land and the Kikuyu," p. 133.
14. Brett, *Colonialism*, p. 170.
15. Leakey, *Mau Mau and the Kikuyu*.
16. Kenyatta, *Facing Mt. Kenya*, p. 39.
17. Kilson, "Land and the Kikuyu," p. 114.
18. Ingham, *History*, p. 206.
19. Barnett and Njama, *Mau Mau;* Berman, "Bureaucracy."
20. Brett, *Colonialism*, p. 67.
21. Sorrenson, *Origins*, p. 254.
22. Hobsbawm, *Industry*, pp. 201–2.
23. Brett, *Colonialism*, pp. 167–68.
24. Van Zwanenberg, "Development."
25. Kilson, "Land and the Kikuyi," p. 128.
26. Ingham, *History*, p. 219.

27. Leys, *Underdevelopment*, p. 171.
28. Dinesen, *Out of Africa*, p. 9.
29. Kilson, "Land and the Kikuyu," p. 124.
30. Brett, *Colonialism*, p. 71.
31. Hobsbawm, *Industry*, pp. 191–92.
32. Brett, *Colonialism*, pp. 73–74.
33. Berman, "Bureaucracy."
34. Van Zwanenberg, "Development."
35. Leys, *Underdevelopment*.
36. Brett, "Bureaucracy," pp. 192–93.
37. Rosberg and Nottingham, *Myth*, p. 42.
38. *Ibid.*
39. Kenyatta, *Facing Mt. Kenya*.
40. Rosberg and Nottingham, *Myth*, p. 139.
41. *Ibid.*, p. 164.
42. Sorrenson, *Origins*, pp. 241–55.
43. Brett, *Colonialism*, ch. 2.
44. Singh, *History*.
45. Berman, "Bureaucracy," p. 159.
46. Rosberg and Nottingham, *Myth*, pp. 203–4.
47. Kilson, "Land and the Kikuyu," p. 123.
48. Sorrenson, *Land Reform*, p. 75.
49. Furedi, "Social Composition," p. 493.
50. Sorrenson, *Land Reform*, pp. 80–85.
51. *Ibid.*, pp. 84–85.
52. Rosberg and Nottingham, *Myth*, p. 208.
53. Furedi, "African Crowd," p. 281.
54. Sorrenson, *Land Reform*, p. 85.
55. Barnett and Njama, *Mau Mau*, pp. 28–30.
56. Mboya, *Freedom and After*.
57. Singh, *History*.
58. Sorrenson, *Land Reform*, pp. 86–87.
59. Rosberg and Nottingham, *Myth*, p. 214.
60. Sorrenson, *Land Reform*, p. 89.
61. Berman, "Bureaucracy," p. 165.
62. Rosberg and Nottingham, *Myth*, p. 233.
63. Furedi, "African Crowd," p. 282.
64. *Ibid.*, p. 285.
65. *Rosberg and Nottingham, Myth*, p. 270.
66. *Ibid.*, p. 248.
67. E.g., Corfield, *Historical Survey*.
68. Thompson, *English Working Class*, e.g., pp. 170, 477, 510.
69. Sorrenson, *Land Reform*, p. 100.
70. Berman, "Bureaucracy," p. 167.
71. *Ibid.*
72. *Ibid.*, p. 170.
73. Kilson, "Land and Politics," p. 578.
74. Rosberg and Nottingham, *Myth*, pp. 278–79.
75. Greene, *Ways of Escape*, pp. 195–202.
76. Rosberg and Nottingham, *Myth*, p. 292.
77. Arnold, *Kenyatta*, p. 110.
78. *Ibid.*
79. Leys, *Underdevelopment*, pp. 198–206.
80. *Ibid.*, p. 63.
81. *Ibid.*, p. 73.
82. *Ibid.*, p. 65.

83. Furedi, "Social Composition."
84. Leys, *Underdevelopment*, pp. 63–64.
85. *Ibid.*, p. 115.
86. *Ibid.*, p. 149.
87. Rothchild, *Racial Bargaining*.
88. Swainson, *Corporate Capitalism*.
89. *Ibid.*, pp. 17–18.
90. Lichauco, "Lichauco Paper."
91. Leys, *Underdevelopment*, p. 255.
92. Saul, "African Socialism"; Shivji et al., *The Silent Class Struggle*.

CHAPTER FIVE

Explaining Revolutionary Situations

IN KEEPING WITH the framework developed in chapter 1, the analytic task of this chapter and the next is to explain, respectively, revolutionary situations and revolutionary outcomes. In this chapter the task may be further subdivided. Drawing on the detailed historical evidence from the case studies, it will be useful, first, to characterize the kinds and "degrees" of revolutionary situations presented. Second, the major thrust of the chapter explains how a revolutionary situation arises out of the general conditions of underdevelopment. Finally, we can return to the question of the nature of national revolts and their proper theoretical understanding.

Recalling the scheme developed in the introduction, a revolutionary situation is identified by the condition of *multiple sovereignty*—a government that has become the object of competing claims to rightful power by two or more political groupings. In addition to these *claims*, of course, multiple sovereignty becomes a political reality only when they are honored by a significant part of the subject population:

The revolutionary moment arrives when previously acquiescent members of that population find themselves confronted with strictly incompatible demands from the government and from an alternative body claiming control over the government, or claiming to *be* the

government . . . and those previously acquiescent people obey the
alternative body.''[1]

A revolutionary situation occurred in each country, distinguishing these three cases of national revolt from lesser instances of protest
and localized rebellion. In the Philippines, the clearest example of
multiple sovereignty in recent history occurred during the Japanese
occupation when the original Huks assumed peacekeeping functions
and began to introduce principles of social democracy among peasant
cultivators. At this time the shadow government of the Huks clearly
enjoyed the allegiance of the people. During the postwar revolt the
situation was more ambiguous and loyalties compromised. The HMB
did not claim to control or be the government, although it was probably true that much of the rural population recognized its authority
above Manila and longed for the days of local autonomy. Moreover,
the HMB organized civilian branches and effectively controlled areas
of Central Luzon. But the political program of the rebels was not
"strictly incompatible" since it began with a concerted effort to join
the government of independence (through the Democratic Alliance)
and ended with a defensive struggle for the rights of peasants and
workers that they felt the government owed them according to the
norms of the polity itself. A revolutionary situation existed in different ways at successive times, but it never was far advanced.

The Colombian case is intermediate. Historically rival sover-
eignties existed in the areas dominated by the Liberal and Conservative parties. The geographical isolation of regions interacted with political rivalries to prompt a series of civil wars during the nineteenth
century and to temper severely the authority of the central government later. The Violencia rekindled to an uncontrollable blaze regional and political rivalries fronted by their separate police and
armies. The purest examples of multiple sovereignty were the
independent republics that multiplied from an earlier precedent during
the Violencia with their own rustic governments, distinctive names,
and announced autonomy from the nation. This situation fell short of
the "revolutionary moment" only in the sense that the alternative
polities did not claim to be *the* government, except within their local
confines—within the historic reaches of the polity they were uncoordinated and sometimes sharply divided. Stated differently, a revolutionary situation was fully developed but did not progress to the moment of coalescence in a unified alternative polity.

Several historical and demographic facts explain why Kenya's
revolutionary situation was most advanced. Obviously the white set-

tlers and their colonial government comprised a small fraction of the population, and attempts to coopt a broader following through the "native" governance ordinances and loyalist chiefs (i.e., indirect rule) foundered on the democratic traditions of tribal organization. Prior to Mau Mau, and among its causes, the African population had ignored or defied colonial authority in countless ways such as the refusal to obey bans on customary practices like female circumcision, settler contracts, labor registration, property laws, and loyalist native councils. Overwhelmingly, African traditions of authority commanded allegiance under conditions of increasing political consciousness with the maturation of the nationalist movement. Where the latter was clearly dominated by the Kikuyu and intertribal questions of sovereignty were real issues, these schisms were steadily ameliorated in the years leading up to the revolt. When the revolutionary moment was prompted by the Emergency, mass loyalty was largely on the side of the nationalist movement, and the variegated forms of participation in the revolt were simply the consequence of colonial efforts to destroy its organizational base. In Kenya a revolutionary situation, in this sense, had existed from the earliest British encroachments. African traditions of law and social organization had always been the basis of nationalist claims, especially on the critical land question. These claims and allegiances became more effective in tandem with the rise and coalescence of the nationalist movement.

In summary, incipient to full-blown revolutionary situations existed at the inception of the national revolts. Visualizing the diagram and continuum reproduced as figure 1.1 in the introductory chapter, one might impressionistically place the Philippines somewhere in the middle of the horizontal axis, Colombia further along, and Kenya well within the range of "irrevocable split." If this lends some clarification to the revolutionary situation as an object of explanation, greater interest attaches to the explanation itself.

Historical Antecedents

The national revolts analyzed in these pages are doubtless complex objects, and their explanation must operate at many levels while retaining a sensitivity to the logic of multiple and cumulative causation. Similarly, the arrangement of historical narrative must be distinguished from the dynamics of causal process, rather than seductively implying the latter through strategic choices about the former.[2] Yet it is not the intention here to shirk the claims and responsibilities of a causal analysis once that is properly understood in the multiple, reciprocal, and cumulative—in short, holistic—sense. On the contrary, the objective of these conclusions is to explain why the revolts occurred and why they led to diverse consequences. This is best accomplished by moving from the most general and historical conditions to the more proximate and circumstantial.

First, the revolts grew out of long histories of grievance and protest attendant to the misanthropic practices of colonialism. By the 1920s (or roughly thirty years before the revolutionary risings) they had taken the form of modern political protest organization in national associations (e.g., the EAA and KA in Kenya), political parties (the UNIR in Colombia and the Sakdal party in the Philippines), and strikes and labor confederations (in all three cases). These were organized political responses to new forms of exploitation superseding "primary resistance movements"[3] and aimed at more than parochial objectives—as in the transtribal orientation of the EAA in Kenya and the rural and urban appeal of the Philippine Sakdal party.

The events immediately preceding the revolts were not only part of a continuous historical stream, they were in some ways not especially distinct from earlier events in the sense of their seriousness or imminent threat to the established regime. For instance, Sakdalism as a political movement and insurrection in the 1930s was on a par with the Democratic Alliance and unrest in the Philippines in 1946. The United Fruit strike and rural protest in Colombia around 1930 were in the same league with rural unrest and the urban Bogotazo of the late 1940s. The level or quality of protest and violence was not closely correlated with revolutionary outbreak in the crude sense of a mounting tide that finally overflowed its banks. As we shall see, other ingredients were required, particularly ones associated with the state and the reasons for its choice to define as "revolt" and to respond in certain ways to a given set of events at a given time. Incidents of protest and violence, however serious, are not inherently revolutionary apart from the context of reaction; "revolt" and "revolution" are socially constructed categories whose interpretation cannot be conceptually divorced from the political struggle.[4]

The continuity of political organization and protest is not without its own causes. Critical in the historical sequences observed here was the incorporation of "traditional" societies of the "external arena" into the world economic system.[5] Nevertheless, incorporation does not happen all at once or with the initial annexation of territories into a colonial system. Colombia, the Philippines, and even Kenya for the brief period 1880–1905 had experienced various forms of colonialism prior to the beginning of structural changes that laid the bases for their modern revolutions. The decisive pass came with efforts to convert these colonies (using the term metaphorically in the Colombian case) into profitably exploitable, *essential* elements in the global capitalist system and division of labor. The colonies came to be viewed as something more than opportunities for adventurism and military or missionary zeal. As Wallerstein characterizes the elimination of the external arena, the peripheral societies themselves became dependent upon trade with core countries for their very survival, and not simply for luxuries and windfall income.[6] Conversely, and closer to the roots of revolutionary causation, they became essential suppliers, markets, and investment opportunities in a calculated economic and military design of metropolitan countries concerned with their own competitive positions in the world system.

The United States was initially attracted to the Philippines as a military outpost in the Far East and a platform from which to enter new markets for its rapidly expanding home industry. Colombia attracted foreign mining companies and subsequently multinational agribusiness. White settlement and the railroad (with its own investment to be recouped) in Kenya coincided with severe economic dislocations in British society that the colonies were now expected to alleviate through the purchase of manufactures and the supply of cheap raw materials. The changing global political economy required that core states make effective use of these incorporated areas.

In these cases the resources that the metropolitan countries sought to exploit were, at first, mainly agricultural and commercial. As a consequence, the salient form of penetration was agricultural production for export, which introduced a familiar chain of events: monoculture of export crops; sugar and coffee plantations; emphasis on greater export productivity through commercialized and industrialized agriculture; pressures on the land; efforts to eliminate tenants and small-holders; land alienation, coerced cash-crop labor and proletarianization of the rural labor force; monetization of the economy; repressive monetary taxation to encourage wage labor; reduction of the opportunities for adequate subsistence and petty commodity production—in short, all of the mechanisms of primitive accumulation that began to destroy agrarian social organization and the moral economy of the peasantry.

The case studies are rich in substantiation of this chain reaction of growing exploitation. Given its unusually high rates of tenancy, Central Luzon was a battleground in the war of commercializing and industrializing landlords and small-holders and tenants trying to retain their farms. Rural struggles in Colombia flared along the boundaries between coffee *fincas* and the plantations, as well as between the plantations and tenant plots where workers tried to grow their own coffee and truck crops. Kenya's White Highlands included large farms and plantations devoted to export production and the mixed farms that relied critically on this source of money income enough to urge official banning of African competition. The Africans had to be made to work on the European farms and plantations even if it took starvation on the overcrowded reserves to convince them of that economic necessity.

Land alienation was a fundamental tool of commercial agriculture in every case, although its magnitude in Kenya was unparalleled. Yet, important as it was, even more basic as the rationale behind land alienation was the effort to coerce wage labor (at this stage land was still relatively abundant in each case). The critical demand for wage labor in export agriculture produced a plethora of incentives (e.g., tax exemptions) and, ultimately, coercive measures (e.g., regressive monetary taxes, labor registration, denial of credit and fair crop-shares, elimination of family subsistence production, legalized foreclosure). With all its implications, the creation of a wage labor force was the farthest-reaching transformation that resulted from incorporation.

The general similarities in these conditions of incorporation and agricultural commercialization for the export economy should not blind us, however, to variation or beguile us into simplifications that treat the peasantry residually and undifferentiatingly as a powder keg of "structurally given insurrectionary potential."[7] The exploitation of agrarian society varied, first, with time: all of the mechanisms discussed were introduced with incorporation, but the tempo of their implementation depnded upon the demand for land and labor. During certain periods of rural unrest, wartime generally, and the Japanese occupation of the Philippines in particular, their enforcement lapsed. Second, there are important differences across societies in the form taken by "capitalist penetration." This is precisely the point Moore makes in his comparative explanation of bourgeois revolutions and, specifically, of the French revolutionary violence: "In contrast to England, commercial influences as they penetrated into the French countryside did not undermine and destroy the feudal framework."[8] There are striking parallels between Moore's analysis and the differences in the degree to which revolutionary situations obtained in the three cases here. In the Philippines, where the revolutionary stiuation was least advanced, destruction of tenancy arrangements and the moral economy of the peasantry was more extensive. But in Kenya's irrevocable revolutionary situation, "underdevelopment had taken a form which did not wholly destroy the Kikuyu social and economic structure; it transformed and compressed it, like a wound-up coil-spring, which expanded again with tremendous energy when the pressure was finally released at independence."[9]

Simultaneously, penetration of the agrarian sector carried equally decisive consequences for the urban areas and the society as a whole. In each of the cases urban migration accelerated in the 1920s and 1930s, giving rise to an urban proletariat that suffered from poor wages and working conditions in export-related industries and services (e.g., railroad workers in all three countries, dock workers in Kenya, and the Philippine sugar mill and cigar workers) or survived precariously by their wits in the overcrowded tertiary sector and the informal economy. Urban migration was almost wholly a consequence of "rural push factors" such as land alienation, deterioriating tenancy arrangements, and the drudgery of low-wage rural labor. Migrants crowded into slums and squatter settlements surviving in underemployment through personal services, petty commerce, hustling, and sundry vices—mainly theft and prostitution. In this fashion an "informal economy" was created that subsidized the upper classes and capital-intensive industries through cheap labor and services.[10] As a proportion of the urban labor force the underemployed grew larger, although sometimes in absolute terms the "aristocracy" of labor also grew in the modernized (typically foreign) industrial and commercial enterprises. Yet even here wages were low and at best only kept up with inflationary living costs, while efforts to unionize were legally and forcibly resisted. Workers were housed in slums and paid in sums adequate to their reproduction in numbers sufficient to serve industry and ensure low-cost services.

Theoretically what is important about these observations is that the immiseration of the urban working class stemmed from the same root cause as the exploitation of the peasantry: the expansion and penetration of the global capitalist political economy. Theories of peasant revolution correctly identify these influences but trace their effects no further than the agrarian sectors, despite the overwhelming blight of urban poverty and the vocal connection between the two. Across sectors and strata of colonial society the impacts of the international economy are interrelated, though differentially felt. In turn, the modalities of resistance and protest documented in the case studies varied (e.g., peasant risings and land invasions, wage and tenancy grievances, labor strikes), but their causes were of a piece—a fact not lost on the organizers of protest movements who were sometimes successful in fashioning rural–urban coalitions.

Antecedents in Geography, Class, Economy, and Politics

In each of the cases there was a regional focus of unrest, explained to a considerable extent by economic and geographic factors. Western Colombia was the center of coffee production, Central Luzon one key area of sugar industrialization, and Kikuyu country the best arable land available. And all three regions were within close proximity of their national capitals. These were "natural" foci of economic exploitation and consequent grievance. But several qualifications should be quickly added to this hint of deterministic economic geography. First, protest incidents, even in the early stages, were not confined to these areas (e.g., the banana strikes in Colombia, the Giriama revolt in Kenya, and the many urban activities in all three cases, were outside the hotbeds) and with the outbreak of revolution the movements embraced large sections of each country. Second, besides the economic features of these regions there were additional factors conducive to protest: cultural factors such as the unique organization of the Kikuyu that made invasion of their land and indirect rule particularly devastating; social factors such as the internal colonization of Colombia's coffee regions and the middle class it partially created; and ecological factors such as the high density and rates of tenancy in Central Luzon. Economic and geographic considerations are powerful but not sufficient explanations of the ecology of revolution.

By contrast to the theory of peasant revolt, each case reflected strategically important links between town and country in their revolutionary movements. Much of the general explanation for this lies in the differential yet interrelated impacts of the global economy discussed a moment ago. More concretely, however, there were additional institutional mechanisms illustrated in the three cases that linked various sectors in a national movement. Persistent, rather than abruptly severed, rural–urban ties were maintained through return migration—prototypically in the Kipande labor registration system in Kenya whereby temporary urban workers were assigned to residences on the reserves. Another institutional factor was the peculiar structure of Philippine labor that officially and organizationally combined agricultural and urban industrial workers. Also, in Colombia and the Philippines absentee landlords were common, and cultivators were constantly reminded of the urban origins of their exploitation and destinations of their surplus. Finally, in Kenya and the Philippines there was a significant stratum of petty traders with frequent, even daily, contact between town and country, making them important channels of communication and, some adduce, key revolutionary recruits.[11]

Like European revolutions, national revolts have their origin in the interplay of rural and urban conditions. Peasants seldom lead revolutions, yet revolutions seldom happen without their active support. The development of a revolutionary situation requires coalition, "the possibility of a fusion between peasant grievances and those of other strata."[12] The three case studies of national revolt agree unequivocally, despite the fact that assorted accounts have described each as a peasant rebellion. Although rural–urban linkages were present in the Violencia, they were less effective than elsewhere, constituting something more in the nature of parallel movements than truly integrated bases of a single movement. That fact, in turn, owes much to Colombian regionalism, geography, and, fundamentally, to the unspoken agreement among elite protagonists that their urban domains be exempted from retaliatory violence. The Huk rebellion demonstrated a closely knit rural–urban coalition implemented through the peasant, labor, and political associations. Although the rural-based organizations more often led this coalition, the urban participants made vital independent contributions through the exercise of their own initiative and strategic support for allied and coterminous organizations. The Mau Mau revolt exhibits a comparably high level of rural–urban integration with leadership roles slightly reversed. The Kenyan nationalist movement was centered in Nairobi from its inception. It was animated, of course, by local concerns throughout the society with rural problems often enjoying prominence. Nevertheless, protest demonstrations and political demands intersected in the city, and schisms between moderates of the nationalist movement and the urban labor militants prompted actions leading to the declared Emergency. Only after the urban leaders of the nationalist movement were interned and the resistance driven into the forests did Mau Mau become a rural rebellion.

Theory and case study evidence suggest several generalizations about rural–urban conditions. In the first instance, these alliances did not rise from the astute designs of political organizers but were guaranteed by institutional mechanisms—built into the organizational arrangements for managing underdevelopment. This fundamental fact is best illustrated in Kenya and the Philippines with the practices of officially combining rural and urban labor matters, the system of labor registration, absentee landlords, and interregional trading networks. All of this "proto-urbanization" brought the peasantry into closer contact with urban political influences and urban markets, whose fluctuations depended, in turn, on international forces.[13] The factual question is not how, despite the odds, incompatible rural and urban interests are harmonized, but how the state and economy chain them together in the unhappy circumstance of joint exploitation. Ironically, Marx, who once stated in the *Manifesto* that "the proletariat alone is a really revolutionary class," later arrived at precisely this insight when analyzing the condition of the French peasantry in the 1850s. In the early nineteenth century Napoleonic reforms eliminated feudal obligations and created a class of peasant freeholders identified with the bourgeois state. "But in the course of the nineteenth century the feudal lords were replaced by urban usurers; the feudal obligation that went with land was replaced by the mortgage" and as the mortgage debt burden increased by mid-century "the interests of the peasants, therefore, are no longer, as under Napoleon, in accord with, but in opposition to the interests of the bourgeoisie, to capital. Hence the peasants find their natural ally and leader in the *urban proletariat*, whose task is the overthrow of the bourgeois order."[14] This remarkable passage from Marx's historical work indicates that he understood long ago the revolutionary role of a peasant–worker alliance.

Second, once urban and rural interests became linked they facilitated mobilization because they lay on the same axis of grievance that the sectors experienced separately. Urban migration, for example, did not provide a safety valve tempering rural unrest (as has been the case in other experiences of uneven development where industry and commerce absorbed and allowed mobility for the migrating rural poor), but added to it new methods of exploitation. The alliances were conjunctural. Third, in an ironic full circle, the rural–urban links were mobilized in part because of the opportunities the state proffered for political participation—the elections, labor organizations, native councils, and similar organizations designed, often mistakenly, for cooptative purposes. For instrumental reasons the popular movement mobilized to avail itself of the seemingly genuine opportunities, only to find later that success brought usurpation. In sum, effective rural–urban coalitions developed where there was an extant institutional basis, correlated grievances, and a small but legitimate hope of redress through mobilization at this node. Peasants and proletarians became "natural allies," not least because they were sometimes the same people attempting to survive in different locales.

In a related vein, some information can be derived concerning the social class composition of the revolutionary movements. With respect to support in the rural areas, every indication from this study is in line with the "middle peasantry" hypothesis of Wolf and Alavi— as, for example, in the militance of the Colombian small-holding coffee farmers, the Philippine small-holders and tenants, and the more prosperous Kenyan farmers and traders.[15]

Urban class support for rebellion has not been as carefully researched and, in any event, may be a tougher and less generalizable problem.[16] Hobsbawm's European historical investigations of this constituency suggest that

> it was a combination of wage-earners, small property-owners and the unclassifiable urban poor. . . . They consisted of the porters, a riot-leading class even in other cities—presumably they include the dockers—and the apprentices and journeymen of the lower trades and crafts such as rope-makers, smiths, brass-workers, tin and lock-smiths, tanners, tailors and shoemakers. The wool and silkworkers, woodworkers, gold and silversmiths and the jewelers as well as the servants in well-to-do houses. . . . We must obviously also add the mass of hawkers and unclassifiable small dealers and people making ends meet which filled pre-industrial cities.[17]

Although a long list, it seems to be summarized by "the ordinary urban poor, and not simply the scum"[18]—artisans, transport workers, and petty traders. Evidence from the case studies supports this generalization: Kenya's traders and Mombasa dockworkers, Philippine stevedores and skilled workers,[19] and Colombian labor in transportation and construction all were among the militants. There were, however, two new classes in the peripheral setting that played an even more important role: subaltern functionaries in the colonial government (e.g., at one time Thuku and Kenyatta in Kenya, Ramos in the Philippines, and Gaitán in Columbia); and the leaders of the incipient labor movement (e.g., Mboya in Kenya and Taruc in the Philippines).

These latter two groups represented the *new cosmopolitans* on their way up the narrow ladder of intended cooptation provided by the colonial governments. In Kenya and the Philippines kindred forms of indirect rule required native authorities and personnel. Bureaucratic functionaries were awarded some authority and, more important, the opportunity to inherit important positions with independence. The fact accounted for much of the domestic jockeying for position that dovetailed with colonial bequests setting the agenda of pre-independence politics and the structures of post-independence. The other new cosmopolitans, of course, were the labor leaders, whose politics were typically more militant than the civil servants, yet whose cooperation was subsequently won through labor reforms. Nevertheless, during the days of the nationalist movement and the revolutionary struggle, all of these classes were relatively unified through coincident interests. To the extent that there is an "urban equivalent" to the middle peasantry, it is found in the new cosmopolitans of labor and public service allied with artisans and traders.

All of these considerations bring us closer to the "revolutionary moment" or the more immediate causes of national revolt. One of the more striking regularities in the historical studies was the fact that immediately prior to the revolutionary outbreak there was a redoubling of economic and political deprivation (absolutely, not to mention relatively). Economically, a condition of chronic austerity and inequality rapidly deteriorated through inflation and regressive policy measures. Politically, earlier gains were stalemated or purloined.

After the ironically prosperous years of Japanese occupation, Philippine peasants met abrupt reversals with the return of landlords. Opposition to more equitable crop-shares was supported by the military and police in their efforts to reimpose old arrangements. With the general economy in chaos it is reasonable to infer that urban workers also experienced setbacks. In Colombia the data show a precipitate and across-the-board decline in real income—most dramatic for urban workers but also visited upon the rural workers and cultivators, with the exception of those independent coffee growers who did not rely on supplemental income from wages. Similarly, reliable evidence for Kenya shows an abrupt decline in rural incomes, while urban wages barely kept pace with the rapidly rising cost of living. In each case the causes of these economic reversals included varying combinations of postwar inflation, the reimposition of landlordism, the intensification of export production, a new wave of migration accelerating urban unemployment (e.g., of dispossessed agriculturalists and ex-servicemen), and a general failure to provide sufficient new sources of employment—or even protect old ones—with the maturation of peripheral capitalism.

As theorists occasionally point out, it is the abruptness of economic reversals, as opposed to an equally austere situation that develops gradually, that transforms class consciousness to revolutionary consciousness.[20] Closely related to these abrupt reversals is another general circumstance that Tilly cites as one of several possible "proximate causes of revolutionary situations . . . [namely] the sudden failure of government to meet specific obligations which members of the subject populations regarded as well established and crucial to their welfare . . . [or] a rapid or unexpected increase in the government's demand for surrender of resources by its subject population."[21] The inflationary setbacks and reimposed forms of paternalism at this juncture provide concrete illustrations of this "demand for surrender" as it contributed to the revolutionary situations.

Equally dramatic was the deterioration of the political situation and the abrupt reversal of gains expected or actually achieved. Immediately prior to the revolutionary outbreak the popular movement in each country was fully committed to legitimate constitutional methods of redress, and the postwar climate seemed to promise that these would succeed. When Gaitán's assassination precipitated the Bogotazo he was regrouping the left of the Liberal party for a probable presidential bid in 1950. Indeed, the portent of such a victory loomed large in the strategizing of the traditional elite parties. In the Philippines the Democratic Alliance was actively organized and enjoying the first fruits of electoral victory. In Kenya, the nationalist movement had returned from its wartime banishment and was pressing for greater representation within the Legislative Council.

Indeed, it was the very success of these constitutional methods that led to the suppression of civil order. The most blatant repression of the new enthusiasm for legitimate politics was in the Philippines, where electoral victories by the Democratic Alliance in 1946 were capriciously canceled. In Colombia the Liberal majority had been denied victory when the party split internally in 1946, but beyond this tactical error the Conservatives returned with a vengeance. Repression of liberal programs and rural communities actually initiated violence prior to the cataclysm of 1948. With the formation in Kenya of the KAU in 1944 and its growing importance by 1947, the new initiative in legitimate politics was belittled, patronized, and circumvented.

In each case there was a short period (two to five years) of constitutional political advocacy that accomplished a great deal for the encouragement and organization of the nationalist movement but was firmly confronted with official intransigence and forcible repression. In varying degrees this helped to radicalize the movements and to justify their more militant elements (the 40 Group and EATUC in Kenya, the socialist–communist alliance in the Philippines, Gaitán's Liberals in Colombia).

Theoretical Reprise: Inevitability and Organization

From a theoretical vantage this crucial period witnessed a growing conviction in the popular movement that there was a concrete and feasible alternative to their oppression. Things did not *have* to be the way they had. As Moore has recently and elegantly argued, limits of obedience are extremely broad. Societies not only tolerate the most heinous forms of injustice, they even cooperate with its agents to make it more effective and insidious. Perhaps the fundamental question is not why people rebel but why acquiescence to injustice is so much more pervasive. The general answer he gives is that "suffering and submission come to these people with such a powerful aura of moral authority that they take pride and pleasure in their pain."[22] The essential ingredient for revolt, therefore, is a dawning awareness that the established order of things in all its authority is not inevitable. How this denial of inevitability appears, of course, is an empirical as much as a theoretical question.

Noninevitability is a concept that illuminates the role of political consciousness and culture. In tandem with all the economic aspects of underdevelopment, the maturation of a nationalistic political consciousness provided an equally important foundation for national revolt. In these cases political consciousness grew with, and was the product of, the interaction of traditional concerns and colonially (or, in Colombia, elite-) imposed political arrangements. In a sense, the political structures with which the popular movements had to negotiate were "external" and alien—the British-inspired native council and Colonial Office, the Philippine tutelary legislature, and the extended franchise and model of labor organization proffered by the Colombian political elites during the Revolución en Marcha. The very contrast between these alien structures and popular grievances expressed in cultural forms stimulated a keen political sense in the nationalist movements. Immense frustrations arose from attempts to present, for example, traditional principles of landownership within the "rational–legal" confines of colonial bureaucracy. And when such efforts inevitably failed, political awareness turned to conscious militance.

Jomo Kenyatta relates a marvelous allegory in this connection. A man living in the jungle befriended an elephant who one day sought shelter in the man's hut during a rainstorm. Pointing out that the hut was too small for both of them the man allowed that the elephant put his trunk under shelter. But once having gained this entree, the elephant pushed his head in and threw the man out in the rain. His complaints attracted the other animals of the jungle, and its king, the lion, who wanted above all peace and tranquility in his kingdom. To that end the lion appointed an impartial Commission of Enquiry composed of Messrs. Rhinoceros, Buffalo, Alligator, and so forth. When the man protested that no one of his persuasion was included, "he was told that it was impossible, since no one from his side was well enough educated to understand the intricacy of jungle law," but that he had nothing to fear from such an honorable and impartial panel. Appearing before the commission, the elephant began, "Gentlemen of the jungle," and went on the explain that the man "invited me to save his hut from being blown away by a hurricane. As the hurricane had gained access owing to the unoccupied space in the hut, I considered it necessary, in my friend's own interests, to turn the undeveloped space to a more economic use by sitting in it myself." Persuaded by this logic, the commission insisted that the man, who testified next, confine himself to the issue "whether the undeveloped space in your hut was occupied by anyone else before Mr. Elephant assumed his position?" Forced to answer "no," the man brought justice upon himself. The commission decided that the elephant was merely protecting his interests and making the best use of space that the man had not yet grown to require.[23]

As Kenyatta's story laconically suggests, this "traditional" point of view is as compellingly rational as colonial policy no doubt seemed to the government. It was the confrontation of such logics that led the national movements to something approaching the desperation of the man in the tale at the same time that it engendered in them a more sophisticated political consciousness. Bad faith clothed in the robes of justice and the collective interest probably did more to mobilize the popular movement than simple intransigence.

If this interpretation convincingly equates the sense of noninevitability with political consciousness, then both have their origins in cultural practice. The studies show that cultural traditions provided both the content and organizational nexus of quite "modern" political movements. To say the same thing in another way, cultural nationalism was a key contributor to each national revolt. The African case has received a good deal of attention on this score in connection with land disputes, tribal social and political organization that revolved around rights of land, social customs such as female circumcision, and the demand for independent African schools. Philippine nationalism, longer in germination, was expressed with equal vigor by the lay brotherhoods of the Tabayas and Colorum revolts, the campaign for secularization and (later) a Philippine Independent church, the ethnic and linguistic bonds of the Tagalog communities of tenants and small-holders in Luzon, and the various mestizo groups.

Regionalism, more than unalloyed nationalism, in Colombia had its expression in the individual ethos of the Antiqueño coffee planters and the frontier traditions of the eastern plains. Yet Colombian nationalism was forcefully expressed in connection with the Panama dispute and the depression aftermath of the "dance of the millions," lending, on both occasions, greater passion to the organizing efforts of the popular movement.

Theories of revolution that ignore political consciousness on the assumption that the potential for rebellion is "structurally given" or that the "rational peasant"[24] bases political action exclusively on some economic calculus seriously underestimate the cultural basis of political organization. Similarly, the useful idea of primary "export regions" in peripheral societies as foci of rebellion[25] can be readily countered with cultural (separatist) enclaves, but a combination of these (as in Luzon, the Kikuyu–White Highlands, and the Colombian coffee regions) promises a more general and fertile explanation. About England, Thompson says, "The making of the working class is a fact of political and cultural, as much as economic, history. It was not the spontaneous generation of the factory-system."[26] The same is true with the making of revolution, which does not follow spontaneously from the system of underdevelopment or the machinations of the state. It is only as these interact with cultural practice that political consciousness finds its theme and expressive vehicle. Revolutionary movements are successfully organized in proportion to the strength and relative unity of their cultural bases.

What became crucial, therefore, was the manner in which cultural nationalism and political consciousness became mobilized immediately prior to the revolts. An irony with many historical precedents was that the state had previously mobilized large indigenous forces (in Kenya and the Philippines) during World War II, forces steeped in military organization and now looking expectantly to their peacetime rewards. Even more important, perhaps, was a growing sense of political efficacy in all three countries. The resurgent nationalists and the people's movements had all demonstrated their electoral strength. The possibility of popular rule, and with it the end of exploitation, emerged as a palpable reality.

The Final Pass

The national revolts began in the years immediately following World War II, years that witnessed the emergence of an economic contradiction that may also be a prescription for revolution: a "rapid improvement in a society's capacity to produce goods and services," so that it now appears possible to solve the problem of poverty, and "a marked increase in the suffering of the lower strata."[27] All three cases demonstrate these twin processes in the postwar boom of export production and in the rapidly deteriorating economic situation of the working classes. The societies were, indeed, producing more goods and services during and immediately after World War II, but rather than solving the problem of poverty, the way that production was organized exacerbated it through narrowly distributed profits and inflation.

In the specific sense of accumulating inequalities and contradictions, in each case the state faced a "crisis of modernization" attendant to the full-scale implementation of dependent capitalism. Upper-class prosperity and the promise of a great deal more in the opportunities presented by neocolonialism combined with increasing and vocal discontent. The old order and its easy transformation to the new was materially threatened by the popular movement. Insurgent groups made "excessive" demands for equity incompatible with the elite-perceived direction of development (e.g., demands for a larger peasant share of land and agricultural surplus versus the requirements of more profitable export; demands for urban jobs and better wages versus capital-intensive foreign investment). As these demands became more militant they threatened to sabotage development strategies, the best example being the threat of the Democratic Alliance to the Bell Trade Act and profitable U.S. alliances with the dependent bourgeoisie.

These circumstances produced important *shifts in elite coalitions* as elements of the rural and urban, industrial and landed upper classes joined ranks and distanced themselves from the popular movement. Dramatically, in Colombia many of the former supporters of the Liberal coalition of the 1930s—industrial and commercial classes—joined with landowners and Conservatives under the threat of the mass movement and with the incentive of new alternatives for capitalist development emanating from the metropole. With export markets booming for commercial agriculture and in-pouring foreign investment in industry, the old split between Conservative landowners and the Liberal national bourgeoisie was healed. These groups were presented the opportunity to become agribusiness exporters or industrial allies of the foreign investors—as well as to merge with one another. In the Philippines the Roxas regime and its U.S. sponsors brought together the new industrialists and the formerly divided sugar interests (the millers and planters). The stakes of politically conditional reconstruction aid and new trade opportunities were too high to be lost in domestic squabbling. In Kenya the divisions between settlers and colonial administrators were temporarily healed with postwar prosperity and in the face of the KAU. Other elite factions resisted the new coalition, producing some splits in the upper classes, for example, the left Colombian Liberals and the Filipino economic nationalists. But the defections were minor.

Revolution was precipitated in this precarious situation of economic contradiction, tentative coalitional realignment, and popular militancy. Specifically, and strikingly in all cases, the violent revolution was officially initiated in an effort by the state and the incipient elite coalition to secure their position and developmental plans through the destruction of the popular movement. The movement now represented a very tangible threat to the objectives of dependent capitalism in all of its social and political manifestations. The use of force against the popular threat to the fragile coalition attested to the weakness of the state—which was simply the other side of multiple sovereignty and the growing strength of the popular movement. The state lacked the capacity, the willingness, or the imagination to address the contradiction in other ways. The state was weak for having lost the masses to the nationalist movement and placed its economic fortunes in the hands of foreign interests. In a classical symptom, its armies and police were divided in their loyalties (especially in Colombia and the Philippines). A nervous elite grabbed at the straw of preemptive violence to still its opposition and to consolidate its coalitional alliance. In the Philippines the police and military began to hunt down, kill, and imprison "ex-Huks" and "Huk sympathizers," who in effect were the opponents of a new landlordism. In Colombia the resurgent Conservatives mounted police and military attacks on Liberal farms and villages. And in Kenya the declared Emergency provided the pretext for a military and political campaign against the Kikuyu and the KAU organization. Conversely, in each case the violent revolution began in a defensive reaction by elements of the popular movement, though it soon outgrew these limits.

The core discovery challenges the widely accepted imagery of revolutionary struggles in which desperate insurgents mount a clandestinely coordinated assault on the state that, like Marie Antoinette, has lost touch with the needs of the people or fumbled the olive branch. I doubt the characterization is overdrawn since it seems implicit in so much misdirected theorizing that asks "What is it that brings people to revolt?" I also doubt many revolutions start that way. The advantage of the interpretation here, beyond the limited evidence from the studies, is that it also makes intuitive sense. Revolution is less a blind leap into the hands of violence than a miscalculated use of violence within the political process—one need not look outside the arena of social and political struggle in which the participants have invested so much of their effort. If we look, then, to the political process [28] for an explanation of the revolutionary outbreak, the salient fact is that the state is institutionally weak and floundering in the wake of unprecedented circumstances. The powerful classes are divided (though endeavoring to heal those divisions), mainly between the modernizing industrialists bent on national production and the landed oligarchy producing agricultural exports. The commercial classes have ties to both of these factions, but they are also segregated junior partners, particularly to the extent that they are comprised of ethnic minorities. The popular movement is less an awesome rival of state power than a precocious nuisance that keeps the conventional political process in turmoil, thus denying the state remedies for its new difficulties. But the state faces a growing contradiction in the economy that is probably beyond any procedural remedy. The society's goods-producing capacity has increased apace with social inequality. The winners and losers in peripheral capitalist development are beginning to recognize their circumstance and its causes. The state lacks the financial resources, institutional mechanisms, and ideas to solve the crisis. Stalemated and impatient, it myopically concludes that a dramatic move to suppress the popular movement will eliminate its most troublesome opposition at the same time that it wins back powerful allies.

This incumbent or elite violence miscalculated in the belief that a strategically aimed and decisive thrust could bring to a quick end the nationalist threat. In fact, the violence got way out of hand and required a costly revolutionary war lasting for roughly five years of pitched conflict, more in the gradual subsiding, and an inconclusive short-run victory for the official side. In a strict sense the actual violent revolution was less the creation of aggrieved and insurgent popular forces than a preemptive strike by the state attempting not to *preserve* the old order but to *consolidate* the new political and class bases of uneven development within a weak state.

The new developmentalist coalition was distinctively characterized by industrialists and (comprador) commercial classes joining hands with export agribusiness—itself replacing the landed oligarchs and settlers. Of course, there were many lesser allied classes among the incipient rural bourgeoisie, higher wage laborers, and the urban commercial and real estate interests. Several circumstances that had not been present previously (e.g., in the 1930s) helped effect this coalition. First was the tangible and imminent threat that the popular movement would impede their plans. Second was the need to consolidate a new class state in order to pursue the path of peripheral capitalist development. Third, to pursue that new path a relatively explicit *choice* presented itself—a policy decision on whether to tie national development to the ministrations of the global economy (e.g., the Bell Trade Act in exchange for development assistance in the Philippines). The state now took recourse to official violence both to cement the coalition itself and to thwart opposition that had not been pacified by simpler and tried methods (e.g., resettlement, better crop-shares, the right to unionize).

Fundamentally, of course, these maneuvers of the popular movement and developmentalist coalition were orchestrated—indeed, produced—by the influence and changing interests in the world system. More specifically, Britain and the United States presented to their dependent satellites the policy choices just mentioned because of their own changing neocolonial roles. As Kenya and the Philippines demonstrate, the old colonial arrangements had become costly and troublesome, both in the colonies and at home among domestic interests (e.g., British humanitarians and American farmers). By contrast to the late nineteenth-century policies based on territorial acquisition and a stable flow of raw materials, what the metropolitan powers now saw as to their greater advantage were stable and growing internal markets for metropolitan exports and multinational corporate investments (and in cases like the Philippines, military outposts). Provision of these required domestic peace and adequate state control to implement the new policies—incomes and distributive policies that would stimulate the internal market. These local and global circumstances provided the crucial intersection at which the revolution and struggle over the aims of development took shape.

This, finally, is the sense in which the national revolts may be understood as developmental (and "modernizing") revolutions. At the root of the political calculation, class division, and economic contradiction were policy issues over how development should proceed from the watershed years of the late 1940s: Who should direct and directly benefit from the new economy? What role should the state assume in alliance with its senior partners at home and abroad? These considerations provided the framework for thinking about particular solutions to the contradiction between the capacity to produce surplus and inequality. Some species of land reform, for example, might take the edge off rural inequality, but it would have to exempt agribusiness and proceed from a state possessed of the finances and political support necessary to redistribute land claimed by the gentry. Similarly, urban jobs provided an avenue for mollifying the proletariat but required reforms that the state would have to wrest from industrial employers and merchant monopolies. These were realistic options assuming the state could rebuild a powerful modernizing coalition.

Theoretical Summary

The preceding discussion has endeavored to explain through a synthesis of the case studies the causes of revolutionary situations that contribute to national revolts. It remains for us to summarize these causes and to consider their implications for a theoretical understanding of the nature of protest and revolution. This summary can be accomplished by isolating four general and interrelated processes: (1) the context of uneven development; (2) the conditions of protest mobilization; (3) modernization crises and coalitions; and (4) the role of the state. Although in some senses these are sequentially related, they are not intended as a natural history, since the processes are also partly contemporaneous and fundamentally dialectical.

Uneven development is generated in the first instance by the penetration of global capitalism into precapitalist societies that vary widely in their resources and forms of social organization. The immediate impact of this penetration is affected by a number of considerations, including what the peripheral society has to offer (e.g., mineral or agricultural resources, commercial or military bases), the motives of the colonizer (e.g., for domains, plunder, trade, investment), the timing of incorporation (e.g., during periods of empire building or commercial competition), and the potential for internal resistance. In combination these conditions produce a multiplicity of initial effects ranging from relatively benign annexation (as in the very early contact between European explorers and the people of East Africa and the Philippines) to wholesale destruction of indigenous groups (as in much of Latin America). Nevertheless, with the passage of time and the closer integration of the periphery as a zone of the world economy, characteristic features of underdevelopment appear. The peripheral society is "developed" not for its own sake but as a complement to the economic and military needs of the core power: systematic inequalities between the two are created and perpetuated, constituting the first sense of uneven development. Typically this entails fostering export agriculture and an internal market for the consumption of imports from the core. These, in turn, often require land alienation, coerced wage labor, and an export-oriented commercial (comprador) sector. Similarly, it is necessary to generate (unequally) national income in this process to ensure purchasing power for imports. Accordingly, the peripheral economy is unevenly developed in a second sense of internal class and sectoral disparities. All this produces a massive transformation of the indigenous economy that entices or forces the population into new forms of wage labor and service to the international system or leaves it behind to starve as traditional forms of subsistence are eliminated or rendered unprofitable.[29]

These new forms of inequality are implemented in law and economic policies that become the focus of local grievance and, later, nationalistic protest. Two broad constituencies articulate the grievances in distinct yet related forms. First, the "peasantry," or the various agrarian classes (small-holders, tenants, rural wage workers, and traders), protest against the loss of their land, deteriorating conditions of tenancy, withdrawal of commons privileges, exclusion from the market, coerced wage labor under conditions of low pay and onerous work, imposition of a monetary economy (e.g., via taxation), land-grabbing and land concentration, rising unemployment, and, generally, the destruction of their customary world and moral economy. Second, the "urban proletariat," representing another ensemble of classes (petty traders, informal sector workers in commerce and services, public functionaries, industrial workers), aim their grievances at underemployment, low wages and the cost of living, restrictions on organization and residence or movement, the conditions of housing and public services.

Protest against these inequalities does not require a long period of germination. In the historical studies it appeared almost coincident with the imposition of exploitative practices, albeit in rustic and localized forms, yet quite apart from the maturation of organizational mechanisms. Indeed, the nationalist movement was born early out of these conditions based on traditional forms of culture and society. Conversely, however, this protest may go on for a long time achieving no satisfactory result. With superior military and economic weapons colonial society resists accommodation save through occasional ameliorative changes in response to massive unrest. Independently the threats that the two class aggregates can mount fall short of endangering the basis of the political economy.

Nevertheless, a popular or nationalistic movement will flourish under these conditions. That movement begins to acquire the tools of potential effectiveness to the extent that it incorporates urban and rural discontent within a political association or party:

> **The country struggles over control of the land, the city over control of labor. The interests of the "subaltern classes" of town and country are necessarily different, though they are not necessarily contradictory. The two are likely to act in concert only when united (a) by some linking organization and (b) by a common opposition to the dominant classes and to their instrument, the state.**[30]

As we have seen, linking organization may be facilitated by state and institutional mechanisms for labor regulation, migration control, absentee ownership, or segregation of the rural (in reserves or tenant zones) and urban (in slums or native quarters) population. The coalition for popular rebellion is fostered to the extent that rural and urban grievances are merged in the routine operation of the economy (e.g., in the circle of traders or the urban and return migration from impoverished rural areas to the conditions of underemployment in the urban slums). Fundamentally, the alliances are encouraged by an expanding national market that ties the fortunes of urbanites, traders in the provincial capitals, and rural producers together in an export economy. These developments in twentieth-century peripheral societies have historical precedents such as the insurrection of French peasants in 1851, which

> **marked the dramatic entry of tens of thousands of peasants into an urban-based movement for social democracy. This movement derived strength from the economic and social links between towns and villages, not from their mutual isolation, it acquired shape and direction through conspiratorial . . . organizations, which used traditional forms of culture for new political purposes.**[31]

And as in the French case, these links were not invariably the product of economic hardship, as opposed to the multifaceted experience of modernization in which winners *and* losers appeared once the dust had settled. To extend that to a related issue, the rhythms of revolutionary organization were less in tune with economic fluctuations than with political fortunes.

What is different about peripheral countries is the assist given to the rural–urban coalition by the inability of the dominant classes to divide and rule by making urban society a refuge for displaced rural populations (e.g., through a vital urban economy of expanding industry and jobs). To a large extent peripheral underdevelopment forecloses this possibility through export–import dependence that provides very limited local industrial growth or jobs, under capital-intensive conditions, while simultaneously requiring a low industrial wage and informal economy to subsidize foreign investors and local comprador classes. In the context of nonindustrial, peripheral under-development, the rural–urban contrast is qualitatively different from that in the European experience of industrialization—rural and urban distinctions are more recent, more permeable. In the absence of effective methods to divide it, essentially by making urban society a safety valve, this fundamentally subversive coalition grows naturally. Long traditions of permanent urban residence are absent, making it difficult to turn this segment against rural producers as in the Great Fear preceding the French Revolution. Urban and rural populations are in flux, closely connected through kinship networks, and coping with conditions sufficiently similar that their casual connection can be readily perceived—especially through the lenses of the nationalist movements that actively court recruits.

A final assist to the political alliance of city and countryside comes with weakening ties between old local oligarchs, mainly land-lords, and the central government. In most underdeveloped agrarian societies

> **a single local elite controls the major links between any particular rural area and the national structure of power. Most often it is the landowning elite. So long as the elite is in place and has effective ties to the national structure, no large mobilization of the countryside occurs without the elite's collaboration. . . . When the ties of the local elite weaken—however that happens—the costs of independent mobilization go down as its possible benefits rise.**[32]

The historical studies show how this principle works out in different settings. British indirect rule through village councils in Kenya un-dermined local democratic forms without transferring authority to the loyalists. The Japanese occupation of the Philippines proved that the peasantry could survive and prosper without the landlords and their village police. Liberal and Conservative local bosses lost influence in the Colombian export economy and ultimately were pitted against one another in a national political war. In each case the influence of local elites paled in the face of stimulants to the national movements that took as axiomatic the importance of rural–urban coalition.

Moving from the context of uneven development to the conditions of protest mobilization (the second summary process), a vital development is the organizational articulation of political conscious-ness. As we have seen, cultural nationalism played an important part in this process. Material achievements, however unequally distributed, helped promote the recognition that poverty could be eliminated, thereby fostering the sense of noninevitability. These forces provided the catalyst for the nationalist movement. But the key to understanding this movement, particularly its maturation from localized and traditional forms to an expression of modern political nationalism, lies in the very mechanisms that colonial society employed in vain attempts at cooptation. It was the dominant society that provided the opening, the opportunity to participate in seemingly sanctioned ways, that coalesced the popular movement. The new legal norms designed to promote innocuous participation of popular classes in the elite plan for modernization failed to mystify as they provided a platform and vehicle for subversion. As Thompson notes from a distant setting,

> **People are not as stupid as some structuralist philosophers believe them to be. They will not be mystified by the first man who puts on a wig. . . . Most men have a strong sense of justice, at least with regard to their own interests. If the law is evidently partial and unjust, then it will mask nothing, legitimize nothing, contribute nothing to any class's hegemony. . . . As such law has not only been imposed *upon* men from above: it has also been a medium within which other conflicts have been fought out.[33]**

Concretely, the legitimation and cooperation of the local population was sought through a tutelary legislature in the Philippines, the native councils and Legislative Council in Kenya, and, in a slightly different sense, through Colombia's political reforms of the 1930s, which invited broader participation in elite management. As the studies show (and Kenyatta's allegory illustrates), the first result of this new franchise was the frustration of popular expressions, which led to more sophisticated forms of political consciousness and militant action. Soon utter frustration with patronizing gestures enabled the popular movement to become more successful at organizational protest. Local revolts took place, winning some concessions and adding fuel to the movement. The critical pass came in the late 1940s with the postwar resurgence of civil politics. Coincident in time were the Philippine congressional elections, the formation of the Kenyan African Unity organization as a vehicle for, among other things, obtaining African representation in the Legislative Council, and the impressive showing in defeat by the left Liberals in Colombia's presidential election. In each case these were major victories for the popular movement—certainly the greatest achievements in their struggle to that point. The Democratic Alliance had elected six representatives to the Philippine congress, which would decide critical postwar issues such as the future of neocolonialism. The Colombian left, based on a growing urban constituency, was fast becoming a social movement with the power to wrest the presidency from the traditional Liberal–Conservative elite alliance. The KAU was becoming a true political party with national (and intertribal) support and symbolic gains in Leg Co.

Tragically, of course, mobilization reached its pinnacle when these political gains were perfunctorily canceled and a new campaign of repression instituted against the movement precisely because it had played the game of conventional politics too well. Revolutionary mobilization was generated from the success that was won and taken away. In that sense the mood was all the more revolutionary than under earlier sufferance of the objective conditions of exploitation or the fancy of something never achieved. This helps explain why the revolutionary movement came when it did. For, although the violence was initiated from the other side, this time the popular movement would fight back.

Finally, it must be recalled that the economic reversals accompanying these political events were equally sharp and regressive. Growing inequality and the absolute deprivation of peasants and workers provided some of the key mobilizing issues for the political movement. Yet this was far from a case of "base" and "superstructure" combining to produce revolutionary mobilization. Economic grievance had been as severe in times past. The two obviously combined, but it was the political situation that was unique and most critical at this moment.

Third among the summary points was the crisis of coalition and modernization among the elites. The first two points help describe the situation confronting the dominant groups. The popular movement was making substantial gains within their bailiwick just as the contradictions of uneven development were becoming fetters on the continued smooth operation of the system. The threats to the dominant classes went far beyond their own lively imaginations. Whether the demands were for land, the rights of labor, or the nationalistic economic interest, they were sharply antagonistic with all of the premises of dependent development negotiated between the elite and foreign interests. At the same time the dominant economic interests were presented with opportunities for greater profit through new and even closer alliances with the metropolitan economy in the postwar boom.

These circumstances combined to urge on the dominant classes a new coalition more faithful to the changing dimensions of interest under dependent capitalism and multinationalism. Some of the previous elite fractures were anachronistic (e.g., between landed oligarchs and commercial-industrial classes) as agribusiness sought allies in export commerce and industrial investment associated with multinational corporations. Where these affinities were not clear, the clamor of the popular movement often forced them. In the end a new elite coalition was formed, and its initially tentative alliances were cemented with the attack on the popular movement. These revolutions cannot be explained through an exclusive emphasis on either the economic plight of the populace or the collapse of state control: "Violence is a by-product of an interaction rather than a direct expression of the propensities of one of the participants . . . the interaction of contenders for power . . . that are engaged in disputes over rights and justice."[34]

This introduces the final summary point on the role of the state. In these cases the state attempted to consolidate its wandering class base by recourse to what was quickly proven an act of desperation. The singular explanation of this act was the objective weaknesses of the state as it had become compromised between foreign and national interests and harried by the popular movement. Its domestic support, from the various upper classes and through the army, was badly split and flagging. Its social base was constricted, and even with the imagination to fashion alternative responses to the economic crisis, it is doubtful that the state could have marshaled the resources to pursue another plan for development. For example, to promote a policy of political independence and economic nationalism, the state would have needed broad popular support—a willingness for self-sacrifice to defer consumption in the interests of new forms of nationally financed production. Conversely, in order to buy off popular discontent through rapid modernization, it would have needed much more extensive foreign aid than its international allies were willing to offer at this stage (although, ironically, not after the violence). From a more detached standpoint, other alternatives come readily to mind long after the fact. At the time, however, a preemptive strike against the opposition may actually have seemed a promising solution to some and to others a calculated risk—more attractive than vague alternatives from the legacy of a state wedded so long to elitist and colonial interests.

This response was a matter of constrained choice rather than necessity. Faced with the same choice, but different resource combinations, other states have taken alternative roads. Most common, perhaps, has been effective repression relying on the means of force in those states that enjoyed a strong and unified military or external intervention (e.g., South Africa, Argentina, the Dominican Republic). Another route has been limited concession combined with new class and ethnic group alliances based on special privilege (e.g., Peru, Brazil, Malaya). Nicaragua provides an interesting transitional case, in which the Sandinista movement met with only limited success as long as the Somoza regime had the support of the domestic bourgeoisie and the United States. It gathered momentum as the dictator's monopolization of the economy began to alienate the former and his inability to control the violence lost the latter. Internally, political disaster followed on natural disaster when, after the 1972 earthquake in Managua, Somoza used the occasion for his own profit. Downtown Managua was cordoned off for several years following under the pretense of rebuilding on firmer ground. The ground in question, however, turned out to be a suburban extension of the city with similar seismological properties and concentrated ownership by Somoza and his inner circle. Since the scheme for great speculative profits on the new land was dependent on the elimination of the old commercial center crowded with small businesses, it was correctly perceived as a callous form of expropriation of the petty bourgeoisie and service economy—one of the few sources of income that Somoza did not already control. In short, Somoza lost a critical constituency to the rebels. In all of these cases, successful avoidance of revolt depended on strategic strengths (e.g., military) or negotiated new ones (e.g., class and ethnic alliances). The abjectly weak states in this comparison lacked such opportunities and inventiveness.

The role of the state involved more than an unmediated expression of metropolitan designs. It would not act as the mere instrument of foreign interests even had it aspired to do so, which it certainly did not. The internal and external constraints on the state require more subtle treatment, and in that connection Marx's study of *The Eighteenth Brumaire of Louis Bonaparte* is instructive. Drawing these parallels, Leys remarks,

> **It is no accident that Marx's discussion of the situation in France in the 1850s is so full of clues to the situation in most of sub-Saharan Africa in the 1960s. In spite of obvious differences, the two situations have something fundamental in common: a complex and fluid class structure corresponding to the still incompletely evolved interrelationship of the capitalist and non-capitalist modes of production.**[35]

In Kenya and the Philippines (though to a lesser extent in Colombia), the postcolonial state was relatively autonomous with respect to control by a single class. The key to its weakness lay in the fact that, although it was not dominated by any single class, "in practice it could not prevent its policies fostering the interests of certain classes, even if it wished to. Yet this enhanced the political power of these classes, and so undermined its own independence of action."[36] In short, the state was predicated on its own contradiction that restricted the range of action and threatened its temporary autonomy. Any action (or for that matter, inaction) would play to certain class interests, and the pursuit of any developmental strategy would require a social base. Faced with this dilemma the states involved chose the pragmatic course of siding with the most potent foreign and (allied) domestic groups in a policy of rapid economic development, which, orthodoxy promised, would also assuage the condition of the masses. The choice meant that the state traded the weakness of a kind of "autonomy" for that of a narrow but potent, foreign and domestic, bourgeois class base.

In the light of this analysis of the causes of revolutionary situations, we can return to some of the broad theoretical issues posed in the introductory chapter. National revolts were conceived as protracted nonlocal conflicts in underdeveloped societies having recourse to violence. They involve political and socioeconomic issues arising out of the penetration of indigenous social formations by the global political economy. And they result in the engagement of popular classes and the response of the state in a struggle over developmental goals that qualitatively transforms state and society. The historical studies attest to the utility of this definition.

The Huk, Violencia, and Mau Mau movements were far more than transient eruptions or parochial instances of localized, peasant rebelliousness—although the old regimes labored to so define them. They were integral parts of continuous struggles that began to take on definable features at the turn of the century (and definite ones by the 1920s) in response to the socioeconomic inequalities and dislocations produced by the incorporation of local and largely precapitalist societies into the global economy. They involved the use of violence, typically as a defensive strategy, but evolved mainly as class-based political movements making equity claims on the state and its developmental policies. When the state failed to respond to (indeed, exacerbated) those claims, a pitched struggle ensued over the aims and beneficiaries of development that transformed the state and society in fundamental if diverse ways.

Conceptually, therefore, national revolts rival their celebrated revolutionary cousins in gravity and scope. Yet concepts are also hypotheses, and the purpose of those advanced goes beyond a pleading that national revolts deserve more historical respect and scholarly status. Rather the claim is that they belong in the same theoretical field with the revolutions and related forms of protest suggested in the introductory scheme in chapter 1. Bluntly, I claim they have the same general causes. Although pieces of the complete argument await the concluding chapter on revolutionary consequences, from the "causal side" the evidence provided suggests an exception to the claim "that successful social revolutions probably emerge from different macrostructural and historical contexts than do either failed social revolutions or political transformations that are not accompanied by transformations of class relations."[37]

The issue, of course, is empirical. The foregoing summary of causes of revolutionary situations (i.e., uneven development, repression and the political mobilization of classes, crises and elite coalitions, and the action of weak states) represents the prelude to national revolt. These causes are precisely the stuff of revolution as it has been explained in the exemplary social histories—explanations based on the penetration of agrarian society, on the peasantry in export agriculture, on rural–urban coalitions, and on the state as an actor in the process.

The failure to notice and examine these connections stems from several circumstances. First, it simply has not been done in a comparative frame that would suggest generalization from the many extraordinary social histories of revolt. Second, analyses of "classical revolutions" have tended to become creatures of their own venerated historical past, failing to appreciate the parallel character and context of modern revolutions. Third, and in a related sense, social scientists have tended to accept at face value the terminology of victorious contemporaries in the revolutionary struggle, not appreciating that those very categories are a *part* of the struggle and designed to accomplish political purposes quite unrelated to conceptual purity—as was graphically shown in the postrevolutionary denial of Mau Mau in the interests of reconciliation. The language of politics deserves its own analysis and, in this instance, reveals something otherwise obscured about the character of revolts.

In search of the appropriate theory and understanding of national revolts, the foregoing analysis helps to sort false and promising leads. An important step involves the demonstration that revolution is not the singular accomplishment of the peasantry or urban proletariat. Theories that counterpose these class ensembles are belied by a great deal of evidence and reason spuriously by virtue of their failure to recognize the common origins and differential political expressions of rural and urban dislocations following from incorporation. Conversely, proceeding from the perspective of a competitive and changing world economy, these transformations are illuminated in the workings of uneven development. If that perspective provides an understanding of the general condition of inequality and the grievances of the periphery, it is nevertheless true that these are necessary but not sufficient for the promotion of revolt. It is here that the merger of revolutionary and underdevelopment theory must be effected—or the dangers of "economistic" explanations avoided. Concretely, the analysis shows that the sufficient conditions of revolt lie in cultural expressions of the political process—the situational contours of uneven development that breed political crises and coalitions prompting and shaping actions of the state.

Notes

1. Tilly, *From Mobilization to Revolution*, p. 192.
2. Stinchcombe, *Theoretical Methods*.
3. Ranger, "Connexions."
4. Edelman, *Symbolic Uses;* Wuthnow, "On Suffering, Rebellion, and the Moral Order."
5. Wallerstein, *Modern World-System*.
6. *Ibid.*, ch. 6.
7. Skocpol, *States and Social Revolutions*, ch. 1.
8. Moore, *Social Origins*, p. 55.
9. Leys, *Underdevelopment*, p. 201.
10. Portes and Walton, *Labor, Class, and the International System*.
11. Furedi, "Social Composition."
12. Moore, *Social Origins*, p. 479.
13. Margadant, *French Peasants*, pp. 55ff.
14. Marx, *The Eighteenth Brumaire of Louis Napoleon*, pp. 127–28.
15. Wolf, *Peasant Wars;* Alavi, "Peasants and Revolution"; Hirschman, *Journeys;* DeRoux, "Social Basis"; Kerkvliet, *Huk Rebellion;* Furedi, "Social Composition."
16. Walton, "Accumulation."
17. Hobsbawm, *Primitive Rebels*, p. 133.
18. *Ibid.*, p. 114.
19. Furedi, "African Crowd"; Pomeroy, "Philippine Peasantry."
20. Giddens, *Class Structure;* Moore, *Injustice*.
21. Tilly, *Mobilization*, pp. 204–5.
22. Moore, *Injustice*, p. 50.
23. Kenyatta, *Facing Mt. Kenya*, pp. 47–51.
24. Skocpol, *States and Social Revolutions;* Popkin, *Rational Peasant*.
25. Paige, *Agrarian Revolution*.
26. Thompson, *English Working Class*, p. 194.
27. Moore, *Injustice*, p. 468.
28. Cumings, "Interest and Ideology."
29. De Janvry, *Agrarian Question*.
30. Tilly, "Town and Country," p. 273.
31. Margadant, *French Peasants*, pp. xxii–xxiii.
32. Tilly, "Town and Country," p. 293.

33. Thompson, *Whigs and Hunters*, pp. 262, 263, 267.
34. Tilly, "Town and Country," p. 283.
35. Leys, *Underdevelopment*, p. 209.
36. *Ibid.*, p. 207.
37. Skocpol, *States and Social Revolutions*, p. 5.

CHAPTER SIX

The Consequences
of National Revolts

THE QUESTION THAT remains is whether revolution makes a difference. The answer will be developed in several steps following the framework that has guided us this far. First, the "outcomes" of the national revolts are evaluated and, in combination with earlier conclusions about revolutionary situations, a typological contrast of the three cases is provided. Second, we shall explore the legacies of the revolts in the more general sense of long-term changes that they helped to initiate. Finally, we shall return once more to the question of what constitutes a "successful" revolution and how various answers to this question affect our theoretical thinking about the revolutions of the past and struggles of the present.

Aiming at the kind of conceptual precision that distinguishes the direct consequences of revolt from all the rest of a society's post-revolutionary history, the scheme introduced earlier conceives of revolutionary outcomes as the displacement of power holders and, especially, of policies. Although the objective here is narrow, it is a useful first step. Parenthetically, it should be recalled that there is no necessary correlation between revolutionary situations and outcomes. On the contrary, historical interpretation and revolutionary criticism suggest that these may be disparate—as in the (big) revolution "betrayed" or the (little) revolution by stealth. In what follows the connection receives a fresh empirical treatment.

In the historical studies, and as a matter of fact rather than contrivance or prediction, the scope of the outcomes assumes the same ordinal scaling as the severity of revolutionary situations. In the Philippines the amount of "displacement" produced by the Huk rebellion was minimal. Indeed, the earlier displacement of six members of the National Congress, produced by electoral victories of the Democratic Alliance in 1946 and then nullified, loomed among the immediate causes of the revolt. Subsequently, as the revolutionary violence gradually subsided, there was no perceptible effort to incorporate (or even "coopt") members of the nationalist movement in positions of power. Within the compass of national politics some of the leaders who rose to key posts, notably Raman Magsaysay, enjoyed reputations for progressivism and the common touch, but their rise owed little to popular preferences. Far from any displacement or leavening of the ruling alliance, the Huk rebellion led to a retrenchment of power and of its military and economic alliances with the United States.

Nowhere is a direct connection between revolt and political change more evident than in the Colombian case. The Rojas dictatorship and the more enduring National Front government that replaced it were designed specifically to bring an end to the Violencia. By any standard the new political system represented a major transformation of the state. True, an earlier precedent existed for the National Front, and during peaceful interludes in the past the Liberal and Conservative party elites had practiced coexistence. The National Front, however, went much further by guaranteeing a sixteen-year period of shared leadership and rotating command that included a role for splinter groups within the party alliances and a greater voice for labor organizations. Amnesty was granted to the participants in regional struggles, and many of them took up posts in local government. Nevertheless, what the Violencia did not accomplish in terms of displacement was a change in the composition of the ruling groups themselves. The more unified Liberal–Conservative coalition continued to reflect the interests of the upper class, although they made genuine efforts to incorporate others (e.g., labor) and respond to the needs of the masses (e.g., with land reform). Some of the new leaders, like Carlos Lleras Restrepo, were unusually gifted politicians and developmentalists. Yet the transformation was largely of the system and style of governance rather than its class bases and principal beneficiaries.

The connection between the Mau Mau revolt and the government of independent Kenya was at once more convoluted and more transformative. The revolt set in motion a chain of circumstances that led to independence, despite the fact that its influence was played down for purposes of reconciliation, as we have seen. Yet it was also true that the days of the British colony in East Africa were numbered after World War II and developments around the world (e.g., India). Although the result was not imminent in 1952 when the revolt began, independence would have come to Kenya before long had it never been for Mau Mau. One consequence of the revolt, therefore, was to hasten independence, but more important was the effect it had on the nature of the transition and the contours of the postcolonial state. The fact of the revolt persuaded the British that reforms (e.g., of land) were urgent if Kenya was to become a healthy economic ally, and it helped to win political concessions (e.g., majority rule) that gave complete self-governance to Africans. Without the revolt the Rhodesian "model" could have been Kenya's fate. Mau Mau did more than speed the inevitable. The displacement brought by independence was complete, albeit restricted in the sense of who held power. Kenyatta's government represented the essence of the nationalist movement in power, and it defeated British efforts to neutralize some of that power through thinly veiled efforts to promote "multiracial government" or tribalism. Although there are important evaluative issues to be pursued about the quality of the transformation, at this juncture it can be concluded that the revolt produced a far-reaching change in the set of power holders and policies.

To summarize with respect to the formulation in chapter 1 and figure 1.1, Kenya approached the conditions of "irrevocable split" and "complete displacement"; Colombia earned respectable marks on both; and the Philippines reflected only a modest amount of multiple sovereignty with little displacement. If it helps, one might graphically imagine a line on the figure that begins at the lower reaches of the middle of the box (Philippines), passes through the intersecting ovals of civil war and insurrection (Colombia), and ends somewhere in the upper righthand portion (Kenya). If the spatial representation does not help, no matter—our interest centers more on understanding national revolts than on classifying them. In that sense the formulation does enhance an appreciation for the continuous quality and the causal unity of events that make for insurrection, civil war, and anticolonial revolution in the historical studies. The point is clear and helps launch a substantive analysis of differential consequences.

Generally, each of the contemporary societies treated in these pages can be described as an instance of peripheral underdevelopment within the capitalist world economy, instances in which predominantly precapitalist societies and localized economies devoted to petty commodity production and regional trade were penetrated by and converted to the needs of an international system dominated by the metropolitan core. For example, in varying degrees each reflects a condition of agricultural production for export rather than indigenous needs (i.e., monoculture), land alienation and wage labor coercion, rapid urbanization associated with underemployment and informal sector immiseration, and a local bourgeoisie subservient to foreign commerce and industry—all conditions that figured in the national revolts as cause and consequence. Nevertheless, this description takes in a lot of territory (from Brazil and Nigeria to Surinam and Malawi) and, at this level, obscures societal differences that are much more determinant of the way people conduct their daily lives. Accordingly, any assessment of revolutionary consequences requires a more exacting description of the kinds of political and economic underdevelopment we want to explain.

Kenya is a *postcolonial state* dominated by an emergent national bourgeoisie based on a one-party political bureaucracy allied with foreign capital. The new privileged classes are a clear minority of landed, commercial, and political interests, but their elevation to this position reflects a good deal of social mobility by contrast to the recent colonial past. The state, with external support, has engineered important reforms in the agrarian sector that have deepened the floor of economic survival. Land and labor reforms favored the middle classes or "aristocratic" segments of the mass, sometimes at the expense of ethnic minorities and the truly poor. In another critical area of reform, the nation has asserted a measure of autonomy and economic nationalism in efforts to control foreign investment. The class structure is more diversified than before, and at the same time those (new) groups at the top enjoy greater privilege.

Colombia is an *associated-dependent state* whose narrowly based upper class and (highly coincident) political elite have not been greatly altered through the process of national revolt in either their social composition or proportionate share of the largesse. Gains, and recurring, painful setbacks, have been made in stabilizing democratic procedures and a broader franchise. Reforms of land and labor have accomplished more in the increase than in the redistribution of the social product. The landed classes have generally evaded reform through more intensive land use, and labor has received the cooptative blandishments of additional jobs and minimum wages. Some autonomy has been asserted with respect to foreign influence on monetary policy and through currency controls, but without coercive efforts to regulate multinational capital. The class structure, although unchanged in its general outlines, is more inclusive, mobile, and subject to political mediation.

The Philippines is an unalloyed *neocolonial state* based on agribusiness, multinational corporate, and military domination. Recently, and related to the Huk rebellion, martial law and the suppression of political expression have been necessary to safeguard the system of social inequality. The United States maintains an enormous multinational corporate and military presence, and the national economy has passed into virtual receivership in the hands of the World Bank and International Monetary Fund. The political leadership is heavily dependent on these sources of support and its near-complete alienation from domestic groups (including the Roman Catholic hierarchy) is reflected in the deportation of priests and jailing of prominent members of the national bourgeoisie and elite political opposition. The present dictatorship is surviving on huge infusions of capital from the World Bank. The political situation is precarious, and it invites a new mass revolt (beyond continuing guerrilla activities) or at least, a coup that could buy time for the initiation of real reforms. Needless to add, the class structure has grown more inegalitarian and oppressive.

When these typological and substantive characterizations are combined, an obvious generalization comes to the fore. Namely, the degree of development and progressive change in these three cases is regularly associated with the extensiveness of their national revolts: "the more extensive the revolutionary situation, the greater the likelihood of an extensive transfer of power."[1] Although that fact is worth noting, it is not advanced as an empirical generalization that would stretch the bounds of historically informed, comparative method. The "generalization" holds in these cases, but it is among the many and interrelated circumstances that explain the connections that more fruitful generalizations should be sought—that is, in the middle range that connects particular conditions of underdevelopment or regional and class alliance with revolutionary action.

Explaining the Consequences of Revolt

Obviously, the first explanatory point about the consequences of revolt harks back to the nature of the revolutionary situation. These two aspects of the revolutionary process are closely related in fact, although they are not tautologically defined or hopelessly confounded. It is the reasoning behind the connection that attracts our interest, as Tilly goes on to suggest:

> **The more extensive the revolutionary situation, the harder it is for any organized group or segment of the population to avoid committing itself to one side or the other. That commitment makes it more difficult for any contender to reconstitute its old multiple alliances in the postrevolutionary settlement. The more extensive the revolutionary situation, the more experience the revolutionary coalition will have in forging its own instruments of government independent of the existing holders of power."** [2]

In the Kenyan case these suppositions are most compelling. During the Emergency the African and settler society was sharply polarized, especially by punitive sanctions on noncombatants (e.g., internment and cessation of economic activity). The oaths were the archetype of commitment. Once the fighting was over, a renewed commitment to labor, investment, and civilian authority could only be encouraged by a respected nationalist movement that, nevertheless, guaranteed the rights of Europeans. A more militant revolutionary government could have attracted mass allegiance, save for the choice to promote rapid economic development. Clearly impossible was any return to colonial politics. The Mau Mau Emergency had convinced Great Britain to pull out in an orderly fashion that protected its investment and trade, which, in turn, meant appeasing nationalist demands that were all the more insistent. African instruments of government had existed for a long time and become more sophisticated in the ways of European custom during the long struggle for parliamentary power.

The revolutionary situation in the Philippines was quite another story. The revolt was more contained socially and geographically. Although the HMB activists and sympathizers came from a broad spectrum of social classes, the movement's leadership was organizationally fragmented. Most important, the movement was both defensive and respectful of the general precepts of the state. Unlike Mau Mau, it did not deny the legitimacy of the institutional state or demand its replacement with another system of authority closer to the people. The effective instruments of government that the movement developed during the occupation and the revolt, it felt, would also work under normal circumstances save for malevolent landlords and employers. Once defeated militarily, the Huks had few choices other than to rejoin the polity and hope for the best from the appealing promises of reform.

In this contrast, the Violencia was closest to the Huk rebellion. The fighting was carried out by extended but geographically isolated groups with even less organizational representation and national coordination. Similarly, apart from regional autonomy (independent republics), the protagonists had no plans for the transformation of the state or alternative standards of national legitimacy—central authority had always been tenuous in Colombia history. The kind of transformation of the state desired was one that would end the political party wars and their staging on local terrain and ensure agrarian and working-class reform—in short, what the National Front promised and, to some extent, delivered.

These contrasts in the aims of the revolutionary situation must be understood, of course, in terms of state-initiated violence. None of the popular movements had prepared for a revolutionary takeover, and their aspirations for a settlement varied according to the previous aims of protest and legitimate political activity as well as the degree of irrevocability brought on by the struggle. The reluctant rebels could hardly be faulted for failing to win a revolution they had not planned. On the contrary, what is impressive is the amount of transformation that was garnered from the struggles begun under such disadvantageous terms. To explain that, we must look again at a set of internal and external circumstances that collectively characterize the revolts.

Internally, the fundamental consideration is the extent to which class power was altered by the revolt itself and the terms of its settlement. In the Philippines the significance of class power is demonstrated in the fact that the domination of the landlords and their control, in alliance with export interests, over the national Congress was never broken. If anything, by the mid-1950s the landlords were stronger than in 1940 by virtue of their ties to multinational agribusiness and to the state, which had pursued palliative methods of land reform. Similarly, labor reforms based on collective bargaining played into the hands of foreign industries and their local partners at the expense of workers and the national bourgeoisie. Splits between the new entrepreneurial classes were looked upon with favor by landed export interests and translated into smoothly effected congressional action on labor relations that deepened the division between the national and internationally linked business communities. The transformation of class power was ultimately regressive.

The changes in Colombia and Kenya, by contrast, were progressive. The transformation in Colombia's class power was slight, involving a broader-based elite whose compromises (e.g., on land reform) produced some fallout for the lower classes, which were also provided greater accessibility to the centers of decision (e.g., in electoral reforms). Class domination was alloyed with the concessions necessary to quell the violence. In Kenya, an authentic rupture in class power took place as the colonial government withdrew and the settlers who stayed were reduced to a powerful class fraction (rather than a dominant force) along with the emerging African bourgeoisie. Although a new agrarian bourgeoisie, comprador commercial class, and state bureaucratic sector all combined in a pattern of stratification that was far from egalitarian, that should not obscure a cold calculation of the impressive amount of structural transformation.

The external bases of the outcomes are equally important, recognizing that internal–external distinctions are only useful fictions. One way to think about the external contribution to revolutionary success is as "a tolerant or permissive World context."[3] Here again the Philippines is an extreme case. As a neocolony, the Philippines had (and still has) great value to the United States. Its internal market, cheap labor, and service as an export platform of manufactures to Asia make it a critical economic asset in U.S. international strategy—such as the intensive effort to keep abreast of Japan's widening role in international markets. This helps to explain the inordinate attention of the World Bank to Philippine "stability," yet it is only half the story. The Philippines provides the major base of U.S. military operations and influence in Asia. The United States has invested countless millions in air and naval installations on the islands from which its perceived vital security interests in Asia and the Pacific are maintained. All of this explains the far-sighted and critical assistance of the United States in the defeat of the Huk rebellion and the dominant foreign presence ever since. Unlike the stakes of Britain in East Africa, this was one colony that simply could not be lost or endangered by the nationalist left.

Colombia and Kenya, once again, share similarities in this regard and are mild instances of the international stake in neocolonialism. In both cases external support was lent to the defeat of the revolt, but the metropolitan powers wanted most a peaceful settlement under liberalized conditions that would stabilize investments and trade opportunities on a new basis. Although direct manipulation of the postrevolutionary situation occurred in Kenya, in both these cases the greater influence flowed from the opportunity that the metropolitan power extended to national elites to finance their reforms and restructure their coalitions. These more benign opportunity structures meant that domestic political groups could realign their own bases and incentives for participation in a state that dovetailed neatly in a dependent alliance with the changing requirements of the international system and new core power interests.

In all three cases the extensiveness of postrevolutionary changes and the peculiar nature of the social and economic transformations in the periphery were closely connected with metropolitan stakes. A final and obvious consideration still deserves mention, namely the power of the core powers involved. By 1960, of course, Britain's status as a major power in the international economy was long past. It had very little long-term leverage in East Africa apart from what the Kenyan leadership chose to grant in connection with its own developmental designs. Had Kenyans been willing to pay the domestic costs of economic nationalism (a la Tanzania), there is no reason to suppose that Britain could have prevented it. The situation of the United States, at the apogee of its international influence, was quite different with respect to its ability to affect the domestic arrangements of developing countries like Colombia and the Philippines when it chose to do so. As we have seen, in the Philippine case, where its national interests were perceived as vital, it employed a wide range of interventionist policies (e.g., counterinsurgency, economic and military aid, support of approved political candidates, corporate investment, domestic policy "advice" on labor and monetary policy) with the aim of complete control of the domestic situation. Colombia, by contrast, was more peripheral to the vital interests of the United States in Latin America. It was neither a "model democracy" to be promoted (like Costa Rica) nor a hotbed of subversion to be "stabilized" (like Argentina, Uruguay, Chile). Within limits, it could make its own arrangements, provided they continued in some form the beneficial dependent alliance. To summarize using a notion advanced by theorists,[4] both Kenya and Colombia enjoyed the social space in which they could fashion their own developmental policies and statecraft.

The internal and external influences on revolutionary outcomes are unified in the state and the manner in which it was transformed. In the actual process of state building these forces and the class interests they represent are worked out in the context of national traditions and circumstantial exigencies that are to some extent independent of strict "structural determination"—the process is emergent, though not without explanation based on a conjunction of influences. This emphasis is one of the strengths of Skocpol's treatment of classical revolutions.

Having established that state building may be a fruitful thread to follow in analyzing social revolutions, it remains to clarify what such an emphasis entails. One thing it means is that the political leaderships involved in revolutions must be regarded as actors struggling to assert and make good their claims to state sovereignty. This may sound obvious, but it is not the usual way in which political leaderships in revolutions are analyzed. Typically, such leaderships in revolutions are analyzed. Typically, such leaderships are treated as representatives of classes or social groups, struggling to realize economic or status interests, and/or as actors attempting to implement a certain ideological vision of the ideal social order. . . . What tends to be missed in all of this is that which political leaderships in revolutionary crises are above all *doing*—claiming and struggling to maintain state power. During revolutionary interregnums, political leaderships rise and fall according to how successful they are in creating and using political arrangements within the crisis circumstances that they face.[5]

Although this activity is often mystified in ideological discussions of the "relative autonomy" of the state, it can be concretely located here in the manner in which governments respond to demands within the constraints of class forces and the exigencies of organizational survival. Illustratively, those who came to power in the postwar Philippines found their room to maneuver constricted on one side by powerful agrarian export interests and by metropolitan interests on the other. Within this restricted space they had very few resources of their own. There was very little slack in the system that they could appropriate for the purpose of state building; most of the choices they could make placed them on one side or another of a well-defined constellation of interests. In this connection it is important to recall that the country had never enjoyed a period of self-government. Among the few traditions of national independence that it could draw upon from 400 years of colonialism were those episodes of defiance of the Spaniards and Japanese that, tellingly, were greatly vaunted in the recorded heritage but provided a few practical lessons for state building. As a result, state building threaded the narrow opening between power blocs represented in palliative land and labor reforms and programs of economic nationalism that penalized ethnic minorities. There was simply little space for innovation in state building, and when the contradictions of underdevelopment reached crisis proportions, the draconian measures of martial law (made possible by external support) provided the only avenue of survival.

This obviously extreme situation contrasts sharply with Colombian activities of statecraft. Colombia has a rich historical legacy of democratic self-government—some of it hypocritical owing to upper-class domination based on a restrictive franchise, and some of it genuine, arising from colonization of internal areas and progressive reformism (especially in Antioquia). Colombians pride themselves—along with the purity of their Spanish and their "blood"—on the sophistication of their nineteenth-century liberalism and twentieth-century record of democratic government. Indeed, prior to 1948 the country was regarded in many quarters as an enviable democracy. What is important here is that these civic traditions were drawn upon heavily in state-building activities designed to end the Violencia. The army intervened at two critical junctures to restore some sanity to the political process, yet chose not to assume any permanent role. The specific mechanisms governing the National Front were drawn from the heritage of nineteenth-century politics and effectively revised to suit the contemporary crisis. The rebuilding of the state was an elaborate and intricate process of negotiation. To be sure, it was guided by elite hands and interests, but progressive liberalism scored many gains in the negotiation process. The Violencia nightmare preyed on everyone's mind and induced a mood of compromise that liberal politicians used skillfully. State building operated on a broad compass marked by incursions into elite privilege and metropolitan preference.

In a different manner state building in Kenya enjoyed a wide latitude among structural and class constraints since a state was being created for the first time on the basis of a variety of traditional and colonial legacies. Many of the formal trappings of British rule were continued after independence (e.g., a National Assembly), their legal properties lending themselves to a continuation of class rule. But as Leys instructs, "The neo-colonial state does not represent the interests of a dominant national bourgeoisie, and consequently these institutions, which developed for that purpose, function badly, if at all. Their utility is largely ideological; in reality they tend to atrophy."[6] Rather, authority and effective decision making were exercised in "Kenyatta's court," which blended elements of tribal tradition with the practical demands of public policy.

The court system served several purposes. The district and tribal delegations, with their gifts and dances and protestations of loyalty, and with their marked element of competition for attention, both reinforced and integrated the ethnic dimension of politics, which flowed from and lent immunity to neo-colonialism. Kenyatta on these occasions was the Father of the Nation, "making people happy within the frame of bourgeois society." At the same time it helped to systematize clientelism, providing a sequence and protocol for the seeking

of favors . . . the basic significance of all this attendance at court should not be lost sight of: it worked because it was Kenyatta, along with the inner court, who could make any important political decision.[7]

In this way the new political leadership was able to bring indigenous groups into the political process in a forum that also aggrandized its power, veiled other compromises, and provided the flexibility necessary for linking patronage to instrumental purpose. All of this enhanced Kenyatta's heroic figure and his ability to dictate certain terms to foreign investors and to share with his family a large slice of the largesse.

In varying degrees the process of state building introduced an additional element of independence into the determination of revolutionary outcomes. It provided the tone and coloration of national policies as these were experienced by the population. But it also contributed unique influences to the extent and quality of the outcomes.

The Success of Revolutions

After all the appropriate clarifying distinctions have been made and the causal argumentation aligned accordingly, the more fundamental question that still haunts is whether revolutions make a difference and, indeed, a difference for the better. In the context of this work the question can be divided into two: whether the events described here can be weighed on the same scale of consequences with others typically evoked as instances of "revolution" in the question; and whether any of these makes a difference. Answers to the questions require that we begin on a note of sobriety and perspective such as Merleau-Ponty strikes in the observation,

It is no accident that all known revolutions have degenerated: it is because as established regimes they can never be what they were as movements; precisely because it succeeded and ended up as an institution, the historical movement is no longer itself: it "betrays" and "disfigures" itself in accomplishing itself. Revolutions are true as movements and false as regimes.[8]

On the first question, one major thrust of this work is to demonstrate that the national revolts belong in the same category of phenomena with revolutions and kindred forms of protest mobilization (insurrections, etc.) that are united in the facts of historical development and the explanations of causal theory. Assuming an adequate case has been made for this position from the standpoint of the causes of revolutionary situations, it follows that an evaluation of revolt consequences can proceed on the basis of comparison with a broad historical selection of revolutionary outcomes. That conclusion is more plausible if we contrast the mixed results of the national revolts described earlier with Moore's appraisal of European revolutions.

The rising commercial and industrial leaders in the towns did not make the revolutionary surges. . . . Once the dust had settled they were the main beneficiaries of the political changes that were the result of these revolutions. Furthermore, commercial and manufacturing interests were also the main agents of the economic changes without which it would have been impossible to apply the new ideas in practice. The new principles were egalitarian only in the sense that they were directed against older forms of privilege.[9]

In the present context this suggests that many of the less-than-cataclysmic consequences of national revolt also characterize events that we have come to define as classically revolutionary—that the "betrayal" or degradation of revolutions *cum* postrevolutionary states assumes similar forms in both instances. This is not to suggest any denigration of revolutionary consequences in a studied appraisal. On the contrary, understanding those as "major transformations" in many qualified senses, the revolts described here demonstrate equally impressive gains. Some focused comparisons illuminate the point.

Illustratively, do the consequences of revolt in Kenya and, say, the Mexican revolution suggest that we are dealing here with distinct objects of explanation? In the last chapter I argued the unity of causes in comparative historical movements such as these. What about consequences? As in Kenya, perhaps the central historical problem that animated the Mexican revolution was land. The revolution led to land reform that started slowly but was implemented on a broad national scale in the 1930s. Ultimately a vast amount of land was expropriated for collective farms (*ejidos*) and small-holders: there was a "major transformation" of the agrarian sector. Nevertheless, it was also true that the reforms exempted large tracts devoted to export production (especially in the northwest) and the extensive holdings of important political figures and former revolutionary generals or local *caciques*. The properties reformed were often the poorer and unused portions of large haciendas. Even in this instance evasion was practiced through various subterfuges such as registering continuous tracts of the maximum legal size for a single individual in the names of spouses, children, and so forth, meaning that many large estates were only slightly diminished if at all. Reform was most effective in cases of enemies of the revolution. Subsequently, the reformed sector continued to labor under great handicaps owing to the limitations on rural credit (including preferential treatment of large-holders by official banks) and national agricultural development policies that emphasized large-scale commercial farming. The case could be pursued in a lengthy comparison, but the inescapable conclusion is that Mexico's revolutionary land reform bears essential similarities to Kenya's, both characterized by limited and low-cost concessions to the poor peasant (taking the edge off), the creation of a rural bourgeoisie, and the continuation of large commercial farming.

The same evaluation obtains in the case of labor reforms. As in Kenya, the militant labor movement that contributed to the revolutionary situation was subsequently incorporated into a series of national syndicates that were integral parts of the political party structure (the workers "sector" of the Partido Revolucionario Institucional, or PRI).[10] Like Kenya's Tripartite Agreement, labor demands were regulated by the state, and labor mobility was closely tied to political patronage.

In fact, there are a great many more parallels between the one-party political bureaucracies of PRI in Mexico and KANU in Kenya. Mexico's "revolutionary family" at the top of PRI and the government systematizes clientelism in ways reminiscent of Kenyatta's court. The public sector is a major employer absorbing many of the contradictions generated in the private economy. In both countries party and government are indistinguishable as the central dispensers of patronage. Going one step further, the national class structures are similar in the domination of a national bourgeoisie in close league with the party state.

Finally, in Mexico and Kenya dependence on metropolitan power and extensive foreign investment in key sectors of the agricultural and industrial economy are far advanced. Nationalistic rhetoric notwithstanding, the control of the Mexican economy by U.S. corporations is extreme and easily on a par with British and U.S. investment in Kenya. And it should be noted that these compromises of the Mexican revolution are not recent reversals of a once progressive policy in the 1920s and 1930s (although the implementation of redistributive programs such as land reform has certainly slowed). The cooptation of peasants and workers in the party state began with the earliest reforms. All of this is not to say that the differences between the Mexican Porfiriato, Britain's Kenya Colony, and today's reality in the two countries are to be minimized even in terms of the welfare of the poor. They represent major transformations—and tellingly similar ones at that.

I want to carefully avoid any misunderstanding on this point. No systematic comparison of the two revolutionary experiences is intended; their causes and historical contexts are different in many ways. Comparisons on that score would have to be inferred from the argument of chapter 5. For the moment the comparison involves only a strict accounting of the magnitude and redistributive consequences of the revolutions. These, too, are different, but the argument is that they are not different in ways that readily divide into the minor effects of a mere revolt and the major accomplishments of a genuine revolution. Like the causes, they are qualitatively of the same fabric and belong in the same theoretical field.

The Mexico–Kenya contrast is not a unique or far-fetched example of limiting considerations. On the contrary, it is the fundamental lesson of most comparisons of national revolts and historical revolutions. Consider briefly, for example, the experience of Algeria, which some exponents of classical revolutionary exclusivity classify approvingly. Chaliand, who distinguishes between this type of "national revolution" and truly transformative socialist revolutions, says of Algeria,

The basic political direction chosen by the Boumedienne regime shows up in the type of development undertaken in the late 1960s, an industrialization creating a limited sector of heavy industry, but not jobs. . . . Basically, only two major developments can be observed in Algeria: the building of a state, and the formation of an administrative bourgeoisie to run it. . . . So the Algerian Revolution has remained a national revolution; it has not overturned the structures of society. This state of affairs has its roots in Algeria's history and in the nature of its nationalist movement. As we have seen from 1920 to 1954 the petty bourgeoisie which initiated the nationalist movement had virtually no perspective beyond its legal opposition to Algeria's status as a colony. Never once during the seven years of the war for national liberation did an ideologically revolutionary leadership form, capable of preparing the social content of independence. It is true that the peasants, especially those in the mountains, played an important role, but they were never mobilized to fight for the social objectives concerning themselves, in particular, as well as the national cause.[11]

Virtually every point in the description of this "revolution" could be applied with equal cogency to the cases of national revolt in Kenya, Colombia, and the Philippines. The comparisons could be extended further (e.g., to "borderline" cases such as Angola, Bolivia, Egypt,

Ethiopia, Iran, Peru), where the available evidence suggests the same general conclusion.[12]

Here the skeptic would probably counter, "How about China and Cuba?" The question deserves extended historical and comparative treatment, but several points suggest that it does not imply a refutation of the argument. First, as we have seen, a persuasive argument can be made for the unity of revolutionary causation in these two cases and others of national revolt suggesting that the results of those causes are probably best derived from a unified analysis. Second, the egalitarian outcomes of these two revolutions also have their critics, suggesting that their special status may be a case of "only me and thee." That is, even respectful observers suggest that Cuba is troubled by new forms of inequality associated with party membership and that China is steadily inclining to bourgeois practices. Third, China and Cuba (along with Vietnam and North Korea) are no doubt special with respect to their socialistic consequences and, accordingly, it would be valuable to pursue the same kind of comparative analysis developed here in a more refined effort to explain the differences between "nationalist" and socialist revolutions. Chaliand has begun this kind of analysis by locating the true contemporary, socialist, revolutions in "Sinized Asia" (Cuba aside), where international exploitation has met with strong traditions of secular culture and the national state, themselves healthy in proportion to their physical and cultural distance from Europe and the United States.[13] More exacting work on this issue would be especially useful. But recall that the exponents of revolutionary exclusivity themselves include France, Mexico, Algeria, Angola, and others within the same universe of "revolution in general" along with Russia, China, Cuba, and so forth. This study recommends the ecumenical value of that course with respect to revolutionary causation and the broadly transformative consequences that, doubtless, deserve more refined treatment. Finally, what we have been able to explain about the differential consequences of revolt here suggests that the most fertile avenue toward greater refinement lies not with the conceptual premise of separate universes but along the same road of continuity marked by differences associated with the nature of the revolutionary situation, class structure, and world system impact.

Revolution and Nonrevolution

Having argued that national revolts and revolutions produce comparable results, we open ourselves to skepticism from another quarter.

Namely, does any of this make a difference? Was the revolution necessary to accomplish the transformation, or would the same kind of change have come through gradual means as the histories of certain nonrevolutionary societies show? Strictly speaking the question is moot since there is no direct way of knowing how these postrevolutionary societies would have been organized had they not experienced a violent transition. Yet the point is also fascinating and suggests comparative methods for drawing some inferences about what might have been. Barrington Moore pursues one of these under the heading "suppressed historical alternatives," suggesting how history might have been different had revolution succeeded in Germany during the 1920s.[14] Another method apropos of this study is more direct comparison of what was accomplished in the revolutionary societies by contrast to their more tranquil neighbors or countries that shared similar conditions of underdevelopment and managed to overcome some of them through nonrevolutionary means.[15]

I shall consider the main question in a fashion that melds these two comparative strategies. Direct comparisons of "similar" countries are informative but inadequate alone since countries are never directly comparable and such comparisons minimize the special circumstances each contends with—how much they accomplish given what they have to overcome. Accordingly, beyond those contrasts, and reversing Moore's question, I shall go on to ask what might have been had the revolution not succeeded. Two provisos inform the remarks that follow. First, I do not trust the logic of quasi-experimental research designs in comparative history. They strike me as mechanical, misleading, and, more important, unnecessary to all who reject positivism in social science. This, of course, is not to say that we should avoid sensitive comparisons in a dialectical mode. Second, the question Does revolution produce better societies than routine transitions? also strikes me as far too simplistic—and the implication, for that matter, untrue. Revolutions may produce better societies, they may do so for a while, they may in some ways, and they may not (as the case studies and, particularly, the Philippine example suggest). This does not mean that generalizations are impossible, only that they must be formulated, as Weber stressed, within more historically specific limits. To pose the comparative questions in other ways, I shall conclude, misconstrues the revolutionary process by expecting too much of it.

Among the few nonrevolutionary Asian societies, Thailand suggests itself as a contrast to the Philippines. Both countries have been predominantly agricultural, relying in varied degrees on wet paddy rice cultivation and export. Both have been dominated by a single urbanizing capital city, experienced the commercial penetration of ethnic Chinese, were the object of European colonial ambition, and later were drawn into hot and cold wars by a strong U.S. military presence. Yet Thailand had no revolution—or better, its revolution of 1932 was a relatively peaceful transition from royal absolutism to constitutional monarchy. Why the difference?

First, Thailand did not figure as prominently in European colonization of the Far East as did the Philippines or the immediate neighbors of the ancient kingdom of Siam: Burma, Indochina, and Malaya. "The geographic position of Burma adjacent to the Indian Empire, as contrasted with the more remote position of Siam, around the great bend of the Malay peninsula and not necessarily a port of call on voyages to the Far East, suggests that Burma may have been subjected to greater external pressure than Siam."[16] Britain and France, preoccupied also with overland routes to southwest China, focused on the Burma Road rather than indirect avenues through Siam. Nevertheless, the British and French did covet Siamese territory adjacent to their colonies. In the latter half of the nineteenth century Thailand was forced to cede large areas of the kingdom, but this was done by treaty rather than conquest, and several of the treaties were on occasion renegotiated as the traditional state became more sophisticated in the ways of European diplomacy, seeking above all to preserve the kingdom's independence. Colonial penetration was notably incomplete and often came on the terms that pragmatically far-sighted rulers themselves drafted.

Great importance attaches to the fact that Thailand never experienced the peasant problem characteristic of so many colonial societies. Europeans did not come to settle or to alienate large tracts of land similar to the friar estates in the Philippines, and there was always plenty of land for domestic producers. Beginning in 1855 Thailand did enter into restrictive trade agreements with England and was thus dragged into the world economy through export of rice, forest products, rubber, and tin. But the changes that followed were gradual and less traumatic:

> **First, the government of the kingdom by means of a consistently conservative economic policy has been reasonably successful in mitigating the impact of new economic forces. Secondly, the abundance of land has permitted both the absorption of increased population and the realization of increased production without doing violence to social relations. Therefore severe pressure of population on the land and the related problems of peasant indebtedness, landlord–tenant conflict, and impoverishment of the rural population have occurred rarely in Thailand.[17]**

After geographical good fortune, what explains the manner in which Thailand was able to develop somewhat autonomously was the central role of the absolutist state and its indigenously sponsored transition to a modernizing bureaucracy. Unlike the Philippines, Thailand was a self-governing kingdom with deeply rooted social and economic practices before the colonialists arrived. When its incorporation of sorts came, foreign trade was assumed as a monopoly of the king. Conservative state policy resisted commercial exploitation and sought to protect the freeholder economy through "an enlightened land policy which has in fact strengthened the cultivator's title and secured his status."[18] As modern enterprise developed, the state assumed not only the management of basic services (e.g., electricity, railways), but established itself as the owner of key industrial enterprises such as in tobacco, sugar refining, distilleries, and textile and paper mills.

Thai society has had its political torments. In some instances it was forced to cede concessions to colonialism, and the military coup of 1932, as well as subsequent transitions by the same means, was in part a result of developmental tensions stemming from Western penetration. The military and civilian bureaucracies have struggled repeatedly for control of the state, and left-wing politicians and the ethnic Chinese have been used as scapegoats for developmental failures. The economy has not made great strides under state management and has been described as "modernization without development."[19] Yet development is more equitable if less spectacular than in the Philippines. Thailand had no revolution in part because it did not need one, and it had no counterrevolution of the sort that oppresses the Philippines today.

Turning from Asia to Latin America, intersocietal comparisons are more direct. For a brief period following independence Colombia and Venezuela were united as one Gran Colombia. Although Simón Bolívar's dream of a single state extending to Ecuador fell apart in the mid-1820s, the two countries were born siamese and share much in common. Venezuela developed initially on a pattern of large capitalist estates and export agriculture, trading in coffee, cacao, tobacco, sugar, cotton, and cattle. The Federalist War of the 1860s, although briefer, rivaled Colombia's nineteenth-century civil wars. Foreign investment and neocolonialism arrived in Venezuela with the twentieth century. In the late 1920s liberal modernizers began to organize politically, providing the leaders of the democratic left after World War II. Although Venezuela did not produce a national revolt of Colombian proportions, it had its own self-proclaimed democratic "revolutions" of 1945 and 1958, which installed progressive regimes through the agency of military coups with broad popular support. And by the 1960s disaffected radicals had taken up a guerrilla campaign for liberation in the cities and countryside. Yet, with all these similarities, Venezuelan politics were distinctive in the longevity of dictatorial regimes based on military force and the unique contribution of the petroleum industry.

To judiciously simplify a complex history, Venezuela was governed by a series of military dictators, regional *caudillos,* and aggrandizing modernizers from the termination of the Federalist War in 1870 until the first democratic revolution of 1945. The army grew synergistically, with large estates and export agriculture providing the bases of successively notorious tyrannies. Yet the tyrants were also modernizers of a sort and bolstered their regimes with conservative reforms in fiscal policy, infrastructure development, and encouragement of foreign investment. The spectacular instance, of course, was development of the petroleum industry that began in earnest after 1910, when Mexico's revolution forced international companies to look to new fields. Venezuela was more than hospitable. "In 1918 [then President] Gómez allowed the companies to draft the kind of petroleum legislation under which they wished to operate and then decreed it law of the land."[20] Enormous by any standard, the revenues from oil enriched the foreign firms, the military, the political bosses, and their regional, often agrarian, supporters and financed huge public works projects, including the glamorization of Caracas. The Venezuelan people benefited indirectly if at all. The oil boom produced inflation and declining real wages, leading in turn to an exodus of rural families in search of jobs in the cities and oil fields. Declines in agricultural production and growing income inequality soon trapped the middle classes and new urban groups in the same austerity of uneven development as plagued the rural poor.

Protest and organized opposition began to take shape among university students in 1928 and with riotous urban masses in 1935, when Gómez's death unleased an insurgent challenge, promptly met by the oligarchy and military. But once again, the military rulers were forced to make reforms, now allowing political party organization and a better national share of oil revenues. The new Democratic Action party capitalized on the initiative urging more rapid and thorough reforms for its constituents among the new urban groups (industrial workers, merchants, professionals) and segments of the peasantry. The first revolution (of 1945) came when the junior officers of the army decided to cast their fortune with the new popular movement. The revolution was relatively short-lived, ending in 1948 as the Democratic

Action government began too many reforms for its military supporters, who had moved up a notch in the transition, and was succeeded
by the dictatorship of Pérez Jiménez. But the democratic reform
movement had won the future and returned in a more cautious mood
in 1958 amidst a general strike and new military defection.

Venezuela and Columbia experienced quite similar modernizing
influences from the outset of the twentieth century and critically in
the 1930s: foreign investment, commercial agriculture, urbanization,
and the appearance of a new middle class of industrial workers, civil
servants, professionals, and commercial occupations. In Columbia
liberal reformers came to power through elections and began serious
programs for labor and for a more aggrieved peasantry that lacked
the option of migration to jobs in the oil fields. These policies endangered Colombia's more entrenched oligarchy, and without Venezuela's army to mediate and impose a resolution, the conservative reaction set in with a vengeance. Venezuela had the army and it had the
oil. As the wealth poured into selected pockets, urban and industrial
jobs grew into political bases in proportion to the decline of the agrarian elites and the rural labor force. The dictators read these changes
as studiously as did the democratic left and the ambitious junior officers. And the latter coalition took power, at first tentatively and
later more permanently in 1958, through a blend of broad popular
agitation, electoral gambits, and coup. Venezuela accomplished what
Gaitán's election to the presidency in Colombia might have. Failing
that alternative so opprobrious to the Conservative elite, Colombia
lapsed into the Violencia, while Venezuela's military and Democratic
Action tactfully used their oil revenues to purchase land reform and
social programs for the new industrial working class. Venezuela was
less divided by class and political tensions. Its military forces could
and did prevent national revolt with fiercely repressive measures when
they were required. Yet, as the old order was transformed by the oil
industry, urbanization, the growing power of labor, and the pragmatic arguments for reform, the military was gradually converted to
Democratic Action, and together they redirected state patrimony by
"sowing the oil" on new urban and rural terrain. Revolution could
be avoided.

And Venezuela developed, albeit in ways that steadily compromised the reformist goals of the first democratic revolution. Land
reform was accomplished through handsome compensation of the
agrarian bourgeoisie. Average incomes climbed with their unequal
distribution in favor of petroleum workers and the new middle class.
Housing projects and health services blossomed at a rate exceeded

only by the growth of the urban population. When the new inequities were decried by the left of Democratic Action, those dissidents were expelled from the party and formed the nucleus of a new guerrilla movement. "Acción Democrática has followed a strategy of socio-economic development mainly oriented toward the promotion of the middle class within the political and economic framework established by U.S. and Venezuelan propertied interests. In this it has to a substantial degree succeeded. However, the Democratic-capitalists have not changed Venezuela's semicolonial economic structure."[21] By these standards, and eliminating the artifactual influence of oil profits on national accounts, Colombia has not done worse. On the contrary, with fewer resources at its disposal Colombia has probably come further along the reform road just to keep apace of its more fortunate neighbor.

Finally, comparison of Kenya and Tanzania may proceed on sure footing since the two nations originated from the same British colonial system and share similarities of geography, economy, politics, and population. From the beginning, however, a singular advantage of Tanzania was the fact that it never received the extensive white settlement of Kenya or, accordingly, the same severe problems of land alienation, plantations and mixed farms, indirect rule, or colonially fanned tribal conflicts. To be sure, Tanzania had elements of each, but none in the same degree or combination. Tanzania attracted fewer white settlers, and those that came found the conditions of agricultural production more precarious—and, of course, even in Kenya they required massive state assistance to make a go of it. More important, therefore, was the fact that "these economic disadvantages were paralleled by an official policy commitment to African production which only partially recognized the legitimacy of the expatriate sector and which therefore tended to concentrate productive resources in the former rather than the latter."[22] Although sisal plantations existed at the lower altitudes, Africans in the Kilimanjaro region were encouraged to grow coffee (not banned as in Kenya), sometimes close by European farms. Similarly, the tax system in Tanzania was not used as a coercive means of labor recruitment, and "the encouragement of African cash production in the regions close to the main transportation routes, and the reinvestment of the greater part of African taxation in African areas, tended to keep the price of labour high."[23] Colonial policy created an economy based on peasant production and defended the peasantry against proletarianization along the Kenyan pattern.

Always a relatively poor country, Tanzania enjoyed other social advantages. It lacked Kenya's multiplicity of tribal groupings, a single plurality group as unified as the Kikuyu, and as much linguistic diversity owing to the fact that Swahili was more widely used in Tanzania. But again, political differences provide the sharpest contrast. A unified African political movement took shape earlier in Tanzania. Growing out of a tradition of centralized political activity and two earlier associations, the Tanganyika African National Union (TANU) was founded in 1954 with the gifted Julius Nyerere at its head. Elected African representatives joined Tanzania's Legislative Council at an early date and added to their numbers until they constituted a majority. European wishes to retain a numerical majority by adding council members from their own ranks were not entertained here as they were in Kenya. Popular elections for a multiracial government began in 1958, and independence came first to Tanzania in 1961: "the African population emerged with unexpected rapidity into the forefront of political affairs."[24] As a result of geographical accident, a more benign colonial policy, and a more unified political movement, Tanzania was spared any national tragedy akin to Mau Mau.

Developmental policies of independent Tanzania, of course, have followed the lights of Nyerere's African socialism. Its longstanding poverty has not been dramatically improved, although elaborate infrastructure works (e.g., the Zambian railroad), the villagization reforms (*ujamaa*), parastatal enterprises, and urban property reforms all represent a coherent endeavor to redevelop the country on egalitarian lines. How much the socialist reforms have actually accomplished is a critical question, not least for the left.[25] Without entering that mixed issue, the developmental contrast of Tanzania and Kenya is obvious. Kenya has made quantitative gains on most conventional measures of development, although some inequalities have been tempered only slightly and other new ones have grown. Tanzania's developmental gains are modest indeed, and its ambitious redistributive program has yet to persuade sympathizers.

Considered together the nonrevolutionary countries speak to several generalizations. Thailand, Venezuela, and Tanzania were not colonial prizes. The world economy penetrated slowly and incompletely only in the late nineteenth century. These countries were not misdeveloped politically and underdeveloped economically to the same extent as their revolutionary neighbors. Particularly, they were less tormented with a peasant problem (although Venezuela is a bit exceptional, with the peasant problem mollified later). The nonrevolutionary countries did suffer many of the same strains that led to

violent conflict elsewhere—even had their quiet revolutions that belong more to the category of coup—but each managed a relatively
peaceful modernizing transition in different ways based on available
institutional alternatives (in Thailand through adaptation of the traditional bureaucracy, in Venezuela with a new coalition of the military
and democratic left, and in Tanzania by a unified political party).
Although they may have come close, they were spared revolution
because their political situations did not become as desperate and because alternative methods worked for them where they did not work,
despite enormous effort and good faith, for the revolutionary societies.

In the end, countries that reluctantly took up the revolutionary
struggle do not seem to become more developed systematically—at
least at first glance they are not better off. In the comparisons provided it is not the case that the Philippines, Colombia, and Kenya are
dramatically more developed than their counterparts, and I believe
that the same observation would hold if we somehow enlarged the
samples. But this is not really the point of revolutionary success. No
informed observer of the variety of world revolutions would claim
that once undertaken they ensure material benefit apart from where
they begin and what happens after they make peace. In that sense the
revolutions testify to marked, perhaps valiant, success at redressing
injustices that had few parallels in the cases of nonrevolutionary
transformation. The foregoing comparisons show the more insidious
and exploitative conditions of underdevelopment that the Filipino,
Colombian, and Kenyan revolutionaries stood up to, and with the
lapse of time we can now say that their development is more or less
on a par with other countries often exhibited as showcases of democratic transition. The revolutions accomplished more the hard way.
They introduced developmental reforms unprecedented in their own
histories, and they helped ensure, for example, that Colombia would
avoid the authoritarian path of so many Latin American countries and
that Kenya would not become another Rhodesia. Understanding the
special problems of the continuing Philippine struggle, each revolution succeeded in the sense of having swept away the crudest mechanisms of underdevelopment and caught a glimpse of freedom from
one kind of oppression.

These observations go some distance toward answering the prior
question about the kind of difference revolutions make. Stated baldly,
they make a good deal of difference, occasionally for the better. They
have so far failed to eliminate all social inequality, but they have
certainly mollified its form and rendered it less pernicious. Yet, how-

ever "fundamental," this is perhaps not the best question to raise about revolutions in the absence of raising it about the historical process in general. Ironically, we expect too much from revolutions. The best response to this conjecture comes not from the revolutionary theorist but from those who pay the costs and evaluate for themselves the benefits. In the words of the Filipino peasant, "No rebellion fails . . . protest against injustice always succeeds."

As we near the end of this story there may be an inkling that it sounds a note as inconclusive as the revolutions themselves. Assessments to the effect that little changed—at least for the better—or that things changed by replacing old inequalities with new are both disheartening and vacuous. Yet we cannot avoid certain elements of truth in these simplifications or gloss over them with game assurances that a new and more just social order was achieved in which isolated revolutionary triumphs continue to warm hearts and lend solace to the future. Disappointment in the absence of more tangible progressive changes, apart from the manner in which revolutions are imbedded in a continuing historical process suffused with inequalities of one sort or another, is once again to be beguiled by the mythology of the classical revolution. It rests on the expected denouement rather than "an adequate realization of the brief and fragile nature of revolutionary upsurges."[26]

The rhetoric and study of revolution has misleadingly conveyed the notion that, for all of its complications, the revolution *is* the denouement. The very term suggests that somehow unfortunate events and injustices have finally been put right, that the people have gotten in their licks, and that, even if the revolution is later "betrayed," a legacy of populist freedoms will live as a reminder to would-be kings and irrepressible democrats. While it is pointless to deny, likewise, the elements of truth in this simplification, what we have discovered is that revolution is as much an instrument of those who would preserve and extend inequality as of those who would create a more just society. Revolution is part of the seamless cloth of history and the many influences that shape the development of societies rather than an event that somehow rises above history in rare instances to bring it to heel and set it off in a new direction.

Notes

1. Tilly, *Mobilization*, p. 212.
2. *Ibid.*
3. Goldfrank, "Theories of Revolution," pp. 135ff.

4. Moore, *Injustice*, pp. 472–82.
5. Skocpol, *States and Social Revolutions*, pp. 164–65.
6. Leys, *Underdevelopment in Kenya*, p. 244.
7. *Ibid.*, pp. 248–49.
8. Merleau-Ponty, *Adventures in Dialectic*, p. 207.
9. Moore, *Injustice*, p. 494.
10. For description and references, see Lubeck and Walton, "Urban Class Conflict."
11. Chaliand, *Revolution in the Third World*, pp. 109–10.
12. E.g., *ibid.;* Marcum, *Angolan Revolution;* Malloy, *Bolivia;* Quijano, *Nationalism and Capitalism;* Selassie, *Conflict and Intervention.*
13. Chaliand, *Revolution in the Third World*, pp. 167, 178–84.
14. Moore, *Injustice.*
15. See the instructive example of Eckstein, "Impact of Revolution."
16. Riggs, *Thailand*, p. 63.
17. Wilson, *Politics in Thailand*, p. 38.
18. *Ibid.*, p. 41.
19. Jacobs, *Modernization Without Development.*
20. Lieuwen, *Venezuela*, pp. 47–48.
21. Petras, *Politics*, p. 104.
22. Brett, *Colonialism and Underdevelopment*, p. 223.
23. *Ibid.*, p. 227.
24. Ingham, *History of East Africa*, p. 435.
25. Saul, "African Socialism"; Shivji et al., *Silent Class Struggle.*
26. Moore, *Injustice*, p. 482.

CHAPTER SEVEN

The Revolutionary
Past and Future

WITTINGLY OR OTHERWISE, historical and comparative investigations must confront their own limits. Chronicles of revolution vary widely in ambition, from presumably universal and timeless accounts of collective violence to treatments of selected classical revolutions whose momentous proportions are not likely to grace the annals of modern history. Critical comment has already addressed these positions, but little has been said about the historical boundaries of national revolts. The events of this narrative are contemporary in the twin sense of their relative recency and their parallel development in the 1940s and 1950s. Those years no doubt witnessed a turning point in the modern world system—a brief period of hegemonic influence for the United States and the (sometimes temporary) decline of other world powers such as Britain, Germany, France, and Japan. It was also a period in which a new form of colonialism matured based less on territorial acquisition and commerce than on the multinational corporation, internal markets, and industrialization in the Third World. For these reasons, it is plausible to suppose that the revolutionary processes of the period were distinctive by contrast to their historical predecessors (as I have argued in connection with theories of underdevelopment) and of changing relevance for the concluding decades of the twentieth century.

Analysis of contemporary national revolts in the Third World implies that the movements treated here are lodged in the ample and changing confines of the neo- and anticolonial Western world—of "North Atlantic capitalism." As I have argued, these rebellious events are continuous with the classical revolutionary transformations of other Western societies such as France and Mexico. And I would go a step further by claiming that many of the preconditions for socialist revolutions are the same as those found in the classical bourgeois revolutions and in national revolts. However, this study does not explore the question of why *classical* revolutions diverge along bourgeois and socialist roads.[1] Although this is an important limitation, I shall delve into some of its aspects by asking why *national revolts* divide into socialist and capitalist or neocolonial systems. A second limitation of this analysis is the manner in which it supersedes "primitive rebels" and millenarian movements, although, once more, there are connections.[2] Historically it is useful to posit three general types of insurrection, each with its own species: precapitalist (e.g., millenarian, revivalist, banditry); capitalist (bourgeois, anticolonial); and socialist (independent, internationally aligned). The focus of this inquiry is on contemporary revolutions in the capitalist world system and especially within its neocolonial periphery—the Third World that includes most instances of twentieth-century rebellion. But the analysis also helps to explain why primitive rebellion is superseded and why some anticolonial revolts chose a socialist path.

Above all, primitive rebels are traditionalists. Although their precapitalist movements may be prompted by the depredations of the slave trade, commercialism, or the paternalistic abuses of indigenous ruling elites, their "primary resistance" looks backward or heavenward. Their protest is organized by the brotherhood or millenarian sect and does not challenge the terms of alien exploitation so much as it wishes them away. Primitive revolts differ from national ones by attempting to protect their corner of the old order rather than remaking a place for themselves in the new.[3] The uprisings of Colorum sects in the Philippines, Colombian social bandits, and the defensive revolt of the Giriama in Kenya each shared some of these characteristics and produced only a few recruits for the national movements that followed. Among these rebels, even the heroic social bandits are individualists who "belong to the peasantry" and do not incline to national or guerrilla movements: "Insofar as bandits have a 'programme' it is the defense or restoration of the traditional order of things 'as it should be.' . . . In this sense social bandits are reformers, not revolutionaries."[4] Primitive rebels may survive in pockets isolated from modernization and even make anachronistic appearances, but as a whole, "the bandits' contribution to modern revolutions was thus ambiguous, doubtful and short. That was their tragedy."[5] The interpretive significance of this fact is that capitalist revolutions are less continuous with archaic social movements than a new kind of protest that grows up with incorporation into the world economy and takes its form within and from the modernization process. Tradition, as we have seen, strongly influences this new brand of insurrection, but the latter is not traditional.

Capitalist revolutions, whether classical or anticolonial, are produced under similar circumstances including economic dislocations stemming from the global economy, a peasantry displaced by urbanization and commercialization, urban discontent among artisans and sans-culottes, and a political crisis of the state. Of course, there are important differences, such as the dependent condition and protracted liberation struggle in the Third World, that were treated in the introductory discussion of new and old or center and periphery revolutions. But the similarities are more striking, particularly when revolutionary consequences are compared, and when the revolutions of a Mexico or Cuba are counted among the classical instances with all their parallels to national revolts. Moreover, it is useful to speak of capitalist revolution as a general type when we turn to today's revolutions in the Third World that present instances of both national revolt and emergent forms contoured to the changing global political economy.

This argument will be assisted by a brief recapitulation of how national revolts are understood in light of current thinking about capitalist revolution in general. One important advance in the study of peasant movements has narrowed theoretically to a singular materialistic emphasis on the social relations of export regions and the rationality of individual decision makers.[6] This valuable work deals, nevertheless, with a small segment of the revolutionary process by incorporating the cultural and political bases of collective action (so important in the historical studies) only insofar as they follow from or color presumably essential economic motives. Although laudably parsimonious, such theories are unable to explain why fluctuating economic inequalities produce rebellion on particular occasions (i.e., what other circumstances combine to produce the revolutionary movement), why regions with similar properties vary in potential and mobilization for revolt, the character and concrete aims of revolts, and their relative success (as affected, for example, by their cultural vitality or political contingencies). Sacrificing elegant predictive models, a rival approach to peasant rebellion treats in greater detail the social organization and moral economy of rural society.[7] But despite their complementary attractions each perspective is predicated on the mistaken notion that the peasant is the quintessential revolutionary in developing societies. The political or moral economy is stressed at the expense of political action.[8] A valid, if partial focus on export regions, rational villagers, or patron–client relationships ignores related revolutionary organization in other sectors and thereby understands only the tip of the causal iceberg.

Kindred theories located on a different interpretative axis emphasize the role of exploitation and hardship as the primordial cause of revolution—either as a more or less direct result of economic fluctuations, or through the perceptual prism of relative deprivation.[9] The historical studies lend some support to this view, particularly where they show sharp economic (and political) reversals that precede and fuel rebellions. Yet these economic precursors are more complex and variegated in their causal influence. Prosperity contributes to inequality as much as economic slump; there are winners and losers during periods in which either result may be the "average" consequence. Analogous is Durkheim's counterintuitive discovery that times of boom *and* bust have high suicide rates, the connecting link being a disrupted normative order. Here the underlying cause is found in the inequality spread by the very process of modernization. My own suspicion, informed by other research,[10] is that the net balance of economic hardship produced in the process is less important than the amount of dislocation in people's lives and communities. As in the case of peasant revolts manifestly based on questions of land and labor, economic hardship is simply one important reflection of a deeper and more pervasive cause.

Recent emphasis on the state as an actor (rather than mere arena) in revolutionary struggles is exactly the right remedy for the sectoral and materialistic narrowness of some previous work. The only danger I see in this emendation is a new form of reification, a tendency to regard the state as the "key variable" in a complex of revolutionary causes that somehow fade into the background as "structurally given."[11] Whatever meaning is intended by a "structural explanation" (mainly it seems to mean nonsocial psychological), preoccupation with such hard abstractions can lead to new mechanistic explanations in which the contingencies of the political process become the unwitting catalyst for a set of poised "predispositions." At bottom much of this theorizing comes to grief in its implicit preference for positivistic assurance rather than dialectical understanding.

Theories of capitalist revolution that locate societal processes in the constraining context of the world economy provide another valuable remedy for parochial interpretation. And again, there is a tendency to become too enamored of the causal potency in the "world system." As Thompson notes, this may tell us more about the occasion than the character of revolution.[12] Yet one may even misjudge the occasion and its converging causes by deemphasizing the critically different forms in which the exigencies of peripheral capitalist development are worked out in national settings. For understanding revolution, the world system is less a place to start than a set of potent influences whose character is determined through interaction at the national and regional level. Otherwise one flirts with teleological and refurbished functionalist interpretations: things *had* to work out this way because the advanced capitalist economies required it so.

Explanation of the causes and consequences of national revolts rejects none of these theoretical leads but, on the contrary, finds a strong empirical justification for each. In their interweaving, however, a distinctive result is produced. National revolts occur in the context of modernization crises. They pit a growingly confident popular movement against a weak state whose wandering social bases include anachronistic oligarchies, ambitious bourgeois interests, and opportunistic metropolitan allies. The crisis is compounded of a growing contradiction between the surplus-producing capacity and inequality, on one hand, and new opportunities for solving that crisis proffered by foreign interests on the other. Two interrelated problems stand between the weak state and the solution: the popular movement making more effective demands for a different (redistributive) kind of development; and the absence of a powerful coalitional base for implementing new opportunities (which would damage parts of the old guard as well as the movement). In this schematic portrait, the solution comes in officially initiated, preemptive violence designed to eliminate the threat in the same move that embraces a new supportive coalition. The stratagem fails because its desperate premises never reckon with the actual strength of the popular movement and its rebellious greeting of purloined gains. Revolution follows, transforming in important ways the state and the structure of class power. The consequences of the revolution depend upon the composition and mobilization of national groups, the stake or tolerance of external allies, and practical activities of state building with their own constraints and opportunities. Revolutions often result in a more egalitarian order than the *ancien régime*, but this is not necessarily the case. It depends on the nature of the transformation, who struggles with what resources, and who wins.

If one chooses, as I do, to generalize this explanation, the inferential core lies in the developmental circumstances (and policies) in which political coalitions are reformed. In the historical studies these circumstances included export opportunities, an industrial and commercial sector poised to grab new opportunities in metropolitan alliances, a labor force that needed relocation both to produce for the new economy and to consume some of its goods. But these circumstances will vary in peripheral societies depending upon specific features of underdevelopment, the state, and its social class bases. With this recognition we may hazard generalization to other instances of national revolt and to emerging forms of insurrection.

First, the sources of national revolt described in these pages are not unique to the three cases. During the same period other national revolts were occurring in Africa (Algeria, Angola, Egypt, Ethiopia, Guinea-Bissau, Zimbabwe, Congo), Asia (Sri Lanka, Malaysia, Indonesia, Bangladesh), and Latin America (Argentina, Bolivia, Brazil, Chile, Peru, Uruguay). In varying degrees these conflicts centered on the changing constraints of the global economy on a collision course with nationalist movements germinating in the conditions of uneven development. The same can be said of very recent developments.

The revolution that succeeded in taking power in Nicaragua during the summer of 1979 resembles in many respects the events described here. The revolution was years in the making. It followed an "economic boom [that] increased the social weight of the working class and employees in the cities, the economic downturns marginalized the bourgeoisie, especially those medium and small owners without access to state credits and subsidies." Moreover, it was based on "the uneven nature of capitalist development, its concentration in certain urban/rural areas finds expression in the uneven development of the revolutionary struggle. The insurrectionary struggle in the cities developed far in advance of the struggle in general."[13] Urban and rural groups formed coalitions and advanced the fighting on both fronts. Massive mobilization came in response to official violence provisioned by modern equipment and advice from the United States. Basic grievances stemmed from familiar patterns of uneven development and periods of U.S. occupation beginning in 1912 prompted by efforts at "stabilization" to guarantee international loans and possible canal sites.[14] Similarly, as the consequences of the revolution begin to be recorded, a number of competing interests are at work stemming from the various elements that made up the new state and from abroad. When time allows, more detailed and reflective work may demonstrate that Nicaragua's Sandinista movement is one more replica of continuing national revolts.

Neighboring El Salvador at the time of this writing is in full revolt. As in the historical studies, current events have a long pedigree including a savagely repressed rebellion in 1932. The Salvadorean economy is a classic instance of export monoculture based on coffee plantations whose land was alienated from Indian communities beginning in the 1870s and linked into a national network by a planter elite in collaboration with the military. The rebellion of 1932 was carried out by worker, peasant, and Indian communities that had organized a popular movement around the Regional Federation of Salvadorean Workers and won important electoral victories, which the government refused to recognize.[15] There is some evidence to suggest that the state provoked the violence leading to the revolt in an effort to suppress the movement and its political gains.[16] At all events, government and civilian losses numbering around 100 people elicited a massacre of 30,000 peasants and leftists. The post-war years ushered in a modernizing elite politically organized in the Revolutionary Party of Democratic Unification:

> Sponsored by the military and the modernizing bourgeoisie, it was designed to involve new sectors of society in the "Revolution": professionals, a growing service sector linked to the phenomenal growth of the state, and the proletariat created by industrialization. To attract the latter, industrial unions were legalized but carefully controlled. . . . Developmentalism was the creation of conditions to permit the expansion and modernization of Salvadorean capitalism, largely restricted to agriculture until the 1950s. Reformism was the policy of adjusting existing structures to keep the system one step ahead of its own contradictions.[17]

The United States attempted to direct the course of this dependent development, particularly after the Cuban revolution, through a Central American Common Market and to suppress dissent with the Central American Defense Council. But the military–coffee planter elite was challenged continually at the polls in the 1960s and in 1972 was forced again to invalidate fraudulently an electoral sweep by the United National Opposition that included everyone from the Christian Democrats to the far left. The current revolutionary situation is a violent consequence of efforts by the old elite and the United States to maintain an unpopular and repressive state under the transparent rationale of a centrist junta and contrived elections whose popular support is belied by every development in national politics over the last fifty years. This is a revolution whose progressive fate is being withheld only by U.S. military intervention.

Although contemporary national revolts are not confined to Central America (witness the New People's Army in the Philippines and developments in the Spanish Sahara and Horn of Africa), other recent and dramatic events suggest emergent patterns of revolution. Iran is an obvious example. The Shah's narrow modernizing coalition relied on the royal retinue, multinational industries and oil companies, the army and secret police. The coalition fitted international needs for a petroleum supplier and Western-oriented, Middle Eastern buffer state. It did not include the strange bedfellows of oil field workers (whose strikes showed the state's weakness), the peasantry dispossessed by commercializing land reforms, the educated elite, and, critically, the bazaar merchants and the closely associated *mulas* representing traditional religious communities—all underprivileged groups by contrast to the modernizing coalition. When the army was thrown against this impressive alignment of groups in an effort to end the oil field strikes and popular demonstrations and itself split, the revolution was ensured. Certainly this case defeats speculation that modern revolutions are unlikely owing to the diffusion of sophisticated weaponry and bureaucratic state structures.[18] But its illustrative purpose is to show that modernization crises, political coalitions, and the composition of popular movements may vary widely in character and still combine to produce revolution for the same *general* reasons suggested in the historical studies. These and related instances of generalization require specific interpretation and extension at the level of concrete historical processes rather than fantasies about timeless causes: "Only individual analysis can reveal the specific combination of tensions which make up any given 'explosion,' and attempts to discover exactly the same combination (as distinct from a general family resemblance in the patterns) are likely to be unsuccessful."[19]

So far Iran is the only recent case of revolution in the Middle East, but other states are restive under related conditions of underdevelopment. Rapid modernization has disrupted traditional village life and attracted migrants to new industrial settlements where they mingle with guest workers from Yemen, India, Pakistan, Palestine, Egypt, Indonesia, and even Korea. Ethnic conflicts are rivaled by a dizzying inflation and speculative scramble among Arab middlemen. Protest over these conditions took shape in the occupation of Saudi Arabia's Grand Mosque at Mecca:

Bedouins and imported workers joined forces to occupy the Grand Mosque, in an "act of despair" with religious overtones. Ultimately, however, their despair is certainly rooted in the fact that the streams of oil revenues flowing into the Arabian Peninsula—and landing primarily in the pockets of the rulers and their friends and proteges— are generating a kind of "development" which is destroying the traditional ways of life of both the Bedouins and the settled oasis peasants. These groups are thus being uprooted and degraded to a kind of displaced proletariat.[20]

National revolts of the past, as well as ones of the same type that continue today (e.g., in Central America), stem from a particular circumstance of underdevelopment common to the first and second "development decades" of the postwar years. Among the many familiar characteristics of this experience were the commercialization of agriculture for export, import substitution efforts, joint ventures with multinationals aimed at the domestic market, and expansion of the state and service sectors. We have already traced concrete connections between such conditions and revolt. What we are witnessing today is a condition of underdevelopment that retains some features of the old (e.g., urbanization, the informal economy, multinational industry, and a dependent state) but introduces new ones that may prove decisive for popular protest and elite coalitional reform. Some of these new forms of underdevelopment are the exploitation and limitation of energy resources, the growing number of Third World "export platforms" or assembly plants that produce mainly for re-export, greater competition among core powers for internal markets, and, therefore, the final collapse of import substitution. To extend the reasoning of this inquiry, emergent patterns of underdevelopment will bring new kinds of popular grievance and elite coalition. For example, energy-exporting countries like Mexico and Nigeria have recently been forced to import basic foodstuffs at inflationary costs to working people. Domestic industry is increasingly squeezed by the closed-investment, multinational export platform industries and by foreign competition for domestic markets.

These examples suffice to suggest that new popular alliances (say, between urban consumers and domestic industrialists) may form in opposition to the policies of new elites (say, multinational firms and state authorities that control energy development). The contours of insurrection will shift, and it may be apposite to speak of metanational revolts. The central point, of course, is that although the main actors and the class and status bases of their political coalitions shift, the developmental and modernizing roots of potential revolutions are essentially the same. In the historical process of capitalist revolution that begins with the classical European instances, national revolts are another stage that now shades into new forms that emerge with the international political economy of late capitalism.

We come finally to the question of socialist revolution. It is obvious that the materials of this inquiry cannot be used to speculate on why the classical revolutions in Russia or China chose the socialist path. Yet other insights about the trajectory of national revolts do suggest themselves from the studies and comparisons. I shall take it as evident that the revolutionary circumstances of new socialist states like Cuba, Vietnam, Algeria, and perhaps Nicaragua bear essential similarities to the conditions prompting national revolts.[21] The question, then, is why these societies chose socialism—or at least "existing socialisms," in light of demurs about how pure their socialism is.

If this is a fair question, the obvious answer is that they did not "choose" socialism any more than others opted for peripheral capitalism. Rather, in the process of struggle for independence they alternately experimented with developmental policies and reacted to international pressures and blandishments that set them on a socialist course—and an unsteady course at that. Developmental ideologies mingled with political exigencies at home and abroad. This is not to suggest a question-begging opportunism any more than a predetermining idealism. The revolutions that took the socialist road were inspired by ideas of social justice and more equitable models of development. But so were the national revolts that steadily inclined to peripheral capitalism. A difference, however, was that the pioneering socialists had more room to maneuver and more foreign and domestic support for their experiments.

Cuba is often and properly cited in this context. With all its heroism, the Cuban revolution was no more thoroughgoing or previously committed to egalitarianism than were the national revolts or other revolutions like the Mexican that culminated in dependent capitalism. Indeed, with no disparagement, the Cuban revolution was an easier victory in the face of a demoralized army and middle class under Batista. And following the victory, Castro charted a left reformist course that included the hope of rapprochement with the United States. The United States, of course, rejected these overtures and retaliated with an economic boycott and armed invasion. Cuban reforms of land, urbanization, and nationalization of key industries found support in the Soviet Union, which was also able to provide the equipment and financial assistance made necessary by the U.S. trade embargo. What "made" Cuba socialist was less the course of the revolution itself or the implications of its reform than the international reaction to this first leftist takeover in the hemisphere and, indeed, the exemplary successes of the reforms once they were undertaken with the support of restored trade.

Although Tanzania did not arrive at its socialism by revolutionary avenues, it adds support to the argument. Both Nyerere and Kenyatta fashioned a developmental doctrine of African socialism based on a somewhat mythical precolonial past, but under different political circumstances. At the head of a more unified party, Nyerere encountered less internal division and fewer obstacles inherited from a settler economy. Unlike Kenyatta, he did not have to guarantee British investments or make concessions entrained with development loans. African socialism in Tanzania provided the symbols of political mobilization and the methods of reform in the *ujamaa* villages and parastatal corporations. And, of course, China was willing to help underwrite the experiment. The United States and Britain, with fewer stakes than they had in Kenya, were willing to let Tanzania follow its course and, indeed, found it useful to have an ally among the "front line" states in Southern African conflicts.

Today we see another instance of postrevolutionary "choice" unfolding in Nicaragua. To the extent that the political leadership is able to determine its own path, Sandinismo is the desired course. Where a full and explicit sense of Sandinismo is yet to be discovered, it certainly means national independence from the United States and Cuba, collectivist reforms in agriculture and industry, and, if possible, a continuing trade and aid relation with the United States and with its multinational agribusiness firms, such as banana magnates Castle and Cook. In short, Nicaragua chooses to pursue a set of progressive reforms that fall short of the elimination of private enterprise or a foreign policy faithful to the interests of the Soviet bloc. The question, of course, is how decisive this preference may be in the face of U.S. efforts to "destabilize" the regime and related counterrevolutionary forces from within. As I am writing we simply do not know, although speculation abounds on the consolidation of the revolution, the inexorable course of popular left-wing regimes in Central America, and domestic discontent that plays into counterrevolutionary hands.[22] For present purposes the point is the same, namely, that what determines whether a revolution is socialist depends less on the revolution itself than on the political struggle that follows.

I think that it is mistaken to posit some notion of socialist revolution and then to search the contents of the revolutionary experience in order to discover those "structural forces" or cultural legacies that produced the result. Once again, this kind of thinking proceeds from the wrong imagery of the modern revolutionary process. Yet it is not an amateurish mistake. The sophisticated and quite valuable work of Chaliand steps into this conceptual snare when, asking what produced the efficacious social revolutions in China and Vietnam by contrast to the compromised national revolutions in so many other Third World countries, he begins to muse about "Sinized Asia . . . with their robust traditions still intact."[23] There can be no doubt that physical or social distance from the imperial centers and robust traditions play a part in revolutionary results, but just part of an unfolding experience shaped by the revolution itself and the world it encounters.

If the reasoning developed thus far is persuasive—if today's revolutions may be theoretically connected with the national revolts of mid-century, and they in turn are closely associated with the classical revolutions—then the implication is that a more comprehensive theory of capitalist transformation is possible. This is less a formal implication or grandiose ambition than simply a step in an enormous undertaking already begun by pioneers like Barrington Moore.[24] The next step may be understanding socialist revolution in the twin senses of those changing world conditions that lead more national revolts along a socialist road, as well as the new prospect of revolutions within the existing socialist states.

Rebellions, as in Hungary, during the 1950s anticipated what is now a series of insurrections directed at the socialist world powers and at empire-related conflicts among these states (e.g., in Afghanistan, Vietnam, and Kampuchea). Poland in 1980 and 1981 may provide the classic instance in a new genre of revolution.[25] The social, political, *and* theoretical significance of these new struggles is unprecedented. Whereas

> **all successful twentieth-century revolutions have taken place in countries which were integrated into the international capitalist economy (insofar as they were integrated at all into an order of non-subsistence economic relationships) in a way which disrupted traditional economic adaptations or made future economic progress excessively difficult to achieve. . . . [contemporary developments such as the export of revolution make] it also necessary to realize that one day there may be real and successful modern revolutions directed against regimes with Marxist-Leninist titles and formal political organization.[26]**

To extend the reasoning that introduced this study, new developments in peripheral capitalism and in the existing socialist states may imply that national revolts, like classical revolutions, are historically specific forms of protest—types that evolve based on strong continuities with the past, but shade into new forms and serve less as fixed models of explanation than as ideal types providing the essences and contrasts that inform maturing theories. At best the study of national revolts would provide such a link. But that link and, ironically, the steps ahead, depend on the continuities we may discover with the past. The revolution in Poland bears uncanny resemblances to France in 1789, with its volatile demonstrations over food shortages, or Russia in 1917, with its coordinated strikes by urban workers. Similarly, despite the fact that Poland is the world's tenth largest industrial producer, under Russian domination underdevelopment emphasizes export, leaving the working class and peasantry undernourished in ways analogous to the Third World. The causes of classical revolution and national revolt merge once again, now in harbingers of the revolutionary future.

Notes

1. That, of course, is a central question in studies of classical revolution such as Moore, *Social Origins;* Skocpol, *States and Social Revolutions.*
2. Hobsbawm, *Primitive Rebels.*
3. Adas, *Prophets of Rebellion.*
4. Hobsbawm, *Bandits,* pp. 130, 26.
5. *Ibid.,* p. 108.
6. Paige, *Agrarian Revolution;* Popkin, *Rational Peasant.*
7. Scott, *Moral Economy.*
8. Cumings, "Interest and Ideology."
9. The former view is discussed and challenged in Hobsbawm, "Economic Fluctuations"; Snyder and Tilly, "Hardship." For the latter, see Davies, "Toward a Theory of Revolution."
10. Margadant, *French Peasants;* Snyder and Tilly, "Hardship."
11. Skocpol, *States and Social Revolutions.*
12. Thompson, *English Working Class.*
13. Petras, "Whither the Nicaraguan Revolution?" pp. 4–5.
14. Fagen, "Dateline Nicaragua."
15. Anderson, *Matanza.*
16. See the analysis of Cuenca described by Anderson in *ibid.,* pp. 84–88.
17. Armstrong and Shenk, "El Salvador—Why Revolution?" pp. 8–10.
18. Skocpol, *States and Social Revolutions,* p. 289.
19. Hobsbawm, "Economic Fluctuations," p. 147.
20. Hottinger, "Who Held the Grand Mosque Hostage?" p. 35.
21. On this point many analyses would agree, including the otherwise quite distinct books of Wolf, *Peasant Wars;* Chaliand, *Revolution in the Third World;* Paige, *Agrarian Revolution.*
22. Some of the better analyses include German, "Power and Consolidation"; Burbach, "Nicaragua."
23. Chaliand, *Revolution in the Third World,* p. 168.
24. Moore, *Social Origins.*
25. Szkolny, "Revolution in Poland."
26. Dunn, *Modern Revolutions.*

Acronyms

AMT	General Workers' Union—Philippines
ANDI	National Industrialists Association (Asociación Nacional de Industriales)—Colombia
CLM	Collective Labor Movement—Philippines
CLO	Congress of Labor Organizations—Philippines
CTC	Confederation of Colombian Workers (Confederación de Trabajadores Colombianos)
DA	Democratic Alliance—Philippines
EAA	East African Association—Kenya
EATUC	East African Trades Union Congress—Kenya
EDCOR	Economic Development Corps—Philippines
FENALCO	National Merchants Federation (Federación Nacional de Comerciantes)—Colombia
FFF	Federation of Free Farmers—Philippines
HMB	People's Liberation Army (Hukbong Mapagpalaya ng Bayan)—Philippines
IMF	International Monetary Fund
INCORA	Colombian Institute of Agrarian Reform (Instituto Colombiano de Reforma Agraria)
JUSMAG	Joint U.S. Military Advisory Group
KA	Kikuyu Association—Kenya
KADU	Kenya African Democratic Union
KANU	Kenya African National Union
KAU	Kenya African Union
KCA	Kikuyu Central Association—Kenya
KNCC	Kisumu Native Chamber of Commerce—Kenya
KPA	Kikuyu Provincial Association—Kenya
KPMP	National Society of Peasants of the Philippines
KPU	Kenya People's Union

LTUEA	Labor Trade Union of East Africa—Kenya
MASAKA	Free Farmers Union—Philippines
NPA	New People's Army—Philippines
PC	Philippine Constabulary
PCC	Colombian Communist Party (Partido Comunista Colombiano)
PKM	National Peasants Union—Philippines
PKP	Philippine Communist Party
PRI	Institutional Revolutionary Party (Partido Revolucionario Institucional)—Mexico
TANU	Tanganyika African National Union
UMA	Ukamba Members Association—Kenya
UNIR	National Leftist Revolutionary Union (Unión Nacional Izquierdista Revolucionario)—Colombia
USAFFE	U.S. Armed Forces in the Far East
UTC	Unión de Trabajadores Colombianos

Bibliography

Adas, Michael. *Prophets of Rebellion: Millenarian Protest Movements Against the European Colonial Order*. Chapel Hill: University of North Carolina Press, 1979.

Agpalo, Remigio. *The Political Process and the Nationalization of Retail Trade in the Philippines*. Manila: University of the Philippines, 1962.

Agudelo, Luis E. and Rafael Montoya y Montoya. *Los guerrilleros intelectuales: Cartas, documentos e informaciones que prohibió la censura*. Medellín, Colombia: Publicaciones Agumont, 1957.

Alavi, Hamza. "Peasants and Revolution." In Kathleen Gough and Hari P. Sharma, eds., *Imperialism and Revolution in South Asia*. New York: Monthly Review Press, 1973.

Amin, Samir. *Accumulation on a World Scale*. 2 vols. New York: Monthly Review Press, 1974.

Anderson, Thomas P. *Matanza: El Salvador's Communist Revolt of 1932*. Lincoln: University of Nebraska Press, 1971.

Appleton, Sheldon. "Overseas Chinese and Economic Nationalism in the Philippines." *Journal of Asian Studies* (February 1960) 14(2):151–61.

Armstrong, Robert and Janet Shenk. "El Salvador—Why Revolution?" *NACLA Report on the Americas* (March–April 1980) 14(2):3–35.

Arnold, Guy. *Kenyatta and the Politics of Kenya*. London: J. M. Dent and Sons, 1974.

Aya, Rod. "Theories of Revolution Reconsidered: Contrasting Models of Collective Violence." *Theory and Society* (July 1979) 8(1):39–99.

Baclagón, Aldarico S. *Lessons from the Huk Campaign in the Philippines*. Manila: M. Colcol, 1960.

Bailey, Norman A. "La Violencia in Colombia." *Journal of Inter-American Studies* (1967) 9(4):561–75.

Barnett, Donald L. and Karari Njama. *Mau Mau from Within: An Analysis of Kenya's Peasant Revolt*. New York: Monthly Review Press, 1966.

Bello, Walden. "Marcos and the World Bank." *Pacific Research and World Empire Telegram* (September–October 1976) 7(6):1–16.

Berman, Bruce J. "Bureaucracy and Incumbent Violence: Colonial Administration and the Origins of the 'Mau Mau' Emergency in Kenya." *British Journal of Political Science* (April 1976) 6:143–75.

Brantley, Cynthia. *The Giriama and Colonial Resistance in Kenya, 1800–1920.* Berkeley: University of California Press, 1981.

Brett, E. A. *Colonialism and Underdevelopment in East Africa: The Politics of Economic Change, 1919–1939.* London: Heinemann, 1973.

Burbach, Roger. "Nicaragua: The Course of the Revolution." *Monthly Review* (February 1980) 31(9):28–39.

Burke, Edmund. *Reflections on the Revolution in France.* Rpt. ed. Garden City, N.Y.: Dolphin Books, 1961. (First published in 1790.)

Carroll, John J. "Philippine Labor Unions." *Philippine Studies* (April 1961) 9(2):220–54.

Chaliand, Gerard. *Revolution in the Third World: Myths and Prospects.* New York: Viking, 1977.

Chirot, Daniel and Charles Ragin. "The Market, Tradition, and Peasant Rebellion: The Case of Romania in 1907." *American Sociological Review* (1975) 40(4):428–44.

Constantine, Renato. *A History of the Philippines: From Spanish Colonization to the Second World War.* New York: Monthly Review Press, 1975.

Corfield, F. D. *Historical Survey of the Origins and Growth of Mau Mau.* London: Her Majesty's Stationery Office, 1960.

Crippen, Harlan R. "Philippine Agrarian Unrest: Historical Background." *Science and Society* (Fall 1946) 10(4):337–60.

Crist, Raymond E. *The Cauca Valley, Colombia: Land Tenure and Land Use.* Baltimore: Waverly Press, 1952.

Cumings, Bruce. "Interests and Ideology in the Study of Agrarian Politics." *Politics and Society* (1981) 10(4):467–95.

Currie, Lauchlin. *Bases de un programa de fomento para Colombia.* Bogotá: Banco de la República, 1951.

Davies, James C. "Toward a Theory of Revolution." *American Sociological Review* (February 1962) 27(1):5–19.

de Janvry, Alain. *The Agrarian Question and Reformism in Latin America.* Baltimore: Johns Hopkins University Press, 1981.

DeRoux, Gustavo I. "The Social Basis of Peasant Unrest: A Theoretical Framework with Special Reference to the Colombian Case." Ph. D. dissertation, University of Wisconsin, Madison, 1974.

Dineson, Isak. *Out of Africa.* New York: Vintage Books, 1972. (First published in 1937.)

Dix, Robert H. *Colombia: The Political Dimensions of Change.* New Haven: Yale University Press, 1967.

Dunn, John. *Modern Revolutions: An Introduction to the Analysis of a Political Phenomenon.* Cambridge: Cambridge University Press, 1972.

Eberhard, Wolfram. "Problems in Historical Sociology." In Reinhard Bendix, ed., *State and Society: A Reader in Comparative Political Sociology.* Berkeley: University of California Press, 1968.

Eckstein, Susan. "The Impact of Revolution on Social Welfare in Latin America." *Theory and Society* (January 1982) 11(1):43–94.

Edelman, Murray. *The Symbolic Uses of Politics.* Urbana: University of Illinois Press, 1964.

Fagen, Richard R. "Dateline Nicaragua: The End of the Affair," *Foreign Policy* (Fall 1979) no. 36, pp. 178–91.

Fals Borda, Orlando. *Subversion and Social Change in Colombia.* New York: Columbia University Press, 1969.

Fals Borda, Orlando. "Violence and the Break-Up of Tradition in Colombia." In Claudio Véliz, ed., *Obstacles to Change in Latin America.* Oxford: Oxford University Press, 1965.

Feierabend, Ivo K., Rosalind L. Feierabend, and Betty A. Nesvold. "Social Change and Political Violence: Cross-National Patterns." In Hugh Davis Graham and Ted Robert Gurr, eds., *Violence in America: Historical and Comparative Perspectives.* New York: New American Library, 1969.

Fluharty, Vernon Lee. *Dance of the Millions: Military Rule and the Social Revolution in Colombia, 1930–1956.* Pittsburgh: University of Pittsburgh Press, 1957.

Franco Isaza, Eduardo. *Las guerrillas del Llano: Testimonio de una lucha de cuatro años por la libertad.* Bogotá: Librería Mundial, 1959.

Frank, Andre Gunder. *Capitalism and Underdevelopment in Latin America: Historical Studies of Chile and Brazil.* New York: Monthly Review Press, 1969.

Friend, Theodore. *Between Two Empires: The Ordeal of the Philippines, 1929–1946.* New Haven: Yale University Press, 1965.

Friend, Theodore. "Philippine Sugar Industry and the Politics of Independence, 1929–1935." *Journal of Asian Studies* (February 1963) 22:179–92.

Furedi, Frank. "The African Crowd in Nairobi: Popular Movements and Elite Politics." *Journal of African History* (1973) 14(2):275–90.

Furedi, Frank. "The Social Composition of the Mau Mau Movement in the White Highlands." *Journal of Peasant Studies* (July 1974) 1(4):486–505.

García, Antonio. *Gaitán y el problema de la revolución colombiana.* Bogotá: Cooperativa de Artes Gráficos, 1955.

Giddens, Anthony. *The Class Structure of the Advanced Societies.* New York: Barnes and Noble, 1973.

Gilhodes, Pierre. "Agrarian Struggles in Colombia." In Rudolfo Stavenhagen, ed., *Agrarian Problems and Peasant Movements in Latin America.* Garden City, N.Y.: Anchor Books, 1970.

Golay, Frank H. *The Philippines: Public Policy and National Economic Development.* Ithaca: Cornell University Press, 1961.

Goldfrank, Walter L. "Theories of Revolution and Revolution Without Theory: The Case of Mexico." *Theory and Society* (January/March 1979) 7(1/2):135–65.

Good, Kenneth. "Settler Colonialism: Economic Development and Class Formation." *Journal of Modern African Studies* (1976) 14(4):597–620.

Gorman, Stephen M. "Power and Consolidation in the Nicaraguan Revolution." *Journal of Latin American Studies* (1981) 13(1):133–49.

Gott, Richard. *Guerrilla Movements in Latin America*. Garden City, N.Y.: Anchor Books, 1972.

Graff, Harry F. *American Imperialism and the Philippine Insurrection: Testimony Taken from the Hearings on Affairs in the Philippine Islands Before the Senate Committee on the Philippines—1902*. Boston: Little, Brown, 1969.

Gramsci, Antonio. "The Southern Question." In *The Modern Prince and Other Writings*. London: Laerence and Wishart, 1957.

Greene, Graham. *Ways of Escape: An Autiobiography*. New York: Simon & Schuster, 1980.

Guerrero, Milagros C. "The Colorum Uprisings: 1924–1931." *Asian Studies* (April 1967) 5(1):65–78.

Gurr, Ted. "A Causal Model of Civil Strife: A Comparative Analysis Using New Indices." *American Political Science Review* (December 1968) 68:1104–24.

Guzmán Campos, Germán, Orlando Fals Borda, and Eduardo Umaña Luna. *La Violencia en Colombia: Estudio de un proceso social*. 2 vols. Bogotá: Ediciones Tercer Mundo, 1962.

Hagopian, Mark N. *The Phenomenon of Revolution*. New York: Dodd, Mead, 1974.

Hamilton, Gary G. "Pariah Capitalism: A Paradox of Power and Dependence." *Ethnic Studies* (1978) 2:1–15.

Hartendrop, A.V.H. *History of Industry and Trade of the Philippines*. Manila: American Chamber of Commerce of the Philippines, 1958.

Havens, Eugene A. *Támesis: Estructura y cambio*. Bogotá: Universidad Nacional, 1979.

Hayden, Joseph Ralston. *The Philippines: A Study of National Development*. New York: Macmillan, 1942.

Henao, Jesús María and Gerardo Arrubla. *History of Colombia*. Translated and edited by J. Fred Rippy. Chapel Hill: University of North Carolina Press, 1938.

Hermassi, Elbaki. "Toward a Comparative Study of Revolutions." *Comparative Studies in Society and History* (April 1976) 18(2):211–35.

Hirschman, Albert O. *Journeys Toward Progress: Studies of Economic Policy-Making in Latin America*. Garden City, N.Y.: Anchor Books, 1965.

Hobsbawm, E. J. *The Age of Revolution, 1789–1848*. New York: Mentor, 1962.

Hobsbawm, E. J. "The Anatomy of Violence." *New Society*, April 11, 1963.

Hobsbawm, E. J. *Bandits*. Rev. ed. New York: Pantheon, 1981.

Hobsbawm, E. J. "Economic Fluctuations and Some Social Movements Since 1800." In *Labouring Men: Studies in the History of Labour*. London: Weidenfeld and Nicolson, 1964.

Hobsbawm, E. J. "From Social History to the History of Society." *Daedalus* (Winter 1971) 100(1):20–45.

Hobsbawm, E. J. *Industry and Empire*. London: Pelican Books, 1968.

Hobsbawm, E. J. *Primitive Rebels: Studies in Archaic Forms of Social Movements in the 19th and 20th Centuries*. New York: Norton, 1959.

Hobsbawm, E. J. "The Revolutionary Situation in Colombia." *World Today* (June 1963) 19(6):248–58.

Hopkins, Terence. "World-Systems Analysis: Methodological Issues." In Barbara

Hockey Kaplan, ed., *Social Change in the Capitalist World Economy.* Beverly Hills, Calif.: Sage, 1978.

Hottinger, Arnold. "Who Held the Grand Mosque Hostage?" *New York Review of Books* (March 6, 1980) 26(3):35–36.

Huke, Robert E. *Shadows on the Land: An Economic Geography of the Philippines.* Manila: Bookmark, 1963.

Hunt, Lynn Avery. *Revolution and Urban Politics in Provincial France: Troyes and Reims, 1786–1790.* Stanford: Stanford University Press, 1978.

Ingham, Kenneth. *A History of East Africa.* Rev. ed. New York: Praeger, 1965.

Jacobs, Norman. *Modernization Without Development: Thailand as an Asian Case Study.* New York: Praeger, 1971.

Jacoby, Erick H. *Agrarian Unrest in Southeast Asia.* London: Asia Publishing House, 1961.

Kaplan, Barbara Hockey. *Social Change in the Capitalist World Economy.* Beverly Hills, Calif.: Sage, 1978.

Kariuki, Josiah Mwangi. *"Mau Mau" Detainee: The Account by a Kenya African of His Experience in Detention Camps, 1953–1960.* Nairobi: Oxford University Press, 1963.

Kau, Ying-Mao. "Urban and Rural Strategies in the Chinese Communist Revolution." In John Wilson Lewis, ed., *Peasant Rebellion and Communist Revolution in Asia.* Stanford: Stanford University Press, 1974.

Kenyatta, Jomo. *Facing Mt. Kenya.* New York: Vintage Books, 1965.

Kerkvliet, Ben, J. "Peasant Society and Unrest Prior to the Huk Revolution in the Philippines." *Asian Studies* (August 1971) 9(2):164–213.

Kerkvliet, Benedict J. *The Huk Rebellion: A Study of Peasant Revolt in the Philippines.* Berkeley: University of California Press, 1977.

Kilson, Martin L., Jr. "Land and Politics in Kenya: An Analysis of African Politics in a Plural Society." *Western Political Quarterly* (September 1957) 10(3):559–81.

Kilson, Martin L., Jr. "Land and the Kikuyu: A Study of the Relationship Between Land and Kikuyu Political Movements." *Journal of Negro History* (April 1955) 40(2):103–53.

Kurihara, Kenneth K. *Labor in the Philippine Economy.* Stanford: Stanford University Press, 1945.

Kushner, Gilbert. "An African Revitalization Movement: Mau Mau." *Anthropos* (1965) 60:763–802.

Lachia, Eduardo. *Huk: Philippine Agrarian Society in Revolt.* Manila: Solidarity Publishing House, 1971.

Lansdale, Edward G. *In the Midst of Wars.* New York: Harper & Row, 1972.

Larkin, John A. *The Pampangans: Colonial Society in a Philippine Province.* Berkeley: University of California Press, 1972.

Leakey, L.S.B. *Mau Mau and the Kikuyu.* London: Methuen, 1955.

Le Grand, Catherine C. "Perspectives for the Historical Study of Rural Politics and the Colombian Case: An Overview." *Latin American Research Review* (1977) 13(1):7–36.

Leys, Colin. *Underdevelopment in Kenya: The Political Economy of Neo-Colonialism, 1964–1971*. London: Heonemann, 1975.

Liberman, Victor. "Why the Hukbalahap Movement Failed." *Solidarity* (October–December 1966) 1(4):22–30.

Lichauco, Alejandro. "The Lichauco Paper: Imperialism in the Philippines." *Monthly Review* (special issue, July–August 1973) 25(3):1–111.

Lieuwen, Edwin. *Venezuela*. London: Oxford University Press, 1961.

Lightfoot, Keith. *The Philippines*. London: Ernest Benn, 1973.

López Toro, Alvaro. *Migración y cambio social en Antioquia durante el siglo diez y nueve*. Bogotá: Universidad de los Andes, 1970.

Lubeck, Paul and John Walton. "Urban Class Conflict in Africa and Latin America: Comparative Analyses from a World Systems Perspective." *International Journal of Urban and Regional Research* (March 1979) 3(1):3–28.

McDonald, Angus, W., Jr. *The Urban Origins of Rural Revolution: Elites and the Masses in Human Province China, 1911–1927*. Berkeley: University of California Press, 1978.

McGee, T. G. *The Urbanization Process in the Third World*. London: C. Bell, 1971.

McGreevey, William Paul. *An Economic History of Colombia, 1845–1930*. Cambridge: Cambridge University Press, 1971.

McGreevey, William Paul. "Exportaciones y precios de tabaco y café." In Miguel Urrutia and Mario Arrubla, eds., *Compendio de estadísticas históricas de Colombia*. Bogotá: Universidad Nacional, 1970.

McLennan, Marshall S. "Land and Tenancy in the Central Luzon Plain." *Philippine Studies* (1969) 17(4):651–82.

Mahajani, Usha. *Philippine Nationalism: External Challenge and Filipino Response, 1565–1946*. St. Lucia: University of Queensland Press, 1971.

Malloy, James M. *Bolivia: The Un-Completed Revolution*. Pittsburgh: University of Pittsburgh Press, 1970.

Marcum, John. *The Angolan Revolution*. 2 vols. Cambridge: MIT Press, 1969 and 1978.

Margadant, Ted W. *French Peasants in Revolt: The Insurrection of 1851*. Princeton: Princeton University Press, 1979.

Martz, John O. *Colombia: A Contemporary Political Survey*. Chapel Hill: University of North Carolina Press, 1962.

Marx, Karl, *The Eighteenth Brumaire of Louis Bonaparte*. New York: International Publishers, 1963. (First published in 1852).

Maullin, Richard L. "The Private War of a Guerrilla: Violence, Banditry and Politics on the Colombian Frontier." *Trans-Action* (March 1970) 7(5):45–54.

Maullin, Richard L. *Soldiers, Guerrillas, and Politics in Colombia*. Lexington, Mass.: Lexington Books, 1973.

Mboya, Tom. *Freedom and After*. Boston: Little, Brown, 1963.

Merleau-Ponty, Maurice. *Adventures in Dialectic*. Evanston: Northwestern University Press, 1973.

Miller, Stuart C. "Our Mylai of 1900: Americans in the Philippine Insurrection," *Trans-Action* (September 1970) 7(11):19–28.

Moore, Barrington, Jr. *Injustice: The Social Bases of Obedience and Revolt.* White Plains, N.Y.: M. E. Sharpe, 1978.

Moore, Barrington, Jr. *Social Origins of Dictatorship and Democracy: Lord and Peasant in the Making of the Modern World.* Boston: Beacon Press, 1966.

Moss, Robert. *Urban Guerrillas: The New Face of Political Violence.* London: Temple Smith, 1972.

Murray, Francis J., Jr. "Land Reform in the Philippines: An Overview." *Philippine Sociological Review,* (January/April (1972) 20(1/2):151–68.

Nash, Gary B. *The Urban Crucible: Social Change, Political Consciousness, and the Origins of the American Revolution.* Cambridge: Harvard University Press, 1979.

Ocampo, José F. *Dominio de clase en la ciudad colombiana.* Medellín, Colombia: Oveja Negra, 1972.

Oppenheimer, Martin. *The Urban Guerrilla.* Chicago: Quadrangle Books, 1969.

Oquist, Paul. *Violence, Conflict, and Politics in Colombia.* New York: Academic Press, 1980.

Ospina Vásquez, Luis. *Industria y protección en Colombia 1810–1930.* Medellín, Colombia: Editorial Santa Fe, 1955.

Paige, Jeffrey M. *Agrarian Revolution: Social Movements and Export Agriculture in the Underdeveloped World.* New York: Free Press, 1975.

Parsons, James J. *Antioqueño Colonization in Western Colombia.* Berkeley: University of California Press, 1949.

Petras, James. *Politics and Social Structure in Latin America.* New York: Monthly Review Press, 1970.

Petras, James. "Whither the Nicaraguan Revolution?" *Monthly Review* (October 1979) 31(5):1–22.

Phelan, John Leddy. "Free Versus Compulsory Labor: Mexico and the Philippines 1540–1648." *Comparative Studies in Society and History* (1959) 1(2):189–201.

Phelan, John Leddy. *The Hispanization of the Philippines: Spanish Aims and Filipino Responses, 1565–1700.* Madison: University of Wisconsin Press, 1959.

Phelan, John Leddy. *The People and the King: The Comunero Revolution in Colombia, 1781.* Madison: University of Wisconsin Press, 1978.

Pollock, John C. "Violence, Politics and Elite Performance: The Political Sociology of La Violencia in Colombia." *Studies in Comparative International Development* (1975) 10(2):22–50.

Pomeroy, William J. *An American Made Tragedy: Neo-Colonialism and Dictatorship in the Philippines.* New York: International Publishers, 1974.

Pomeroy, William J. *American Neo-Colonialism: Its Emergence in the Philippines and Asia.* New York: International Publishers, 1970.

Pomeroy, William J. *The Forest: A Personal Record of the Huk Guerrilla Struggle in the Philippines.* New York: International Publishers, 1963.

Pomeroy, William J. "The Philippine Peasantry and the Huk Revolt." *Journal of Peasant Studies* (July 1978) 5(4):497–517.

Popkin, Samuel L. *The Rational Peasant: The Political Economy of Rural Society in Vietnam.* Berkeley: University of California Press, 1979.

Portes, Alejandro and John Walton. *Labor, Class, and the International System.* New York: Academic Press, 1981.

Posada, Francisco. *Colombia: Violencia y subdesarrollo.* Bogota: Universidad Nacional de Colombia, 1968.

Quijano, Aníbal. *Nationalism and Capitalism in Peru: A Study of Neo-Imperialism.* New York: Monthly Review Press, 1971.

Ranger, T. O. "Connexions Between 'Primary Resistance' Movements and Modern Mass Nationalism in East and Central Africa. Parts I and II." *Journal of African History* (1968) 9(3/4):437–53, 631–41.

Riggs, Fred W. *Thailand: The Modernization of a Bureaucratic Polity.* Honolulu: East-West Center Press, 1966.

Rippy, J. Fred. *The Capitalists and Colombia.* New York: Vanguard Press, 1931.

Rosberg, Carl G., Jr., and John Nottingham. *The Myth of "Mau Mau": Nationalism in Kenya.* New York: Praeger, 1966.

Rothchild, Donald. *Racial Bargaining in Independent Kenya: A Study of Minorities and Decolonization.* London: Oxford University Press, 1973.

Rudé, George. *Paris and London in the Eighteenth Century.* New York: Viking Press, 1952.

Safford, Frank. *The Ideal of the Practical.* Austin: University of Texas Press, 1976.

Salmon, Jack O. "The Huk Rebellion." *Solidarity* (December 1968) 2(12):1–30.

Saul, John S. "African Socialism in One Country: Tanzania." In Giovanni Arrighi and John S. Saul, eds., *Essays on the Political Economy of Africa.* New York: Monthly Review Press, 1973.

Scaff, Alvin H. *The Philippine Answer to Communism.* Stanford: Stanford University Press, 1955.

Schurz, William Lytle. *The Manila Galleon.* New York: Dutton, 1959.

Schutte, A. G. "Mau Mau: The Cognitive Restructuring of Socio-Political Action." *African Studies* (1973) 32(4):215–27.

Scott, James. "Hegemony and the Peasantry." *Politics and Society* (1977) 7(3):267–96.

Scott, James. *The Moral Economy of the Peasant: Rebellion and Subsistence in Southeast Asia.* New Haven: Yale University Press, 1976.

Selassie, Bereket Habte. *Conflict and Intervention in the Horn of Africa.* New York: Monthly Review Press, 1980.

Sharpless, Richard E. *Gaitán of Colombia: A Political Biography.* Pittsburgh: University of Pittsburgh Press, 1978.

Shivji, Issa G. et al. *The Silent Class Struggle.* Dar es Salaam: Tanzania Publishing House, 1973.

Singh, D. P. "Mau Mau: A Case Study of Kenyan Nationalism." *African Quarterly* (April–June 1968) 8(1):10–23.

Singh, Makhan. *History of Kenya's Trade Union Movement to 1952.* Nairobi: East African Publishing House, 1969.

Skocpol, Theda. "Explaining Revolutions: In Quest of a Social-Structural Approach." In Lewis A. Coser and Otto N. Larsen, eds., *The Uses of Controversy in Sociology.* New York: Free Press, 1976.

Skocpol, Theda. *States and Social Revolutions: A Comparative Analysis of France, Russia, and China.* Cambridge: Cambridge University Press, 1979.

Slater, David. "Colonialism and the Spatial Structure of Underdevelopment: Outlines of an Alternative Approach, with Special Reference to Tanzania." *Progress in Planning* (1974) vol. 4, part 2, pp. 137–162.

Snyder, David and Charles Tilly. "Hardship and Collective Violence in France, 1830 to 1960," *American Sociological Review* (December 1972) 37(5):520–32.

Sorrenson, M. P. K. *Land Reform in the Kikuyu Country: A Study in Government Policy.* Nairobi: Oxford University Press, 1967.

Sorrenson, M. P. K. *Origins of European Settlement in Kenya.* Nairobi: Oxford University Press, 1968.

Starner, F. L. *Magsaysay and the Philippine Peasantry: The Agrarian Impact of Philippine Politics, 1953–56.* Berkeley: University of California Press, 1961.

Stenson, Michael. "The Ethnic and Urban Bases of Communist Revolt in Malaya." In John Wilson Lewis, ed., *Peasant Rebellion and Communist Revolution in Asia.* Stanford: Stanford University Press, 1974.

Stinchcombe, Arthur L. "Social Structure and Organizations." In James G. March, ed., *Handbook of Organizations.* Chicago: Rand McNally, 1965.

Stinchcombe, Arthur L. *Theoretical Methods in Social History.* New York: Academic Press, 1978.

Sturtevant, David R. "Sakdalism and Philippine Radicalism." *Journal of Asian Studies* (February 1962) 21(2):199–213.

Swainson, Nicola. *The Development of Corporate Capitalism in Kenya 1918–77.* Berkeley: University of California Press, 1980.

Sweet, David. "A Proto-Political Peasant Movement in the Spanish Philippines: The Cofradía de San José and the Tayabas Rebellion of 1841." *Asian Studies* (April 1970) 8(1):94–119.

Szkolny, Michael. "Revolution in Poland." *Monthly Review* (June 1981) 23(2):1–21.

Takahashi, Akira. *Land and Peasants in Central Luzon: Socio-Economic Structure of a Philippine Village.* Honolulu: East-West Center Press, 1969.

Taruc, Luis. *Born of the People.* New York: International Publishers, 1953.

Taruc, Luis. *He Who Rides the Tiger: The Story of an Asian Guerrilla Leader.* New York: Praeger, 1967.

Thiong'O, Ngugi Wa. *Petals of Blood.* London: Dutton, 1978.

Thompson, E. P. *The Making of the English Working Class.* New York: Vintage Books, 1966. (First published in 1963.)

Thompson, E. P. *Whigs and Hunters: The Origin of the Black Act.* New York: Pantheon, 1975.

Tilly, Charles. "Does Modernization Breed Revolution?" *Comparative Politics* (April 1974) 5(3):425–47.

Tilly, Charles. *From Mobilization to Revolution.* New York: Addison-Wesley, 1978.

Tilly, Charles. "Town and Country in Revolution." In John Wilson Lewis, ed., *Peasant Rebellion and Communist Revolution in Asia.* Stanford: Stanford University Press, 1974.

Tilly, Charles, Louise Tilly, and Richard Tilly. *The Rebellious Century, 1830–1930.* Cambridge: Harvard University Press, 1975.

Torres Restrepo, Camilo. "Social Change and Rural Violence in Colombia." *Studies in Comparative International Development* (1968–1969) 4(12):262–82.

Van Zwanenberg, Roger. "The Development of Peasant Commodity Production in Kenya, 1920–40." *Economic History Review* (August 1974) 27(3):442–54.

Wallerstein, Immanuel. *The Modern World-System: Capitalist Agriculture and the Origins of the European World-Economy in the Sixteenth Century.* New York: Academic Press, 1974.

Wallerstein, Immanuel. *The Modern World-System II: Mercantilism and the Consolidation of the European World-Economy, 1600–1750.* New York: Academic Press, 1980.

Walton, John. "Accumulation and Comparative Urban Systems: Theory and Some Tentative Contrasts of Latin America and Africa." *Comparative Urban Research* (1977) 5(1):5–18.

Walton, John. *Elites and Economic Development: Comparative Studies on the Political Economy of Latin American Cities.* Austin: Institute of Latin American Studies, University of Texas Press, 1977.

Walton, John. "Guadalajara: Creating the Divided City." In Wayne A. Cornelius and Robert V. Kemper, eds., *Metropolitan Problems and Governmental Response to Latin America.* Latin American Urban Research, vol. 6. Beverly Hills, Calif.: Sage, 1978.

Walton, John. "Urban Political Movements and Revolutionary Change in the Third World." *Urban Affairs Quarterly* (September 1979) 15(1):3–22.

Weinert, Richard C. "Violence in Pre-Modern Societies: Rural Colombia." *American Political Science Review* (June 1966) 60(2):340–46.

Weinstedt, Frederick L. and J. E. Spencer. *The Philippine Island World: A Physical, Cultural, and Regional Geography.* Berkeley: University of California Press, 1967.

White, Christine Pelzer. "The Vietnamese Revolutionary Alliance: Intellectuals, Workers, and Peasants." In John Wilson Lewis, ed., *Peasant Rebellion and Communist Revolution in Asia.* Stanford: Stanford University Press, 1974.

Wickberg, Edgar. *The Chinese in Philippine Life, 1850–1898.* New Haven: Yale University Press, 1965.

Williamson, Robert C. "Toward a Theory of Political Violence: The Case of Rural Colombia." *Western Political Quarterly* (March 1965) 18(1):35–44.

Wilson, David A. *Politics in Thailand.* Ithaca: Cornell University Press, 1962.

Wolf, Eric R. *Peasant Wars of the Twentieth Century.* New York: Harper & Row, 1969.

Woods, H. D. "Labor Relations and the Administrative Process in the Philippines." *Philippine Quarterly* (March 1957) 5(1):23–44.

Wurfel, David. "Philippine Agrarian Reform Under Magsaysay, Parts I and II." *Far Eastern Survey* (January/February 1958) 27(1/2):7–15, 23–30.

Wurfel, David. "Trade Union Development and Labor Relations Policy in the Philippines." *Industrial and Labor Relations Review* (July 1959) 12(4):582–608.

Wuthnow, Robert. "On Suffering, Rebellion, and the Moral Order." *Contemporary Sociology* (1979) 8(2):212–15.

Zaide, Gregorio. *The Philippines Since Pre-Spanish Times*. Manila: R. P. García, 1949.

Index